THE
ADVANCING SOUTH

THE
ADVANCING SOUTH

Stories of Progress and Reaction

BY

EDWIN MIMS

PROFESSOR OF ENGLISH, VANDERBILT UNIVERSITY
AUTHOR OF
"LIFE OF SIDNEY LANIER"

KENNIKAT PRESS/Port Washington, N.Y.

TO

MY WIFE

THE ADVANCING SOUTH

Copyright 1926 by Doubleday, Page & Company
Reissued 1969 by Kennikat Press
by arrangement with Doubleday & Company, Inc.

Library of Congress Catalog Card No: 68-8212
SBN 8046-0315-4
Manufactured in the United States of America

PREFACE

I HAVE endeavoured in this volume to reveal and interpret the individuals, institutions, and organizations that are now carrying on a veritable war of liberation in the Southern States. What may seem at first glance a series of disconnected essays will prove, I trust, to be related parts of a story of the liberal movement in the South. Nothing more important and significant is happening in this country or in the world to-day than the rise to power and influence of constantly enlarging groups of liberal leaders who are fighting against the conservatism, the sensitiveness to criticism, the lack of freedom that have too long impeded Southern progress. Such a statement may seem exaggerated to those who see only the surface indications of public opinion or who mistake noise for fundamental realities. The reactionary forces, stung to renewed action by evidences of the growth of the progressive spirit, are more outspoken, more belligerent, more apparently victorious, but their citadels are gradually being undermined by the rising tide of liberalism. The South, once so potent in the life of the nation, is passing through, not only a remarkable industrial development, but an even more important and significant intellectual renascence.

Unknown to one another and more frequently unknown to the rest of the country, the liberal leaders of whom I have written are bearing the burden that forward-looking men have always borne. They have the critical intelligence, the courage, the faith of men who are fighting for emancipation from outworn traditions. They are cheered by the vision of a new age and a finer civilization. Their words are not always sufficiently articulate to carry to remote places; their achievements may seem fragmentary and incomplete; but both will assume a deeper significance with the passing of the years. The undercurrents of true and fresh ideas will become the main currents; prophecies will become realities. The section that has made such a fight and won will be in a position to make distinct contributions to the nation and to the world.

To write about the South at all is, some insist, sheer provincialism; the true aim of all Americans ought to be to inculcate a spirit of nationalism which would lose sight of sectional differences and merge all parts of the country into one nation, uniform in its standards, traditions, and ideals. But is nationalism antagonistic to a wholesome provincialism? Is it well that American life should be standardized? The South is still a well-defined section of the country, just as New England is, or the Middle West, or the Far West; it is a unit within a larger unit, made so by certain historic, economic, and social facts. Although many of the conditions that formerly made it a distinct section have passed away and although every state has its own characteristics and traits, there is still a solidarity of opinion on religious as well as on political and social questions. There are temperamental traits that are distinctively Southern. It is a belated section—a fact due not only to the Civil War and Reconstruction but to certain intellectual characteristics that tend to resist

the inevitable progress of modern thought. Southerners themselves do not always see that their backwardness must be reckoned with in their analysis of
actual situations, and Northerners often display a lack
of knowledge and imagination that renders them unsympathetic in their consideration of Southern problems. It may turn out that backwardness is an
advantage as well as a disadvantage, and that the
South may make a real contribution to the nation in
avoiding some of the extreme tendencies of modern
life and thought. Contemporary ancestors may be
more promising than decadent grandchildren.

This is substantially the point of view of such books
as Edgar Gardner Murphy's "The Present South,"
Walter H. Page's "The Rebuilding of Old Commonwealths," and other books that have been written during the past quarter of a century. Articles are
constantly appearing in leading American magazines
and newspapers setting forth the industrial and educational progress of the Southern States as a whole or of
some particular state. An increasing number of men
and women have in prose fiction revealed and interpreted the historical and natural background and the
most significant social and intellectual tendencies. But
the situation is always changing. A younger generation is now at work on the tasks suggested by men like
Page and Murphy. The progress well under way for
two decades and more has awakened the reactionary
forces to new strength and confidence. And the liberal leaders of to-day must gird themselves for a new
struggle.

I have purposely avoided the abstract discussion of
Southern problems and have rather aimed at the con-

crete representation of personalities and events. In suggesting the agricultural and industrial development I have been concerned, not with statistics or summaries, but with men who have applied intelligence and science to the business in hand and who at the same time have seen the relation of such progress to social and intellectual progress. I have omitted the mere facts of educational progress—the increase in buildings, appropriations, endowments—and have emphasized the results of such progress as seen in straight thinking, in true scholarship, and in freedom of investigation. The growth of religious organizations is not so important as the conflict between Fundamentalism and the liberal interpretation of religion in the light of modern science and criticism. Others have written about Southern literature as a chapter in the literary history of America—some with exaggeration and others with condescension; I have chosen to consider literature as an interpretation of social life and as a factor in creative thinking. If I have had little to say of the race problem, it is because much has been written by others; I have sought only to show its effect on conservative and liberal minds and to indicate the contributions that certain groups of men are making to what is becoming more and more a national problem. Without attempting to solve the problem presented by the ever stubborn fact of the Solid South in national politics, I have indicated a group of progressive editors who are showing increasing independence and courage in combating the evils of sectionalism and machine politics.

In writing such a book I have had in mind very dis-

tinct types of possible readers and have not found it
easy to shift the point of emphasis and to maintain a
balanced point of view. As I meet an increasing
number of men and women in other sections of the
country, I am impressed that some of them are prejudiced sometimes to the point of bigotry and snobbish-
ness, and that more of them are ignorant—some of
them hopelessly ignorant—of the more favourable
aspects of Southern life. This ignorance is partly due
to the South's carelessness in revealing its better self
or to the silence of its enlightened minority; but it is
due also to an indifference suggested in the remark of
an observant critic that the people of Cambridge,
Massachusetts, know more about Japan or China than
about Virginia or the Carolinas. Ought one to call
himself a good American who does not now and then
go on a journey of discovery to the various provinces
that make up the nation? He will scarcely find the
South—the real South—at Pinehurst, or Miami, or in
the sensational dispatches of American newspapers.
One may travel along all the main lines of Southern
railroads and never be aware of such centres of light
as Chapel Hill, or Sewanee, or Charlottesville. Many
of the special reporters of the recent Dayton trial
never learned the difference between Dayton and
Nashville; some of their articles gave abundant evidence of ignorance as profound as that of the people
they were criticizing.

The Southern conservative looms large in the national consciousness, and never more so than at this
moment. He has been spoken of, perhaps too often
in this volume, as a demagogue and a reactionary. If

he reads this book at all—he probably will in garbled extracts—he will be sure to furnish further illustrations of some of its major contentions. I think I understand this type of man: he is often honest, attractive, and most assuredly powerful. He uses all the weapons at the command of the Bourbon—ridicule, sentiment, and authority. He too often, as John Morley said of Carlyle, takes for granted all his premises and swears to all his conclusions. Although he has a monopoly of the organs of public opinion, he resents any talking back. He believes in the gospel of silence—for other people. As a politician or a preacher he is a veritable Son of Thunder. He brings heat rather than light to a discussion. He knows nothing of the fine art of making distinctions; the wisdom of the golden mean has never penetrated his mind.

It is for the Southerners who are fighting this potent enemy that I have primarily written. Scattered about in their various provinces they do not know one another and in some cases are fighting one another over a difference of uniform. The largest and best newspapers frequently have only a local influence. Despite the establishment of magazines, there is no organ of opinion that reaches even a respectable minority. Many a battle has been lost in the struggle for liberalism because the progressives did not combine while the conservatives were united and aggressive. There are many groups or centres of liberal thought, but they think of themselves as isolated and often ignore what their comrades are doing in other places.

Now it is not easy to keep one's balance in having these three points of view in mind. At times there is a temptation to keep back something that a reader in another section ought not perhaps to know and that a Southerner ought to know; to indulge in an optimism that is not warranted or in a bit of sentimentalism that obscures the fact. I have tried to discriminate be-tween outside critics who take an unseemly pleasure in rubbing old sores and those who are genuinely interested in the South, and who have a right to be because it is a part of the nation; between critics from the inside who in their reaction from traditions have become radical and destructive and those who are willing to face any fact if thereby they may improve a situation.

Likewise, in some of the subjects touched upon, I have sought to discriminate between freedom and license, progressivism and radicalism, vital tradition and traditionalism, sentiment and sentimentalism, science that is irreverent and intolerant and science that is the basis of a larger and more vital faith. Think of the disaster that has come everywhere, and especially in the South, by not making this last dis-tinction. It is unfortunate that so many people follow Mr. Bryan in making an irrepressible conflict between evolution and Christianity, and equally un-fortunate that Mr. Darrow has given such an oppor-tunity to confuse science and the deterministic or agnostic philosophy.

To speak one personal word, I may say that, like Brer Rabbit, I was born and bred in the brier patch, and that the main source of my happiness has been to teach Southern youth for thirty years. My chief de-sire in writing this book is to help along the cause that is growing in strength and vision. The South is to-day the land of opportunity; not because it has a finished or perfect civilization, but because the task of the present generation is so difficult and yet so inspiring.

I am under obligations to all those about whom I have written for furnishing me with material; to call their names would be superfluous. I am grateful to the *World's Work,* the *Review of Reviews,* and the *South Atlantic Quarterly* for permission to use articles that have appeared in these magazines. I desire to thank my colleagues, Professors Curry, Ransom, Davidson, and Drennon, for reading the manuscript and the proofs. I am under very special obligations to Mr. and Mrs. Lawrence S. Holt, Jr., and to Mr. and Mrs. Stewart L. Mims.

EDWIN MIMS.

Nashville, Tennessee,
December 1, 1925.

PREFACE TO THE FIFTH EDITION

I take advantage of another printing to correct some errors in the first edition. I take this opportunity to say that the attitude of Mr. Daniels as set forth in the story of the Bassett affair at Trinity College (Chapter VI) does not altogether represent his point of view at the present time. It is only fair to say that he has been, as trustee and as editor, one of the main supporters of the liberal policies of the University of North Carolina. A good pendant to the Bassett story is that several years afterward it fell to Mr. Daniels's lot to introduce Dr. Bassett, now Professor of History at Smith College and Secretary of the American Historical Association, at a banquet held at the University of North Carolina. He said to a member of the Faculty at the conclusion, "Don't you think I treated Bassett like a Christian?" "Yes," said the professor, "but I think Bassett was even more of a Christian." It seems well to give this pleasant ending of a bitter controversy. He who runs may read.

EDWIN MIMS.

Nashville, Tennessee,
    September 4, 1926.

CONTENTS

THE ADVANCING
SOUTH

THE ADVANCING SOUTH

CHAPTER I

ON JUDGING PUBLIC OPINION IN THE SOUTH

NO INTERPRETATION of contemporary tendencies in the South would be adequate without some consideration of the past. The conflict between the forces of progress and reaction has been going on ever since Appomattox. The leaders of the progressive movement are conscious that they are the inheritors of the spirit of those who, after the Civil War, rebuilt with courageous faith a shattered social order. Reactionary leaders ought to know that they are the descendants of leaders who pursued a policy of obstruction and of sectionalism.

The conservative Southerner, whether he was the fiery Bourbon or the more balanced protagonist of the old order, failed to understand the meaning of defeat. He interpreted the victory of the North as the triumph of brute force—sheer material prosperity—and comforted himself with the thought that many of the noblest causes had gone down in defeat. He threshed over the arguments of Calhoun with regard to the Constitution of 1787, and maintained that secession was still the right of every sovereign state. He still quoted Scripture in defense of slavery, or tried by legislation to continue slavery in spirit, if not in name. He saw no hope for the Negro, and looked for his speedy deterioration under freedom. Compelled by force of circumstances to acknowledge the supremacy of the Federal Government, he was still dominated by the ideas of separation. He saw no future for the nation. "This once fair temple of liberty," one of them said, "rent from the bottom, desecrated by the orgies of a half-mad crew of fanatics and fools, knaves, Negroes, and Jacobins, abandoned wholly by its original worshippers, stands as Babel did of old, a melancholy monument of the frustrate hopes and heaven-aspiring ambition of its builders."

He magnified the life before the war as the most glorious in the history of the world. He saw none of its defects; he resented criticism, either by Northerners or by his own people. He opposed the public-school system as "Yankeeish and infidel," stoutly championing the system of education which had prevailed under the old order. He recognized no standards. "We fearlessly assert," said an alumnus of the most distinguished of Southern universities, "that in this university, the standard is higher, the education more thorough, and the work done by both teachers and students is far greater, than in Princeton, or Yale, or Harvard, or in any other Northern college or university." If such a man ventured into literary criticism, he maintained that the Old South had a literature equal to that of New England; if he had any doubts upon that subject, he looked forward to a time not far off when the Lost Cause would find monumental expression in a great literature, and he thought that oratory might accomplish that result. If he thought on theological or philosophical subjects, it was in terms of the seventeenth and eighteenth centuries. The watchwords of modern life were so many red flags to him—science the enemy of religion, German philosophy of the Transcendental period a denial of the depravity of man, democracy the product of French infidelity and of false humanitarianism, industrial prosperity the inveterate foe of refinement and culture. To use Sidney Lanier's words, he "failed to perceive the deeper movements under-running the times." Defeated in a long war and inheriting the provincialism and sensitiveness of a feudal order, he remained proud in his isolation. He went to work with a stubborn and unconquered spirit, with the idea that sometime in the future all the principles for which the South had stood would triumph.

Into the hands of such men the Reconstruction governments played. Worse even than the effects of excessive taxation, misgovernment, and despair in the minds of the people was the permanent effect produced on the Southern mind. The prophecies that had been made with regard to the triumph of despotism seemed to be fulfilled; every contention that had been made in 1861 with regard to the dangers of Federal usurpation seemed justified by the acts of the government. The political equality of the Negro, guaranteed by the Fifteenth Amendment, and the attempt to give him social equality, were stubborn facts which seemed to overthrow the more liberal ideas of Lincoln and of those Southern leaders who after the war hoped that the magnanimity of the North would be equal to the great task ahead of the nation. The conservative leaders were invested with a dignity that recalls the popularity of Burke when his predictions with regard to the French Revolution were fulfilled. During all the years that have intervened since Reconstruction, the conservative has harked back to those days and his leadership has thereby been strengthened. The demagogue and the reactionary—enemies of the children of light—have always been able to inflame the populace with appeals to the memories and issues of the past.   Such men have forgot nothing and learned nothing.[1]

How different was the point of view of General Lee!   All his intimate associates have testified to the magnanimity of his spirit, and readers of his "Life and Letters" by his son know that he moved at once out of the shadows of Appomattox to the light of a new day. As he was the consummate flower of the ante-bellum civilization and the great commander who fought a losing battle with the courage and skill shown by others in victory, so he became the leader of the liberal forces that were to make a new order.   There is not a progressive movement in the South to-day that cannot find inspiration in his letters and conversations, and even the very slogans for the battle are his.   When he said, "Abandon all these local animosities and make your sons Americans," he became what Gamiel Bradford has called him, "Lee: the American," who did more for the Union during those five years after the war than any other man of his time.   When he said that "the thorough education of all classes of people is the

---

[1] I have sketched a composite type—the result of a study of the magazines, newspapers, and biographies of the period 1865 to 1880. Alfred T. Bledsoe, editor of the *Southern Review* (Baltimore), Toombs of Georgia, Rev. R. L. Dabney and Dr. J. William Jones of Virginia serve to define the type.

most efficacious means for promoting the prosperity of the South," he placed himself at the head of all educational campaigns which have been held since then. When he said that the great aim of every Southerner should be to unite in "the allayment of passion, the dissipation of prejudice, and the restoration of reason," he rebuked every man who at that time and later made his appeal to passion and prejudice.

The more one studies his life and words during that period, the more he admires the heroism, patience, and faith with which Lee faced the task of educating the young men whose fathers he had led into battle. Yes, he was a great commander in peace as in war.

The late Governor Aycock of North Carolina expressed the real spirit of the man when in the peroration of a strong educational address before the Southern Educational Conference at the University of Georgia he told of Lee's dying words as his mind reverted to one of his generals in the titanic struggle, "Tell Hill he must come up"; he then gave his interpretation of the words for the South of to-day:

We are fighting to-day a more terrific battle with the forces of ignorance than he was fighting then. If I had the right to use the words of this mighty man I should call out to-night and say, "President Alderman, President McIver . . . Chancellor Kirkland, you must come up. Bring up all your corps of truth, and light and power. Open your batteries, for the conflict is now on with the enemy. The powers of ignorance and darkness are arrayed against us, and the fight must be to a finish. 'Tell Hill he must come up.'"

The interpretation is not at all forced. The year after Lee's death another Hill, Senator Ben Hill, an-

swered the call of his commander with an address at
the University of Georgia, in which he said:

> Nor can we afford to waste time and strength in defense of
> theories and systems, however valued in their day, which have been
> swept down by the moving avalanche of actual events. We can
> live neither in nor by the defeated past. . . . We live in one
> of those rare junctures in human affairs when one civilization ends
> and another begins. I feel oppressed with a sense of fear that
> we shall not be equal to the unusual responsibilities which this
> condition imposes, unless we can deal frankly with these events,
> frankly with ourselves, and bravely with our very habits of
> thought.

He understood the meaning of defeat. He attrib-
uted the failure of the South to measure up to other
states to the fact that the Southern labourer was a
slave, a Negro slave, and an ignorant Negro slave.
Labour was looked down upon in the Old South because of its association with slavery. Henceforth, the
South must honour, educate, and elevate labour, and to
that end must establish schools of science. "Nothing
is so costly as ignorance, and nothing so cheap as
knowledge." The address closes with an eloquent
appeal: "Shall we rise, or shall we fall yet lower?
Shall we live, or shall we die? We shall live! we shall
rise! we shall command!"

In 1873 L. Q. C. Lamar in the same spirit delivered
in Congress his well-known tribute to Charles Sum-
ner, the leader of the abolitionists. He closed with the
words, "My countrymen, know one another and you
will love one another." This utterance of a native
Georgian gives point to the statement that in Georgia
the readjustment to new conditions came sooner, partly
by reason of the fact that a more democratic people

lived there. Virginia gave to the nation at the time of the foundation of the Republic a group of statesmen rarely excelled in the history of the world. South Carolina statesmen led in the movement toward secession, but the leadership of the New South was first found in a group of far-seeing, liberal-minded Georgians. The action of the state Legislature in repealing the ordinance of secession and in accepting the emancipation of slaves within one minute was characteristic of her later work. In 1866, Alexander H. Stephens and Benjamin H. Hill—one before the Legislature of Georgia and the other before Tammany Hall—sounded the note of patience, of nationalism, and of hope. "There was a South of slavery and secession," said the latter; "that South is dead. There is a South of Union and freedom; that South, thank God! is living, breathing, growing every hour."

These words became the text of the now celebrated address of a Georgian who, twenty years later, before the New England Club of New York, gave notable expression to the new national spirit. Henry Grady, as editor of the Atlanta *Constitution,* was, after 1876, an exponent of the idea that the future of the South lay primarily not in politics, but in an industrial order which should be the basis of a more enduring civilization. At his advice, as Joel Chandler Harris said, everybody began to take a day off from politics occasionally and devote himself to the upbuilding of the resources of the state. Another Georgian, General John B. Gordon, united with Grady and others in saying "a bold and manly word in behalf of the American Union in the ear of the South, and a bold and manly word in behalf of the South in the ear of the North."

While recounting the last days of the Confederacy, he awoke in Northern hearts an admiration for Lee and in Southern hearts an admiration for Grant, and in all an aspiration toward nationalism.

Atticus G. Haygood, president of Emory College and afterward bishop of the Methodist Episcopal Church, South, voiced the sentiment of the liberal South with regard to the Negro, in a book whose title, "Our Brother in Black," sufficiently indicates the spirit in which it was written. In a Thanksgiving sermon on the New South, delivered in 1881, he criticized severely the croakers and the demagogues who were endeavouring to mislead the people, and reviewed with sympathy the great progress that had been made since the war. He pleaded guilty to the charge of having new light, and said he was glad of it. He pointed out with keen insight the illiteracy of the masses of the Southern people and the lack of educational facilities. A movement for the development of a public-school system in the South was led by J. L. M. Curry, a Confederate soldier of Georgia stock. He became an evangelist in the crusade for public education, announcing before state legislatures the principle upon which a true democratic order might be established. "I am not afraid of the educated masses," he said, in an address before the Georgia Legislature, "I would rather trust the masses than king, priest, aristocracy, or established church. No nation can realize its full possibility unless it builds upon the education of the whole people."

One of the greatest disappointments in reading Southern history is that Georgia, which produced such men and responded to their words, has seemed in later years to lose them from its consciousness. The sceptre of Southern leadership passed to North Carolina. Georgia has failed to support its educational system adequately; has followed politicians who inculcated a bitterness toward the Negro, the Jew, and the Catholic; it is the headquarters of the Ku Klux Klan; it has furnished the leader who more than any other man in the Southern Methodist Church is responsible for the defeat of the unification of the two branches of Methodism and who at the same time has been the foremost exponent of a reactionary theology. On the whole, despite individuals and groups as progressive as any in the country, the state, in all except industrial progress, has in recent years been a laggard in the matter of intellectual and social progress.

What is true of Georgia is true of other Southern states. The stage seems all set for wonderful progress; the obstacles seem to be removed; and then something happens; there is a resurgence of the old reactionary spirit, policies, and ideas. And in some respects the South looks worse to other sections of the country and to its own intelligent minority than it has looked at any time within the last decade or more. A section that is still solid in politics, however issues or candidates may change, that is a fertile ground for all sorts of intolerant ideas, that still gives little evidence that institutions of higher learning, fostered by state and private benevolence, have any appreciable influence on public opinion—surely such a section must seem a disappointment to the country as a whole.

Let one turn, for instance, from some of the superlative statements with which Southern newspapers and commercial bulletins are now filled to books that during the present year have had wide reading: to Skaggs's "Southern Oligarchy," which is a merciless and withal extreme statement of the political situation, past and present; or to "These United States," in which critical judgment of the various states is applied with special severity to all Southern states save one; or to Tannenbaum's "Darker Phases of the South," which leaves one amazed and overwhelmed by the representation of certain social conditions in the South, based in every instance on Southern sources of information; or to Mencken's now notorious essay on "The Sahara of the Bozart," the title of which gives but a faint suggestion of its ruthless analysis of Southern art and thought. Scarcely less severe is the criticism that is springing up in the South itself. I refer to the editorial in the Charleston *News and Courier* which last year was awarded the Pulitzer prize, to a series of articles by Gerald Johnson on "The Battling South," and "Tilting with Southern Windmills," to the *Journal of Social Forces,* published at the University of North Carolina and containing articles covering the whole range of social conditions in the South, or to the brilliant witticisms of a columnist like Nell Battle Lewis in the Raleigh *News and Observer,* or to the novels of Ellen Glasgow and James Branch Cabell. Such criticism and unrest underneath all the apparent prosperity must be duly considered.

Certain uncomfortable questions are being asked. Of what avail is the enormous growth of factories if we are to "bury our Anglo-Saxons" under a system that is paternalistic and feudalistic? If good roads are to connect towns in which Philistinism is raised to the *n*th degree, why rejoice in their extension? What good is the abolition of illiteracy if literacy leads to so meagre results? Why give money to higher institutions of learning if they are threatened, and in some cases actually confronted, by a negation of the very spirit of research and inquiry that scholarship demands, and especially when some of these institutions are supine to the point of conformity and convention? The progress in religion as evidenced by statistics of members and by enormous funds for church building has often been associated with a bigotry and intolerance that take us back to the Middle Ages for a parallel.

All of which is to say that progress at one point does not mean progress at all points. Some of the most prominent manufacturers and best educated lawyers I know are Fundamentalists. The paper that comes near being the organ of the cotton-mill industry of the Piedmont section voices the sentiment of its own city and section in advocating the passage of an Anti-Evolution law. The legislature of Tennessee that made provision for an eight months school term and gave the largest appropriation that it has ever given to its university passed the Anti-Evolution law, and the University did not seem to think that it made any difference. National boards of education that have been generous to Vanderbilt University and Peabody College for Teachers must feel that their efforts are futile when in the very capital city in which these institutions are located such a bill is allowed to become a law without any very aggressive opposition. At about the same time that Mr. J. B. Duke was establishing a foundation to build a real university devoted to research and freedom, the Governor of North Carolina and the Board of Education were declaring and enacting that a textbook in biology adopted by the Textbook Commission should not be taught in the schools of the state because it had a picture of an anthropoid ape and a primitive man on the same page. The Southern Railway is now one of the most prosperous railroads of the country, but its Crescent Limited, the latest thing in construction, passes through wide stretches of territory which are as hostile to new ideas as they were when poverty reigned and illiteracy was like a blot on the scutcheons of old commonwealths. Atlanta, in many ways the most progressive of Southern cities, is the capital of the Invisible Kingdom.

And yet it is my contention in this volume that the situation, bad as it is, is not as bad as it seems. We have been simply too hopeful; Southern people have a way of being over-optimistic as to immediate results. The South has come a long way, but there is still a long way to go before the forces of sound and intelligent public opinion can prevail. There are things being said and done in the South that Northern readers do not know about, and it is just as true that Southern people in some states know nothing about what is happening in their sister states. There is a lack of co-operation among progressives, while the forces of reaction are united and aggressive. One who travels about in the South finds in newspapers, in conversations, in public addresses, evidences that there are circles here and there, institutions of learning, assemblies of various kinds, that are as enlightened and as free as any in the country. It so happened that I first read Tannenbaum's "Darker Phases of the South" in Asheville at a time when the North Carolina Conference for Social Service was holding its annual meeting there. The personnel of this conference and the addresses gave evidence that the people of the state are dealing effectively with the social problems that are presented in that volume. At the same time, the superintendents of county schools were grappling with the question of rural education. None of these figured in Associated Press dispatches, while the Dayton trial was on the front page of every American newspaper.

There are many illustrations of the danger of hasty generalization. The Southern Baptist Church is recognized as the most powerful denomination in country districts; the utterances of most of its conventions have indicated its opposition to science and its espousal of Fundamentalism. Its adoption of a statement of belief at Memphis, following quickly upon a message of congratulation to Governor Peay for signing the Anti-Evolution bill, was a warning to those who were in their colleges holding any sort of liberal opinions. It has carried on a persistent harrowing of its professors by having the presidents of colleges subject them to questionnaires, touching their beliefs on certain moot questions.

All this is true, and yet some of the most liberal leaders in the South are Baptists. Rev. Ashby Jones, one of the noted preachers and citizens of Atlanta, in a recent article in the Atlanta *Constitution,* said, among other things, that the fundamental principle of development is accepted by every reputable physical scientist, and that likewise the spiritual origin of the universe is accepted by the overwhelming majority of philosophers. The "how" of creation is not the question of debate; we must distinguish between science and philosophy. The facts of Geology and Biology cannot be questioned. In the Commencement sermon at the University of North Carolina in June, he went even further:

The hypothesis of the laboratory is not a "guess." It is truth already tested by experiment, plus that which it is believed will have to be true. . . . . The protest of the Church against rationalism, which means reason, has proven a tragedy. An irrational, an unreasonable, faith, is one which rests on insufficient knowledge. . . . Religion says, "I believe in the beginning God created." Concerning the time of that beginning, religion knows nothing. It depends upon science for its knowledge. Of the method of creation religion knows nothing. . . . Religion is not an invitation to certainty, nor to safety. It is a call to a great adventure.

Dr. R. T. Vann, for a long time a leader in the Baptist Church in North Carolina, in a pamphlet entitled, "What have Baptist Colleges to do with Fundamentalism and Modernism?" said recently:

Much of the Bible cannot be taken literally, and was never meant to be so taken. . . . In interpreting the Bible, regard must be had to the fact that the revelation from God was first given thousands of years ago, to an immature race differing widely from us in respect of time, race, intelligence, habits, and language. God's revelation was and is progressive. . . . Our people should be informed that our English Bible was not given to us directly from God, but through some comparatively modern scholars, and no Fundamentalist would contend that those translators were inspired.

The chief protagonist of the liberal forces in the Baptist Church is President W. L. Poteat of Wake Forest College, who for a generation has stood out uncompromisingly as a champion of the theory of evolution. He has never surrendered what he learned as a teacher of Biology. He recently delivered the McNair lectures at the University of North Carolina on the relation of science and religion.[1] The lectures were heard by a thousand people for three consecutive nights; in addition to the faculty and students of the University, scores of people came from Raleigh, Durham, and other nearby towns. Without any dodging or sidestepping, he faced squarely the issue with regard to both science and the interpretation of the Bible. He was discriminating, balanced, and fearless. As one reads the volume which has just come from the press, he feels that it does for the South in this generation what John Fiske's "Destiny of Man" and "Idea of God" did a generation ago for other sections. It may be safely said that with all that has been written during the present controversy nothing has appeared that goes straighter to the heart of the issues involved or that is wiser and bolder.

The lectures were reported for the leading North Carolina newspapers and were cordially approved in editorials in all except one. The Board of Trustees of Wake Forest unanimously approved his position and said that they were glad to have the college take the lead in the controversy; the alumni and student body at Commencement let it be known that they were with their President. As I write these words, he is lecturing on evolution to the preachers and teachers of Asheville and has just repeated the McNair lectures to five hundred college students of the South at the Blue Ridge Conference. It is true that threats have

---

[1]"Can a Man Be a Christian To-day?" (University Press, Chapel Hill, N. C., 1925) is the exact title of the book.

been made that the collections for the college will not be so large as they have been, and the critics of Doctor Poteat are hoping that the big guns of the Baptists in other states will be turned upon him, and that he will at last be routed.   But he is too firmly intrenched to be dislodged.

Such incidents as I have given—and they might be multiplied—show rather conclusively that public opinion in the South is not as static as has been thought, and, furthermore, that it yields to men of courage and vision.   Somehow, the reports of persecution go further and remain longer in the memory.   It was my good fortune to be teaching in two colleges at times when the principle of academic freedom was at stake, and I have told in Chapter V of this volume the stories of what happened at Trinity College (now Duke University) and at Vanderbilt University.

Any analysis of public opinion in the South has to reckon with the influence of outside criticism as an important factor.   More than once have I seen a wholesome and courageous condemnation of an atrocious lynching in the South followed by such a resentment of Northern criticism that the point of emphasis in the local press was entirely shifted to one of defence, and the original crime forgotten.   Talk with intelligent cotton-mill owners about the defects in the present industrial system and you will get frank admissions and remedies; but let some social reformer or government expert write about these same evils, and immediately the operators attribute the criticism to the propaganda of New England mill owners intended to thwart competition, or to the busybody reformers and uplifters of the sentimental type, or even to Bolshevists in Russia.

A more recent illustration of the same tendency is seen in the reaction of many people in Tennessee toward outside criticism of its Anti-Evolution law. The owner of a leading newspaper, who took no stand when the bill was before the Legislature, although he himself regarded the law as a foolish one, afterward published a leading editorial answering the New York *World's* denunciation of the law and proclaiming in vigorous language that Tennessee could attend to its own affairs; the state had a perfect right to say what should be taught or not taught in its schools. Some lawyers who had been opposed to the passage of the law so resented the appearance of Mr. Darrow and Mr. Malone in the case that their point of emphasis shifted to a defense of the old Volunteer state. Mr. Mencken's violent diatribes have strengthened the conservative forces.

Southerners do not realize that the demand that the South be let alone to work out its own problems would be more pertinent if an enlightened public would take aggressive steps to make itself effective. If, in this instance, there had been a quick crystallization of opinion, which would have made itself felt in legislative committees before the question passed to the stage of consideration by the larger body more apt to be affected by popular passion and prejudice, or if after the passage of the law steps had been immediately taken to test its constitutionality and thus obviated the sensational trial at Dayton, in which an outside organization and outside attorneys and witnesses were the main protagonists for a great principle of freedom, then the results would have been far better.

Northern ignorance and prejudice are exasperating,

but a wise man does not let an extremist on the other side throw him off his balance. But it needs to be added that the South resents not only outside criticism, but the criticism of its own citizens, whose motives are impugned and whose facts are denied because forsooth they are said to be writing to win the favour of the people of the North. In a recent edition of the *Manufacturers' Record,* a fling is taken at "a good many Southern speakers and writers who, though Southern-born and claiming to be Southern in sentiment, do as much to misrepresent the South at home and abroad as even the most avowed enemies of the South." The editor continues:

Any Southern orator who desired to win the enthusiastic applause of the Northern press and people could do so at any moment by misrepresenting the activity of the Old South and praising the progress of the present as due to the infusion of Northern ideas. It did not take any great quantity of brains, and certainly very little knowledge of the South, to be able to win public favour in the North by such a course.

To readers of this journal over a period of many years, the indictment has a familiar sound, for, periodically, it has had the habit of republishing in its editorial columns a stereotyped list of quotations from Southern men taken without regard to context or occasion to prove that the work of the Southern Education Board, composed, as it was, of Northern and Southern leaders interested in a great coöperative effort to further education in all the Southern States, was meant to destroy Southern traditions, to inculcate certain ideas with regard to the Negro, and eventually to build up the Republican party in the South. It so happens that some of the men included in this list of Southern "traitors" were Governors Aycock of North Carolina and Montague of Virginia, Walter H. Page, Doctors Alderman, McIver, Dabney, Mitchell, and others now generally recognized as men who took part in one of the greatest educational movements of modern times. The criticism directed toward such men surely recoils upon the heads of its perpetrators, and yet it was repeated by many editors who followed the lead of this foremost exponent of Southern industrial progress and by many of the most prominent manufacturers who look to it for the law and the gospel.

And just the same sort of criticism has been heaped upon Southern scholars, who in writing history have adopted the methods of the scientific historian rather than the demands of sentimental tradition, or who in writing literary criticism have maintained universal standards of judgment rather than parochial or provincial standards. A case in point is the storm of abuse that broke upon Professor W. P. Trent when he wrote the life of William Gillmore Simms, in which he said that Simms, with all his good intentions and his unlimited energy, did not attain to the highest literary excellence, and that his failure was partly due to his environment and to his absorption in the slavery contest. Charlestonians especially resented his characterization of the ante-bellum social life of South Carolina, and, Episcopalians as they were, demanded that the University of the South should get rid of a professor who had so sinned against the established order in the very citadel of the Church. Fortunately, Vice-Chancellor Wiggins had the good sense and the courage to say that if Trent went he would go, too, and there the matter ended. When Professor Trent, after a few years, resigned to accept a professorship at Columbia, his critics were quick to say that he had realized the ambition he had had in writing the book. It never occurred to them that one reason why he went to Columbia was that the Episcopal Church had failed to provide Sewanee with an adequate library and other resources that a scholar needs to do the work he wants to do, and that another reason was that it is difficult to do scholarly work among a people who say in any field of research, "Thus far shalt thou go, and no farther."

Others have gone North, and for the same reason; and some of them, notably William E. Dodd and John Spencer Bassett, have continued their research in various periods of Southern history. Some scholars have worked on in the South with limited facilities in sociology, history, science, and literary criticism, and may be counted upon to play their part in the liberalization of public opinion. They have a way of discovering disagreeable facts, and they have the temerity to publish them, cost what it may.

Whether, then, we think of criticism from without or from within, the trouble is that the Southern States still have a great mass of uneducated people, sensitive, passionate, prejudiced, and another mass of the half-educated who have very little intellectual curiosity or independence of judgment. The demagogue always knows what the masses will think about certain questions. He knows that he holds the whip hand in any ecclesiastical or political struggle; he knows that with ridicule and sentiment and an appeal to long-cherished traditions he can sway the public. He does not need argument or facts to overthrow his opponents.   And the most unfortunate fact of all is, that the enlightened man, be he preacher or editor or scholar or business man, either keeps quiet or is so interested in an institution or organization that he will not endanger his leadership by taking a positive stand for what he knows is right.   The man who says or does nothing salves his conscience by emphasizing the futility of opposition; the man who compromises and equivocates hopes for a better day when he will be able by reason of his staying with the organization to dominate a more favourable situation.   Such men hope that, in some peaceable way, reform in politics or progress in religious thought may come about, while at the same time they may praise the men of the past who had the wisdom and the courage to be pioneers of a new order. There are far too many men of the type which Bunyan had in mind when he drew Mr. Facing-both-Ways and Mr. Faintheart.

Meantime, men in cloistered walls or in quiet studies, cherishing the integrity of their own minds and heroically building at the Temple of Truth, wait patiently for Mr. Valiant-for-Truth and Mr. Greatheart. And sometimes they see the glory of the coming of the Lord as men unsheathe their swords or give forth the call of the bugle.   It may be an Aycock standing before a hostile Democratic Convention ready to pass resolutions denouncing his administration for its support of Negro schools and winning them to his support by the sheer audacity of his flaming faith and eloquence; or a Poteat speaking to a Baptist State Convention assembled to condemn his views on evolution and leaving them so overwhelmed with his sincerity and his spiritual insight that no one dares to speak against him; or a Snyder, with an almost solid delegation from South Carolina against unification around him, pleading with the General Conference of his Church to adopt the plan of unification; or a Kirkland working for a quarter of a century against every sort of opposition for the maintenance of honest standards in Southern colleges, until at last he is crowned as the unquestioned leader of a great movement in Southern education; or a Mooney in editorial after editorial denouncing the Ku Klux Klan in the very capital of the Black Belt; or a Bishop Mouzon in the chapel of Vanderbilt University, outlining the programme of Jesus in a series of lectures that cut the ground out from all false ecclesiasticism of the day— a true prophet of God; or an Alderman, from the vantage ground of thirty years of constructive work in the field of education, interpreting to a critical audience assembled in the Capitol of the nation the life and spirit of Woodrow Wilson in an address notable alike for its comprehensive vision and its stately eloquence.

Such men as these—and there are more of them than most people, North or South, think—are the basis of faith in the growth of a wiser and braver leadership. They are not isolated individuals, but in nearly every case they have behind them institutions and organizations that in whole or in part rally to them. May their tribe increase!

CHAPTER II

THE short interval between the death of Thomas Nelson Page and of Walter Hines Page served to focus attention upon the personalities and the achievements of two of the most distinguished Southerners of their generation. To be sure, they were more than Southerners: they were Americans, filling important rôles, the one as ambassador to Italy, the other as ambassador to Great Britain, during the momentous years of the war. But neither their national nor international fame should obscure the fact that they were born and bred in the South and that they represented two distinct elements in Southern life. They were born within two years of each other, spent their boyhood amid the scenes of the Civil War and Reconstruction, were both educated in struggling colleges of the South, won recognition in the field of literature, and were called to important diplomatic positions abroad. It was eminently fitting that they should have died, the one at Oakland, Virginia, and the other at Aberdeen, North Carolina, which had been associated with some of the fondest memories of their lives and with the achievements of several generations of their ancestors.

The contrasts between their temperaments and their

[1]Reprinted, with revision, from the *South Atlantic Quarterly*, April, 1919.

points of view are much more striking than the parallels. Thomas Nelson Page, with the blood of several generations of Virginia gentlemen and gentlewomen flowing in his veins, was a typical product of the social conditions that prevailed in Virginia under the old régime. His highest ambition was to reveal and to interpret the civilization which he believed to be the "sweetest, purest, and most beautiful" that this country ever had. There was in his essays and short stories the glamour that he associated with his ancestors and their distinctive social life. Walter Hines Page, a typical descendant of what may be called the middle class of pioneers and religious leaders who made the more democratic conditions that prevailed in North Carolina, early in life saw and interpreted the limitations of the old order in the South, and throughout his life, now in addresses, and now in magazine articles, and once in a novel, sought to shatter the false illusions that had gathered about his native section.

The one was distinctively a romantic, looking back upon a vanished age which for him had many of the characteristics of a golden age; the other was a critic, seeing with clear eyes the shortcomings of his people, and attacking with brave heart the barriers that hampered them in their struggle toward a more progressive life. One was an aristocrat, fully conscious of the charm and prestige of the aristocracy whose traditions he had inherited; the other was a democrat, believing in the possibilities that lay in the training of the backward people of the South, for to him democracy was not simply a theory of government but a state of society in which all men might find the opportunity for the development of their distinctive talents.

Two distinct memories of Thomas Nelson Page stand out in my boyhood days. While I was still in preparatory school, I found printed in the leading paper of my state an address delivered by him at Washington and Lee University on "The Old South." I read every word of it with enthusiasm and memorized the best parts of it for a declamation. Upon me, as upon every other Southerner, the tribute to Lee and Washington, the defense of ante-bellum Southern civilization against its critics, the repudiation of "the new South" as an implied protest against the old, the eloquent summary of the great Southerners who had played such a decisive part in the making of the nation, and, above all, the appeal to the young men of the institution that had been presided over by "the foremost soldier, the knightliest gentleman, the noblest man of his race," to guard the memory and maintain the prestige of the civilization of which he was the consummate flower, had something of the effect of "Dixie" when one has not heard it for a long time.

With this address in my mind and with hero-worship strong in my heart, I awaited with breathless interest the author's appearance in Nashville during my early student days at Vanderbilt University. He had just awakened to fame with the publication of "In Ole Virginia." Before an audience of a thousand people he read selections from "Marse Chan," "Meh Lady," and "Unc' Edinburg's Drowndin'." To many in his audience his success was the fulfillment of a long dream, and the vindication in art of a misunderstood people.

Even more memorable in the minds of all who heard it was an address delivered by Walter H. Page at

Birmingham before the Southern Educational Conference in 1904, on "The Unfulfilled Ambition of the
South." He was as enthusiastic as Thomas Nelson
Page in recalling "the large-minded period when
Southern men built the spacious house of our liberty,"
but he raised the question as to why this leadership
had passed away. Every true Southerner would, he
believed, give his work, if he knew how—he would
give his life, if need be—to restore the thought, the
character, and the influence of the South to the commanding position that it had held a hundred years
ago. As men, Southerners could face facts as bravely
as they had faced misfortune, and they are not afraid
of any truth. The loss of leadership was due to two
facts—untrained men and a lack of freedom of
thought and of expression. Training is the thing
that has made the world a new world, that has vindi-
cated democracy, that has opened the door of opportunity for Americans. A comparison of Iowa and
North Carolina—two states of equal area and population—served to illustrate the difference between
trained and untrained labour, between scientific and
unscientific farming. Public opinion in the South was
not "the thought of educated men but the blind push
of untrained men." If the South would develop its
manhood resources, and if public opinion could be
directed in right channels, too much could not be
prophesied as to its future. If it would make its struggle for larger economic resources and for education
and culture, America would then turn to it for leadership. A democracy in its days of trial calls its leaders
from those who struggle last. "When we win this

battle here—over ourselves and over inherited error
—the nation will have need of us."

In these two men, then, we have two supplementary
points of view—one the best representative of what
may be called the Old South, and the other of the New
South. Because I may take for granted a knowledge
of all that is suggested in the former's writings, I prefer to emphasize the latter as a fearless critic and a
real prophet.

It was no mere accident that Walter Hines Page
died in North Carolina and that he was buried at
Aberdeen. No doubt his desire to spend his last days
in the section which he always affectionately referred
to as "the old land" sustained him during his prostra-
tion from overwhelming responsibilities in London and
in his suffering on the high seas. The simple funeral
services held at his grave were a fitting end to his busy,
crowded, and, one may say, romantic life. There
were gathered his partners in business and the representatives of a great magazine, which had made a new
era in periodical literature; and with them his fellow
workers on the national boards which had contributed
so much to Southern development. From London
and Paris came messages to the bereaved family, testi-
fying to the formative work he had done in cementing
the ties that linked the two branches of the English-
speaking people and in the victory of the Allied forces.

But these tributes to his memory could not obscure
the thought in the minds of some that he was one of
the great Southerners of his generation, and that no
man had helped—positively helped—so many individuals, institutions, organizations, and movements that

had as their primary aim the rebuilding of old commonwealths. If, as he once said, he had not literally carried with him wherever he went a pot of his native earth, he had carried with him always what the pot of earth stood for. With him the love of the state and of the section was not a mere sentiment, but, as will appear, an abiding interest that led to words and deeds of far-reaching significance. What he wrote about his friend and fellow worker, Dr. Charles D. McIver, applies to himself:

> But when death startles us and cuts a career short and we must measure the dead man once for all, we find ourselves asking first of all the one question, how true and helpful he was to his friends, to his community, and to human kind; for that is the highest test after all.

At the time when one might well emphasize Mr. Page's Americanism and his cosmopolitanism and when his letters, as edited by Mr. Hendrick, have been recognized as a remarkable contribution to literature, it may seem strange, and indeed provincial, even to suggest the Southern qualities of his character and the work which he did for this section. But it is a striking fact that all of his collected writings relate to the South; and it may be confidently claimed that, however much his alert and receptive mind may have assimilated from his early experiences in the West, or from his life in New England, or from his larger outlook on the international affairs of his time, he had certain qualities that are distinctively Southern. No one ever knew him who was not impressed with his cordiality, his enthusiasm, and his persistent and continuous interest in Southern development. If to be a Southerner is to be sectional in one's feelings, provincial in one's judgments, sentimental in one's attitude to Southern history; if it is to accept blindly all the traditional views of the ante-bellum South, the Civil War, the Negro, and education, then Mr. Page was not a Southerner. But if to be a Southerner is to be born and reared in the South, to possess certain personal qualities characteristic of Southern people, to be a vital leader in every progressive movement in the South, and all the while to have as the object nearest his heart to serve the land of his forbears and contemporaries, then he was a Southerner. By his addresses in all the large centres and colleges of the South, by his constant endeavour to use his publishing house and magazine as media for the revelation and interpretation of the Southern people to themselves and to the nation, by his own writings, and most of all, perhaps, by his friendly and stimulating counsel to individuals and to at least three great national boards—by all these means he established himself in the minds of all thoughtful people as a friend of the South.

What he said and did the younger generation in the South should not willingly let die. Nor should they overlook the fact that much of what he said and did met with criticism that was unjust and misunderstanding that was frequently passionate. I do not allude to these criticisms with any desire to call up unpleasant memories—certainly they can affect him no longer, if, indeed, they ever did. It is well, however, for those who remain to realize just what such a man encountered, and what any other man who does the same sort of work must encounter. From the time that he wrote his "Mummy" articles in the Raleigh *State Chronicle*—surely they will be resurrected sometime —to almost the end of his life, he was the object of the severest criticism. It was no uncommon thing for newspapers and public speakers to refer to him as a traitor to the South, as one who held up to scorn before the eyes of the nation certain traditions and ideas.

This criticism reached its height at the time of the publication of the "Autobiography of a Southerner," which, although published anonymously, was soon rightly accredited to him. Of that book I shall have something to say later, for it cannot be rightly judged except by a consideration of other points involved in his life and writings. Certain garbled quotations and a failure to adopt even the most elementary principles of literary interpretation did the author a grave injustice. Especially is this true of the vigorous attack in a certain magazine that for many years made capital of the prejudices of Southern readers. The article might have died in the pages of this little-read magazine had it not been taken up by many Southern newspapers and aired in the halls of Congress by Southern politicians. The effect was to produce a very widespread prejudice against Mr. Page in the minds of many Southerners who never knew him personally or never read that book or any other book he ever wrote.

It may be admitted that Mr. Page often spoke frankly, and even bluntly, of the defects of the Southern people. He took for granted certain things that traditional Southerners were always emphasizing, and he did not like to carry coals to Newcastle. He punc-

tured with ridicule and sarcasm some of the sophistries
that had long been the stock in trade of demagogues
and sentimentalists.   He often referred to the three
ghosts that haunted the imagination of the South—
the Confederacy, the fear of Negro domination, and
religious orthodoxy.   He said some things in a way
that some of his admirers would not have said them.
But it should be said in all fairness that he attacked
evils in the nation with the same straightforward honesty—for instance, no man ever attacked more per-
sistently and with more overwhelming evidence the
abuses of the pension system.   Furthermore, at the
very time when he was criticizing the South, he was
always suggesting something constructive or, better
still, doing something that had for its aim the development of his people.   He was so patient that he ignored
his critics.

I know of no better illustration of the injustice of
such criticism than the furore which followed his address on "The Forgotten Man" at the Normal and
Industrial College in Greensboro, North Carolina, in
1897.   As one now reads the entire address—so cor-
dial, so suggestive, so constructive—one wonders at
the storm of abuse that broke about his head.   It was
a frank appeal "to accept our own conditions without
illusions, to face our own problems like men, and,
when necessary, with all respect for the past, to lift
dead men's hands from our life."   It is a striking fact
that, despite the criticism of newspapers and publicists
and preachers, North Carolina, for the past twenty-
five years, has been doing the very things pointed out
by him in that address, and that many of its sentences
and phrases have become the slogans of forward-

looking men. Who does not say now that the greatest undeveloped resource in any state is the untrained masses of the people, that a democratic society must be based upon such training, and that "a public-school system generously supported by public sentiment, and generously maintained by both state and local taxation, is the only effective means to develop the forgotten man, and even more surely the only means to develop the forgotten woman"?

One might in the same way consider other addresses and writings of Mr. Page and find that the constructive, the hopeful, the statesmanlike element always outweighs what might be considered incidental, destructive points. I have thought that a more limited study in a more limited field might better set forth the spirit of the man and suggest many ideas and plans that were characteristic of his mind and heart. I was fortunate enough to receive from him during a period of ten years approximately one hundred letters, extracts from which will serve the purpose I have indicated. I have no doubt that others have even more noteworthy letters. He was a prolific letter-writer, undoubtedly one of the best of our time. In his very busy life he found time to write to a wide circle of friends and acquaintances. At a time when the stenographer is said to have destroyed the art of letter writing, he brought to his correspondence the vitality, the charm, and, I believe, the enduring literary quality of the masters of the craft. Necessarily, many of the personal features of his letters cannot be revealed, but I believe the selections herewith given suggest some of the essential points in the story of his life, which, when all his letters have been collected by members of his family, will be one of the interesting human documents of this age.[1]

My correspondence with Mr. Page began as the result of an article which I wrote in 1902, entitled "Some Notable Utterances of Southern Men," in the course of which I referred to a recently published editorial in the *World's Work* as "an attack on the South." He had said, among other things, that the South suffered from preachers who were "herding women and children by the stagnant pools of theology." While not agreeing with Mr. Page in his general indictment, I suggested that it would be well to consider if there was any truth in what he had said, rather than to dismiss it entirely. He rather resented my expression, "attack on the South," and then revealed to me a side of his nature which I came more and more to learn was characteristic of the man. He dismissed the matter in these words: "Now, never give the matter another thought, I pray you. Let's turn to bigger tasks and nobler aims. They can't get us into a silly personal controversy—not on your life! We've too much to do."

The editor of a leading church paper in North Carolina continued the attack on Mr. Page in a most virulent fashion. When some of his friends called attention to these editorials, Mr. Page wrote me:

I have had several letters about an "excoriation" (Great Heavens! what a word!) that somebody in North Carolina has been giving me. I never read these things and don't know what it's all

---

[1] I take some pride in the fact that my prophecy has been more than fulfilled in the publication of his "Life and Letters," by Mr. Burton J. Hendrick. Necessarily in those volumes emphasis was placed on the war period rather than on his formative work in the South.

about—nor do I care. But perhaps you'll be interested in a letter that I wrote an old friend (a lady) who is concerned about it. I enclose a copy of it. I shall never notice any "Excoriator." But if you wish to add to the gaiety of nations, give this copy to some newspaper and let it loose in the state—if you care to do so. We must have patience with these puny and peevish brethren. They've been trained to a false view of life. Heaven knows I bear them no ill-will.

I have forgotten just what this letter was that I gave to the Charlotte *Observer,* but it was a good-natured declination to enter into a controversy when there were so many more interesting things to do, and especially when so many more interesting things were happening in North Carolina. The purport of the letter is expressed in another of May 15, 1904:

What the South has got a chance to do is to lead. There's no use stopping short of that. The effect of the croakers and the critics and all kinds of narrow men, has been to make us forget that we once had leadership. They keep us for ever in the low lands of complaint. Let's keep sounding the note of leadership and the next generation will hear it and take it up and *do* it, praise God!

Because he was always interested in speaking to such potential leaders whenever his business life allowed him an interval of leisure, he accepted an invitation to deliver the principal address at the meeting of the North Carolina Teachers' Assembly in 1902. In anticipation he wrote:

I cannot tell you with what pleasure I shall go to Wrightsville. I shall be glad of the chance to meet so many teachers. They carry the Ark of the Covenant in North Carolina. . . . I had rather go to this meeting than to any other that has been held in

North Carolina in my memory. Just when the educational awakening is at its height I should like to try to picture what it means
to the state—just how the school teachers may make it a new
Commonwealth—keeping all the good qualities to build on. I
see such a revolution in this matter as I think few communities
have ever experienced, and such a rapid advance of the whole
people as could take place nowhere else.

Unfortunately, an important business engagement
at the last minute prevented his going, but the following year he went to a meeting of the Assembly at
Greensboro. The general spirit of the address was
that of his most frequently quoted creed:

I believe in the free public training of both the hands and the
mind of every child born of woman.
I believe that by the right training of men we add to the wealth
of the world.
I believe in the perpetual regeneration of society, in the immor-
tality of democracy and in growth everlasting.

And he closed with these inspiring words:

We who have seen this truth have been changed by it, and we
can never fall away from it. We have an inexhaustible supply of
energy and a boundless hope. We work with joy for the love of
our fellows and for our faith in them. We cannot rest upon the
glory of democracy as it has been revealed to us, for we are caught
in the swing of its orbic movement. And we cannot recant even
at the bidding of all the solemn plausibilities of the world.

For this address he was severely criticized in a leading editorial in the most widely read newspaper of the
state. Another very important issue in which he and
the editor held entirely different points of view was the
attempt to remove Professor Bassett from his chair
at Trinity College, because of certain utterances he

had made in the *South Atlantic Quarterly*. It is all ancient history now, but in 1903 it was a very lively fact that threatened the welfare, not only of an individual, but of an institution.[1] Mr. Page followed with keen interest the progress of the state-wide agitation. It was to him a fight for freedom of speech against what he once characterized as "the unyielding stability of opinion which gives a feeling of despair, the very antithesis of social growth and of social mobility." He had nothing to say about it in public, but two letters will indicate his great concern about the matter.

Writing about one of the trustees he said:

> You may count on —— to the last ditch in a contest like this —to the very last ditch. Don't have any fear about that for one moment, now or hereafter, in this fight for manhood or for any other like it. And he isn't afraid of anybody, nor of anybody's newspapers, nor of any party, nor clique, nor church, nor any kind of organized howl whatever. Depend on that.

Just before the meeting of the Trustees he wrote to me as follows:

> I envy every one of you this chance. It isn't once in a lifetime that this issue is so clearly drawn—the supreme issue of free speech: the very bottom thing in a democracy. The Negro question is one thing, and in comparison with free speech a very little thing. If this fight is won and the college should be closed on account of it, it would be the most important event in the history of North Carolina in our time; for free speech and free teaching will be won for all time to come there.
>
> But, of course, no bad results will follow—not even bad tem-

---

[1] For a full account of this struggle for academic freedom see Chapter V.

porary results. A few people may cry "Republican" or "Nigger" or "Tobacco Trust"—no matter what they cry, the whole academic world will know that there is one home of free men in the South. It will be a great and permanent victory for every one of you; and I congratulate you.

It's a fine fight. It'll be a fine victory for every one of you.

When the trustees by a decisive majority sustained the principle of academic freedom, Mr. Page published in the ensuing number of the *World's Work*, as the leading article, a story of the whole fight and an interpretation of the issues at stake. It was characteristic of the man that he should get from the inside the facts involved and that he should then with enthusiasm put them before the readers of his magazine. He wanted the Northern public to know this good thing that had happened in the South. All of which shows the truth of what Mr. Page once said to me: "Southern public opinion is like a ghost; if you confront it bravely, it will vanish into thin air. That is, if you will give it a little time."

The manner in which Mr. Page played up the Bassett affair in the *World's Work* was typical of his constant efforts to promote the knowledge of the South in the nation at large. In 1907, he wrote:

I have just read the notice in the *South Atlantic Quarterly* of Rowland's "Encyclopedia of Mississippi History" and it occurs to me to ask, if this plan is as good as the *Quarterly* says it is, would it not be possible to make a profitable enterprise of this same plan adapted to Southern history in general. The history of the Southern States has, as you know, been hopelessly neglected.

Suppose material could be got together and an encyclopedia like this made, how big should it be to be fairly complete? Do you think there would be a general sale for it? You see I am always feeling my way toward the utilization of this vast unused material and I wish to make this publishing machinery which centres here *do all the good it possibly can in my lifetime for the old country.*

A little later he wrote more fully of more ambitious projects. There is no statement that could better express his constant desire to bring out material from Southern writers than this:

May I tell you of one hope and ambition that I set great value on, and I shall be very happy if during the coming year I can in some appreciable way further it. I wish to get reduced to some specific shape, if it be possible and if the time be ripe, both magazine matter and books—especially books—which shall be written with such fervour and at such an angle to life as will hasten the broadening of Southern development. While we carry on our trade of putting forth periodical and book literature, of course, I am not content simply to publish books and magazines with this, that, and the other routine thing in them, however good this routine may be; for I regard all this machinery simply as so many tools to be used for furthering great purposes. Of course, one of the very great purposes that men of our time can have is just this —the broadening of Southern development, and I wish I knew enough and could find out enough to reduce this large purpose to some good concrete terms during the coming year.

Can't you help me? If you can think of any treatment of Southern subjects, especially of any subjects for books and effective writers that would give the old land a lift, won't you let me know?

One of his hobbies was that colleges ought to develop writers. When I went to the University of North Carolina in 1909, he wrote me a most enthusiastic letter just before he landed in England. It is an exaggeration, to be sure, and I am not sure that I altogether agree with him, but it is so characteristic of the man that I give it in full:

The state-maintained institution is *the* institution of our democracy and it will grow more and more as the prime servant of the people. Strength to your elbow and success to you in all your plans!

I firmly believe that you could grow a crop of effective writers, start a new, great educational movement, give literary studies a new meaning and a new vitality and put the University at the head of a quickly-widening movement in all this work by working out concretely this fundamental truth: *The way to teach literature is to teach men to write and to talk right*—in a word, not by reading but by practice.

That's the way we teach surgery, engineering, law, farming (Knapp), the mechanical trades. It's the way we teach everything that we really do teach. Latin and Greek and literature, we don't *really* teach by the prevalent method.

You could in five years have every university in the land following you, and "The N. C. Method" of teaching (and of making) literature could become as familiar to the next generation as "Tar, Pitch, and Turpentine" were to the last.

That teaching is a failure which makes it possible for a man to get a degree in English who cannot write an idiomatic speech or speak effectively in the idioms of the people—with dramatic effect and proportion. Simply knowing something in books—that isn't the effective thing.

Most of the men who are teaching English now don't even know this obvious fact. You have a great opportunity. You can work a revolution, if you are free, as I assume you are.

I've been reading by an electric lamp on my pillow these nights since I sailed from New York a book called "The Pilgrim's Progress." What a delight old Bunyan's idioms are! It is language with a spinal cord, with strong muscles. It can grasp, hit, hold. Contrast the "literary" language of our time with it!

You have a virgin field and a boundless opportunity. You have just the right material to work on—boys without "literary" traditions or enervating ideas. They are themselves the idioms of our population.

But Mr. Page did not depend on others to write for him about the South. As editor of the *World's Work* for more than ten years, he published editorials and articles by himself and by others setting forth the rising tide of Southern prosperity. In June, 1907, he published a special Southern number, some two hundred thousand copies of which were distributed in all parts of the country. It is safe to say that no such varied and comprehensive statement has ever been made of the intellectual, social, and industrial progress of the Southern States. The articles written by representative Southerners cover the whole field. The editor himself spent two months and a half visiting every section of the South and gave his impressions in words of generous praise that made the coldest heart thrill with emotion. Surely no enemy of the South could have written the chapter entitled "A Journey through the Southern States," or such an editorial as the introductory "The Arisen South," the first sentence of which was: "The present industrial awakening in the Southern States is the most important economic event in our history since the settlement of the West." The most enthusiastic Southerner could not say more than this:

There is nothing in our contemporaneous life more interesting or more important than this rise of the people in these states, eager to the task of their own development and of the development of this richest region of the Union. This work has now been begun with such vigour that it will go on indefinitely; for natural forces have come into play and the land of "problems" has become a land of progress.

And again:

For the most important change that is taking place is not the development of the wealth—great as that is—but the development of the people, who until now have been isolated, sidetracked, held back, kept out of the highways of life.

The number closes with advice to young men of the country to "go South," for there they will find "a land of old-time courtesy as well as of a newly awakened activity."

This special number of the *World's Work* was not an exception to the editor's policy of proclaiming to the world every new phase of Southern progress. Now it is the state of Louisiana putting forth special efforts in sanitation; now the state of Georgia carrying on in a notable way demonstration farm work; now the state of South Carolina, through its efficient supervisor of rural schools, bringing about a revolution in country life; now the Piedmont section of North Carolina quickened into new life by the development of its water powers. For November, 1911, at least four articles tell stories of Southern advancement.

In the spring of 1911, I received a long letter from him outlining a series of articles on the South, and asking me to write them. It began with his reasons for publishing such a series at that time:

Every year of our lives the new era in the South was just about to begin; but in fact it has only just now begun. With 15- to 18-cent cotton, with profitable manufactures, with the broadening influence of trade, with the results of modern education, the old land is just coming to its own. The next ten years will see such a development as was never seen elsewhere in the world except when the West was settled.

Now this gives—on this fiftieth year since the Civil War—a real chance to write a short series of magazine articles that shall worthily set forth so great a fact—articles that shall have an historical, and one might even hope, a literary value—a general survey and interpretation.

He outlined the nature and difficulty of the task in words that are the key to his own success as a magazine writer and editor:

You'd have to take some typical communities and study them thoroughly; some typical industries and do the same thing; some typical men and their careers; some typical institutions, too; you'd have to find definite typical opportunities and show that it is a land of opportunity.

Most difficult of all, you'd have to weld all these kinds of facts into definite, attractive, cumulative form, and do a great piece of writing, using almost wholly facts. Let *them* tell your doctrines and your conclusions. It is a sort of glorified reporting and interpretation—a real piece of (shall I say "applied"?) literature. In general, the method of writing must be rather the story-teller's than the essayist's! It is a description rather than avowed essay; incident, never argument; pictures rather than opinions.

And then he added some "don'ts" that might well be called his Four Commandments:

Use no history, except very sparingly as a background. Your readers know the history of the South already.

Do not take up the race problem as a separate subject. Do no more with it than you are obliged to do. Your readers have been bored to death with it, and most of them already know the main facts, and they have all formed their opinion.

In general, do not open up (certainly do not dwell on) any violently controversial matter. The real great facts of the South have been buried under controversy for all these fifty years. People know all the old controversies, and they'd like to know the facts.

Don't once mention the war, nor the old nigger mammy, nor the old civilization, nor the poor white trash. Write in the terms the vocabulary of the world of to-day, not of the historical or legendary world. This is necessary to give a new edge to an old subject, and to avoid going over old ground.

I did not at first see that I could write such articles, but his confidence caused me to accept the commission. For two months I travelled through the Southern States enjoying the most interesting human experience I have ever had. Not many days passed without my receiving letters from him that opened up to me new doors of opportunity. His joy over some of my "finds" was like a boy's. The first three articles in the series, which we decided to call "The South Realizing Itself," passed muster and were received by him with increasing satisfaction and hearty praise.

But the fourth, which was to be an article on Southern educational progress, never was published—and for reasons that appear in the following letter. He had finally to admit that the thing could not be done in the way he had imagined. The things that might give colour and *verve* could not at that time—nor now—be told. Perhaps, also, Page was apt to emphasize more than I the industrial aspects of education. At any rate, he magnanimously took away the sting of regret that the series was never completed, in such words as these:

This is the hardest subject that not only you have tackled but that any one can tackle. The moment that you use the word "education" the lay reader puts on rubber heels and runs as if the devil himself were after him. You have got to catch his attention by talking about training. He is interested in training horses or vines or men, but the educational world in its professional talk has been so deadly dull the past twenty years that it has slain a large part of the interest in the subject with the jaw bones of many asses. You must therefore steal a march on the fellow that we are stalking.

You are engaged in the most difficult business known to man, except the writing of immortal verse. Taken altogether you had less trouble with your first three articles than anybody has had in my memory and you are now going through only the normal experience.

I often wondered that he did not feel more keenly the lack of response on the part of Southern people to all his efforts to reveal the South. "How many subscribers to the *World's Work* did you get as the result of the special Southern number?" I once asked him. He only smiled, but later wrote me the following letter, which expresses well the lack of intellectual curiosity and of the reading habit in this section of the country:

It is unfortunate, but it is true, that an infinitesimal part of the population of our Southern States, for the last hundred years at least, has had any intellectual curiosity. If you had the names of all the men you know in North Carolina written down in a book, and you were to go over them one by one, I think you would be astonished to see how few have ever shown this quality. They are content with the knowledge that they have. I don't know whether this is a psychological result of the dogmatism that followed the slavery controversy or whether it is a result of rural life and isolation—or more likely it is the result of physical causes such as hookworm and malaria. But whatever it is the result of, the one thing that differentiates the mass of Southern men from the mass of Massachusetts men, say, is this lack of intellectual curiosity.

Therefore the Southern people don't buy magazines or books— I say "people," mind you. Of course, the few leading minds do. I am therefore not at all surprised that we get no appreciable direct results. I have tried this sort of thing too often to expect much. We published a book on cotton, which is far and away the best book published on the subject. We have tried many plans, and with great persistence, to sell it down South; but the men who grow cotton know more about cotton than the man who wrote the book! In other words, they have no intellectual curiosity.

We have had an awfully hard time making that book pay the printer's bill.

There is no reason for discouragement. I have more and more hope, the older I grow, with the clearing up of the country so that malaria will be banished, and with sanitary improvements and changes in the habits of the people, which will eradicate the hookworm and other debilitating parasites. I expect our people to show at last (I mean a considerable mass of the people) the same intellectual curiosity that a certain number of people show in England and in New England and in our Western States. In other words, the grandchildren or the great-grandchildren of the men that you are now teaching will develop this quality, provided in the meantime the women that they marry are also properly taught. But for this generation, or the next, don't fool yourself. A few people among them read a few books. That is the most you can hope for. Suppose you had an accurate enumeration of all the white people who reached, I will say, the age of thirty or more in North Carolina during the last hundred years, and then a list of the books that had been actually read in the borders of the state, what fraction of a book per person do you suppose it would figure out?

It is a great deal better now than it ever was before. A man here and there will take fire, just as one of your students will take fire here and there permanently. Look back at the students you have had in your classes seven or eight years ago. How many of them do you suppose have read two books of intellectual value since the first of last January?

And a little later he wrote:

I've had a feeling that perhaps I oughtn't to have written to you about the comically slow and prevaricative methods of our easy-speaking, ready-promising Southern public: it may discourage you or perhaps even leave on your mind the feeling that *I* am discouraged—let me correct that. I'm pleased—pleased to death. Much of my life has been given to work that I meant to help the old land and the people thereof, and the rest of it shall be given in the same way. But as for any visible, concrete appreciation or reward—Lord, no, no—no! I've long ages ago got past expecting that—or even caring for it.

It's the same old thing—100 years behind in intellectual curiosity and the oratorical habit of speech which means lying (most
comically) about Religion, Women, and Reading. Funny—very
funny. It reminds me of a rich man in Charlotte who deducted
something from Miss ——'s school-bill for his little girl because
she was absent two days with a cold! The whole bill was only
three dollars. But you don't have to pay for wood or potatoes
you don't get, why the devil should you pay for schoolin' you don't
get!

You don't have to pay for a magazine to talk about an article:
you have read a piece about it in the paper. Why read any more,
then? Reading comes hard to many men that you know: don't
you know it does?

But fifty years hence you fellows will have educated *all* the
people: that's the trick. Only one in a hundred is really educated
to the point of really waking or reading anything. This is proved
by the fact that not a subscriber has come from the town that you
set all the nation to talking about. But it'll all come and it's all
right. I was never so cheerful.

This clear-sighted analysis of one defect in the
Southern people, and yet the hopefulness in the final
outcome, are characteristic of all of Mr. Page's writings. Industry and education, he believed, would
bring about a new order. Time alone would bring
results; in the meantime, patience and unceasing, un-
tiring effort. That is the keynote of his "Rebuilding
of Old Commonwealths." Space does not allow either
a summary or an interpretation of this suggestive little
volume with its three chapters, "The Forgotten Man,"
"The School That Built a Town," and "The Rebuilding of Old Commonwealths." Nearly every page of
it is quotable, and it will more and more be recognized
as the clearest, most illuminating, and most convincing
statement that has yet been made of the principles
which are now guiding all forward-looking Southern

men.   It ought to be read and reread by every Southern man who would understand the significant forces
that are now making a new order of society.   It ought
to be required that every Southern teacher, before receiving his license, should pass an examination upon it.
To be sure, the whole truth about the South is not in
this volume—and the author would have been the first
to say so.   But he who would see the South steadily
and see it whole should supplement other books with
this penetrating and vigorous volume.

Many would agree with what has been said up to
this point but would be ready to ask, "What about the
'Autobiography of a Southerner'?"   To one who
knows the facts, it would be absurd to say that the life
of Nicholas Worth is the life of Mr. Page in all its
details.   It is manifestly unfair to treat any work of
fiction as the autobiography of the author.   It is not
even fair to say that all the opinions expressed in the
book are those of the author.   Some of the critics
seem to lack entirely the sense of humour.   There are
some things in the book that I, for one, wish he had not
written: there is a confusion of periods of history;
there is a lack of balance and discrimination in some of
the characters; there is a failure to recognize the good
of some things that may be, and often are, abused.
But when all this is said, it remains true that many of
the indictments of Southern types and ideals are true.
The manifestly unfair treatment of the novel, however, is that no attention whatever is given by critics to
the constructive forces that are constantly emphasized
throughout the story—the industrial leaders and the
educational reformers who were laying the basis for
the work in which every Southern state is now en-

gaged. The character of Professor Billy—known by all North Carolinians as Doctor McIver—is one that might well distinguish any book. His humour, his epigrams, his common sense, and his enthusiasm for education are portrayed in a masterful way. The conclusion of the story, in which Nicholas Worth and his sons decide that they will live in the South and give themselves to its development, is thoroughly characteristic of the author and is an anticipation of the close of his own life and of the return of at least one of his sons to the old land.

Page's services to his native section have been even more direct and more practical than the writings I have referred to. By reason of his wide acquaintance with Southern leaders and of the confidence in his judgment by Northern philanthropists, he played a leading rôle in the educational development of the Southern States. He did much to direct into proper channels large sums of money, heretofore given indiscriminately and frequently unwisely. Many Southern college presidents, superintendents of public instruction, and practical reformers of country schools would testify to his friendly coöperation and support. As a member of the Southern Education Board and the General Education Board, he attended, not only their meetings, but the larger meetings that were fostered at various Southern points. He was one of the first to see the significance of the fight against the hookworm, and threw himself with characteristic zeal into the work of the Rockefeller Commission, later known as the International Health Board. More significant still was his aggressive and persistent support of the Coöperative Farm Demonstration Work inaugurated by the late Dr. Seaman A. Knapp, under the supervision of the United States Department of Agriculture. He was probably Doctor Knapp's most intimate friend, and it was eminently appropriate that he should have pronounced the eulogy at the funeral of the man who, in his judgment, had done more than any man of his generation to promote the welfare of the South.

Somehow, I always think of him as saying, in connection with all these efforts to improve conditions in the South, what he said at the conclusion of the address at Birmingham already referred to. His words ring with the challenge of a great task, and they show how he always identified himself in thought and in feeling with the Southern people:

Those that sit in soft places and discuss academic propositions (and mistake self-indulgence and criticism for the intellectual life) are welcome to their ease. We would not swap birthrights with them. If we have a rough task, it is a high task. While we are doing it, we shall have the joy of constructive activity. We look forward to a golden age that we may surely help to bring, not back to one that never was.

CHAPTER III

BROOMSEDGE AND LIFE EVERLASTING

MISS GLASGOW'S recently published "Barren Ground" may be considered as an allegory of the South rising from its own barren ground to fruitfulness and beauty. The background of the novel is a backward county of Virginia, where live the "poor whites" and the decadent middle class of the old Scotch-Irish population. With a realistic vividness that reminds one of the old Dutch painters or the Russian novelists, the author sketches the father and mother of Dorinda and their neighbours as they struggle with, or rather submit to, the deteriorating soil and the dull monotony of life. The mother, who has a sort of religious mania of suppressed emotions, succumbs to the animal existence of her husband, who had never known anything but the toil, unavailing toil, of a tenant farmer, and who could neither read nor write; he seemed a member of some affectionate but inarticulate animal kingdom. Their daughter, Dorinda, after a romantic love affair that ends in disillusionment, desertion, sickness, and poverty which would have conquered anybody less resolute, flees to New York City.

After living there a few months, she feels a sudden tenderness for the old soil and the old scenes;

"earlier and deeper associations, rooted there in the earth, drew her across time and space and forgetfulness." She studies scientific farming and unites with her knowledge industry, initiative, vision. She has finished with love, she has abandoned romance, but she finds another kind of love and a new romance. "Armoured with reason," she is ready to meet life on its own terms. She has the audacity and the spirit of adventure to build and restore. She adds acre after acre to her farm, and then another farm. She redeems them from the sassafras and the broomsedge and fills them with growing crops and beautiful cattle. The success that she has, symbolized in the endurance of the pine and the charm of life everlasting, is not the main thing; rather that she is turning the barren ground of her own life into something rich and strange. She has abundant vitality, creative energy, and integrity of vision—the same qualities that had enabled her pioneer ancestors to triumph over difficulties. At the end she finds, if not happiness, blessedness, if not romance, reality that may lead to a deeper romance. She misses the happiness for which she had once longed, but the serenity of mind which is above the conflict of frustrated desires is hers.

Nearly fifty years before Miss Glasgow's novel appeared, Sidney Lanier wrote to his brother, Clifford Lanier:

I cannot contemplate with any patience your stay in the South. In my soberest moments I can perceive no outlook for that land. . . . It really seems as if any prosperity at the South must come long after your time and mine. Our people have failed to perceive the deeper movements under-running the times; they lie wholly off, out of the stream of thought, and whirl their poor dead leaves of recollection round and round, in a piteous eddy that has all the wear and tear of motion without any of the rewards of progress. By the best information I can get, the country is substantially poorer now than when the war closed, and Southern securities have become simply a catchword. . . . Whatever is to be done, you and I can do our part of it far better here than there. Come away.

The very next year, however, he wrote his essay on the "New South," showing a far more hopeful view. Since the writing of "Corn" and earlier dialect poems, he had frequently commented on the future of the South as to be determined largely by an improved agricultural system. To him the best foundation of the enduring character of the new civilization was a democracy, growing out of a vital revolution in the farming economy of the South. "The great rise of the small farmer in the Southern States during the last twenty years," he says, "becomes the notable circumstance of the period, in comparison with which noisier events signify nothing." The hero of the essay is a small farmer "who commenced work after the war with his own hands, not a dollar in his pocket, and now owns his plantation, has it well stocked, no mortgage or debt of any kind on it, and a little money to lend." Lanier clips from newspaper files passages indicating the constantly increasing number of such farmers and a growing diversity of crops. The reader is carried into the country fairs and along the roads and through plantations by a man who had a realistic sense of what was going on in the whole state of Georgia.

Lanier saw that out of this growth in small farming —this agricultural prosperity—would come changes of profound significance. He saw an intimate relation between politics, social life, morality, and art, on the one hand, and the bread-giver earth on the other:

One has only to remember that, particularly here in America, whatever crop we hope to reap in the future—whether it be a crop of poems, of paintings, of symphonies, of constitutional safeguards, of virtuous behaviours, of religious exaltations—we have got to bring it out of the ground with palpable ploughs and with plain farmer's forethought: in order to see that a vital revolution in the farming economy of the South, if it is actually occurring, is necessarily carrying with it all future Southern politics and Southern social relations and Southern art, and that, therefore, such an agricultural change is the one substantial fact upon which any really new South can be predicated.

He had a vision of

the village library, the neighbourhood farmers' club, the amateur Thespian Society, the improvement of the public schools, the village orchestra, all manner of betterments and gentilities and openings out into the universe.

The best agricultural colleges, in their regular instruction and in their extension work, have had much to do with the realization of these visions of Miss Glasgow and Lanier. One illustration will suffice. In Madison County, Virginia, Captain R. S. Walker, the descendant of a long line of gentlemen planters, bought in 1873 the estate of Woodberry Forest, formerly owned by the brother of President Madison.[1] For a while after the war, Captain Walker—one of Mosby's men, distinguished for his bravery in many battles—found it difficult to curb his restless spirit; he would ride through the country as of old, taking venturesome chances with the Federal army still encamped in the region; he endeavoured to work off his

[1]Portions of this chapter appeared in the *World's Work*, November, 1911.

surplus energy by fox chases; he went to Louisville, Kentucky, in obedience to the call of the West, then so compelling to young Southerners. He finally settled upon the Woodberry Forest estate to find a natural outlet for his powers between plough handles and in the management of his farm. One of his sons, Frank, showed a strong disinclination for academic work. From his childhood he had been interested in farming. So the father, instead of giving him a classical education at the University of Virginia, as he gave his other sons, decided that this boy should go to the Virginia Polytechnic Institute. The son objected because it took him away from the farm. As soon as he went to Blacksburg, however, he found that the very subjects which he wished to study were taught there. Besides the regular course in agriculture necessary for his degree, he took extra work in horticulture, veterinary science, and dairying. The days were all too short for him; often, in the afternoons, when others were engaged in athletic sports, he was learning how to graft and spray orchard trees, or making inquiries about the live stock in the college herds. So successful was he in his studies that his professors urged him to become a teacher of agriculture; his fellow students invited him into their ventures in orchards, which were then just becoming extremely profitable in Virginia. But he returned to his father's farm, satisfied now that the education he had received was worth more to him than the bequest of a large plantation.

He took charge of the old farm and bought out the interest of his brothers in their grandfather's farm near by, which had for several years been in the hands of careless renters. On these two farms of more than

a thousand acres he has applied the lessons of his college days—always with the hearty coöperation of his
father, whose long experience in practical farming has
been of invaluable service. He saw at once that he
needed lime to build up the farm; his knowledge of
fertilizers and of their relation to the soil enabled him
to mix his own and thus reduce the costs; he redeemed
the galls and gulleys by sowing legumes and by the
rotation of crops. In one year he raised four thousand bushels of wheat, six thousand bushels of corn,
and three to four hundred tons of alfalfa, clover, and
pea hay. Best of all, however, he has established
a well-equipped live-stock farm, with registered Hol-
steins and Guernseys to supply cream for the markets
of Washington and Richmond, and a herd of fine hogs,
beef cattle, and horses. The farm has become a sort
of unofficial demonstration farm for his neighbours;
at the same time, his maternal uncle, who has a large
orchard at Somerset, profits by his nephew's knowledge of horticulture.

One of his classically trained brothers once said to
him that he would never amount to anything if he
didn't stop following a cow's tail. And yet that
brother, who, with the coöperation of his father and
other brothers, has established on the old place what
many consider the best preparatory school in Virginia,
now reaps the benefit of the income from dairy and
farm, which goes to the equipment and efficiency of
the school. The one hundred and fifty boys who come
there from all sections of the country are provided
with more wholesome milk, vegetables, and meats than
schoolboys generally have. This story, then, is an
illustration of the way in which farming may become

more and more economically profitable and spiritually significant. The neighbouring estate of President Madison has passed into the hands of rich Philadelphians, who have let the land go down while they have remodelled the ancient house in accordance with modern notions of comfort and luxury. But Woodberry Forest, still preserving all that was best and most distinguished in the old régime—the house now stands amid its immemorial trees as stately as when ex-Presidents were wont to stop there on their way from Washington to Monticello—has been made over into a more and more prosperous farm. Nowhere else in the country will one find a better suggestion of what is most beautiful in the scenery and in the home life of rural England.

But the improvement of agricultural conditions in the South is much more than the work of individuals who have exceptional opportunities arising from inheritance, travel, and education. When we consider the deterioration of lands as the result of senseless methods of cultivation, the undeveloped wet lands and sandy regions, when we consider, too, the great masses of untrained and even stolid men, we realize that heroic efforts must be made to overcome inertia and indifference, economic fallacies, and stupid blunders. There must be organized effort on the part of state, nation, and community; the public spirit of masterful leaders; well-equipped institutions of learning—all of these vitally related to all the forces that are making for the improvement of agriculture.

A unique contribution both to agricultural progress and to education has been the farm demonstration work conceived and, with the coöperation of the

United States Government, the General Education Board, and the agricultural colleges, put into operation by the late Dr. Seaman A. Knapp. It is not my purpose to write in detail either of Doctor Knapp or of the system of agricultural education inaugurated by him for the instruction of adult farmers and of boys and girls; for I take it that the reading public is already familiar with both. What I should like to do is to give some idea of the order of demonstration agents now found in nearly every county of the South. One has only to talk with these state and local agents to realize that they are a body of men as noteworthy for their consecration and unselfishness as for their expert and even scientific knowledge. In their aggressiveness and enthusiasm they remind one of some of the religious orders of the Middle Ages.

As an illustration of the state agents, I cite the case of Mr. Gentry of Georgia, who was a farmer in Texas when Doctor Knapp began his demonstrations in that state. On hearing one of Doctor Knapp's lectures, he was so impressed with the personality of the man that he sought an interview; and Doctor Knapp was so impressed with him that he immediately offered him a position as agent. Although he was then making a profit of $3,000 from his farm, he immediately accepted and worked for three years in Texas. In 1907, he was transferred to Georgia, where he began work with six local agents, a number which he afterward increased to nearly a hundred. It is interesting to hear him tell of his experiences, and especially to know of the local agents whom he has secured for various counties. He has, for instance, one farmer in south Georgia who is worth $250,000—the most successful farmer in this section—and who now gives half his time to the demonstration work. "How do you get such men?" asked an agent of the International Harvester Company. "They do it in response to an appeal to their public spirit and because they love the work," answered Mr. Gentry, who has himself refused recently a position as superintendent of farms that would have doubled his salary. The reports of Mr. Gentry and his local agents to the Department of Agriculture make as interesting reading as one could demand; they will be of invaluable service to the historian of the future. Notes like the following, written as the results of observation in different sections of the South, tell the story far better than any statistics:

> One man has cotton six to nine inches high, with roots sixteen to twenty inches long, as the result of deep ploughing in winter, while his neighbours are replanting. . . . As one of the main ways to fight the boll weevil, I have secured from the State Board of Entomology a case of boll weevils and affected squares, which I am taking with me on my rounds. . . . I saw twelve purebred Berkshire sows on vetch and rye pastures. . . . Farm implements doubled in one year in one county as the result of farm tool demonstration on the farm. . . . Where they have been reading agricultural literature, they are now studying it. . . . Farmers have bought over four thousand two-horse ploughs since last fall and are buying harrows faster than men can supply them. . . . Forty cars of farm implements as against two last year were sold by one wholesale dealer as the result of demonstration talk. . . . There has been sold in one county a carload of good Western mares.

Such field notes—and they might be multiplied indefinitely—suggest the transformation of agricultural conditions. While there are literally hundreds of stories that might be told of the definite results of such teaching, I think that two letters, one from a white man and the other from a Negro, will suggest the economic profits and at the same time the new vision of life that have come to the most backward Southern farmers:

STONY, TEXAS,
Nov. 17,1910.

DR. S. A. KNAPP,
        Washington, D. C.
DEAR SIR:

I feel it is my duty, also take it as a privilege, to write to you pertaining to the demonstration work. I can't find words to express my appreciation of what the demonstration work has done for me. When last spring a year ago, Mr. Ganzer preached the gospel of better farming in Decatur, I was one of the men who signed up for the demonstration work because I was convinced that there was something in it.

I was financially involved very deeply. I was owing about $1,250. I did not have a cow or a hog of any kind. I had an old pair of mules 29 years old, and I told Mr. Ganzler that I had to do something better in the way of farming or lose my home of 125 acres, of which 90 acres are in Denton Creek bottom; so I set out to follow instructions on 10 acres each of corn and cotton. I was so pleased with results that it nearly trebled the yield of the crops cultivated the old way. Myself and family were carried away with the results. I followed this year the instructions on my whole crop. The results were overwhelming. I made a bale of cotton per acre and 50 bushels of corn per acre. I paid every dollar of my indebtedness and have $400 on deposit and about 700 bushels of corn. I bought a good span of mules worth $500, 3 cows, and have $300 worth of good hogs.

Now, dear Dr. Knapp, can you blame me when I say that I cannot find words to express my appreciation for what the demonstration work has done for me. I owe my great improved condition to you first, and to Mr. Ganzer, the demonstration agent, next. I hope that this great work you are doing will benefit other farmers as it has benefited me, and it will if they follow instructions.

In regard to the great move you made in organizing the boys' corn clubs to educate them in better farm methods, I will say that it has caused a wonderful awakening among the boys. My son, Archie, 13 years old, has raised 50 bushels of corn to the acre, and was a winner of one of the prizes of Wise County.

Now, Dr. Knapp, the above facts I am fully able to prove by either of the banks of Decatur, or by my neighbours. Myself and family certainly bless the day when the demonstration work was brought to us. I will close by saying that some day I hope to meet you, shake your hand, and thank you more fully.

I remain very respectfully,

(*Signed*) A. L. FOSTER.

I submit the letter of the Negro farmer with the firm conviction that it is vastly more significant than a conventional dialect story of the old-fashioned darkey, or than one of Mr. Cohen's stories of the new-fashioned humourist of the city: he has the good sense and the philosophy of a more famous Washington of his race, and he spells like Artemus Ward:

A.D., 7–16–10.

Sir, Mr. S. A. Knapp, I rite you a few lins in the gards of farming agricultur. I do say that your advice have Ben Folard and your direcksion have Ben o Baid an I find that i am successful in Life. Say, Mr. Knapp, I do know that there is gooder men as you an as fair as you. But o that keen eye ov yourse that watches ever crook in farming, that can tell ever man whichever was to Gro to be successful in Life. On last year I folered your advice an allso yer Before last. On 1908 i made 14 Bails of cotton and 1909, 17 Bails an startid With 1 mule an now I own 3 head ov the great worthies, an thanks to you for your advice a Long that Line an Great success in your occupation to you.

Say, Mr. Knapp, I am a culered man, Live near Graysport, Miss., Corn a plenty, allso make a plenty of Sweet potatoes, but I read your advice a Bout them.

Will close,   Yourse,

(*Signed*) WM. WASHINGTON.

Mr. Will Criss is my agent, visited twice a month.

Another story of the effect produced by Doctor Knapp and his agents is that of a young New York lawyer, who, after graduating at Harvard College and in the Harvard Law School, occupied a cubbyhole of a law office in the city. When he suddenly realized one day that he was run down and miserable, work and play alike tiresome, he induced a friend in Vermont, who had had something of the same experience and was contemplating the purchase of an orchard in the Shenandoah Valley, to go with him to see Doctor Knapp in Washington—"the only real prophet" that he had ever known—and to lay their case before him.

He greeted us [so runs his account[1]], in a spirit of fun and pleasure and help that has kept us going and singing ever since. We told him frankly and gaily that we had never farmed a straw, that Goldsmith was the only authority that we had ever read on the dairy, and that we had no money, and only an academic education—one trained in cosines and the other in legal education.

Doctor Knapp showed them what other men had done as evidenced in monthly reports of his agents, gave them his ten commandments of agriculture, and sent them to the country around Pinehurst, North Carolina.

They rode for a week through a region of sand and little streams and the remnants of a mighty forest. With the advice of the local farm demonstration agent and with the aid of a foreman, they bought a farm of 800 acres at ten dollars an acre; they built shanties, barns, a residence, and fertilizer house, bought twelve horses and mules, cleared forty acres, stumped 230

---

[1]"From a Law Office to a Cotton Farm," by Ralph W. Page, *World's Work*, November, 1911.

acres, bought a complete equipment of machinery and tools, tile-draining, a dam, a tank, and a water supply —all at a cost of $20,000. They later bought 3,000 acres of adjoining land and rented another farm. They put in cotton and corn and cantaloupes and watermelons, and later developed a peach industry in a section that now rivals the best districts in Georgia. The value of the land has increased in fifteen years enormously, and a section of the state that was like a desert with Pinehurst as an oasis for foreigners has become one of the richest in the state. Better schools and all other advantages of an improving rural community have followed.[1]

The making of money is not the point of this story. This young man came back to the land of his fathers and has found the joy of creative activity. He concludes his entrancing story, which I have here abbreviated and mutilated, with the following words:

But this I know: every morning I can spring out of bed at sunrise with a song (because I don't *have* to spring or sing—do you see?) and rejoice at the cheerful ringing of the plantation bell. And I can call Tobe to saddle my mare, Dixie, and ride as a master of the earth, down long green rows of my own, and put my hands to the new cultivator that runs like a sewing machine, and direct the building of a dam, just as though I were a real man, and was already successful. And I get my fun going to seed-corn meetings, and investigating Mr. Price's cotton picker, and in doing what I please. . . . The fact is that I have quit trying to please myself by any future Elysium; but I am now happy and independent and on the way to make all the money I need, and

[2]Aspects of the later development of this community may be found in articles by Mr. Page in the *World's Work*, December, 1914, the *Country Gentleman*, November 20, 1915; the *Red Cross Magazine*, January, 1917. cf. also Roosevelt: "The Foes of Our Own Household," Chapter IX, pp. 202-17.

I have all the time in the world to tell anybody who wishes to try such a life all I have learned about it—you or anybody else.

Such are the agencies and forces and such the individual men who are now reshaping agricultural conditions in the Southern States. But even these are not sufficient to deal adequately with the situation in its entirety. Men who have been primarily interested in the building up of cities and who therefore represent large interests of capital, are making wise and effective plans for the improvement of undeveloped land and for the introduction of desirable immigrants. There is scarcely a section of the South from the coastal regions to the Mississippi bottoms that is not now being exploited and developed. The railroads are taking a most important part in the opening up of these lands. One of the most notable conventions ever held in the South was held a few years ago at Gulfport, Mississippi, with the avowed object of providing for an extensive system of small farms from the cut-over timber lands and the undrained swamps of Mississippi and Louisiana. The leader in this movement is Mr. P. H. Saunders, president of the Commercial Bank & Trust Company of Laurel, Mississippi, and New Orleans, and vice-president of the Gulf States Investment Company. Formerly Professor of Latin and Greek in the University of Mississippi, a man well trained in the best institutions of this country and Germany, he has given himself to the building up of his native state. He is really an industrial statesman, who has spoken with candour and courage of the necessity for the cooperation of all social and industrial forces in the making of a better rural civilization.

Such men are sacrificing mere temporary advantages to the permanent prosperity of coming generations, and are proving once more that the practical plans of enlightened captains of industry are better than the dreams of ineffective philanthropists.

One of the most striking evidences of the intelligent handling of undeveloped regions of the South by men of large commercial vision is the intelligent plan adopted by the Chamber of Commerce of Charleston, South Carolina. While in South Carolina, recently, I made my first visit to the historic city, attracted thereto by its romantic association with American history and literature, and with the words of Owen Wister and Henry James in my mind. After hearing the chimes of St. Michael's from the quiet cemetery—a suggestion of some old cathedral town in England—and after walking along the Battery, famed in legend and song, I entered the Chamber of Commerce, from the walls of whose historic building looked down the portraits of its presidents of a hundred years. It was nearly two hours before I could see the secretary, for his office was filled with busy men and committees. Several years ago some of the most progressive citizens of the town, notably Mayor Rhett and Mr. H. P. Gadsden, determined that they would secure the best secretary for the Chamber of Commerce that was available, regardless of salary. Their choice was Mr. A. M. McKeand, who had been for six years secretary of the Chamber of Commerce of Oklahoma City.

His first observation, after a survey of the field, was that only 2 per cent. of the four counties around Charleston was under cultivation. And his first declaration of policy, readily sanctioned by his Board of Directors, was that, whatever effort might be directed toward the widening and deepening of Charleston Harbour or toward the industrial pros‑ perity of Charleston business concerns, the primary duty was to develop the surrounding land. With his experience gained from the building up of Oklahoma and Kansas, he went to work upon a consistent and in‑ telligent plan of organizing a company for the pur‑ chase of 60,000 acres to be drained and cut up into small farms and provided with all the advantages of the best agricultural communities. Fortunately, at Summerville, just outside of Charleston, Clemson Col‑ lege established about the same time an experimental farm of 300 acres, which has thoroughly demonstrated that land with an average of four inches of water over its surface can be drained and cultivated so that it will, on staple crops, yield a profit of $53 per acre; and that, furthermore, white men can live and work upon such plantations the year round, with the best condi‑ tions of climate and health. Furthermore, the Drain‑ age law, passed by a recent session of the Legislature, providing for the issuance of bonds by drainage dis‑ tricts, is working to the same end.

So that in the next few years one may expect to see that whole section of South Carolina, which has for a long time been considered utterly worthless, re‑ deemed and made an attractive place for men to live and work in. Vulgarization is descending upon King's Port, as Owen Wister sadly observed in "Lady Balti‑ more," but is not material and social well-being partici‑ pated in by an increasing number of people of all classes and from all sections and all nations better than an aristocracy, exclusive in its spirit and reactionary in its policy? That such a change is now coming in all parts of the South—that many districts are becoming fruitful as well as a few favoured spots, and that the people are being brought within the current of the world's activities and within the scope of all the best influences of society and government—that is surely one of the most hopeful, most inspiring tendencies in American life.

The man who best gathers all such stories as I have been telling and who has the keenest eye for the agencies that are now improving agricultural conditions is Clarence H. Poe, editor of the *Progressive Farmer*. The words of Lanier already quoted have been his guiding principle since he first read them. He wields a wholesome influence over a larger number of Southern farmers than any other man. His paper is now published in Raleigh, Birmingham, Dallas, and Memphis, and has 450,000 subscribers. He and his associate editors, for the most part agricultural experts, are teaching farmers the best methods of farming, the right use of farm implements, business management, the necessity of coöperative marketing, and all the other things that make for material success. What is far better, they are interpreting ideals of living which include the education of young and old and the building of better rural communities. With their eyes on every part of the world they are bringing to bear upon Southern agriculture the best that is being thought and done anywhere else. They have made of the paper a financial success, but they have made it also an instrument of civilization; they have lifted whole communities and commonwealths to a higher level, and they are at the beginning of still further development. It is a common saying in the South that you can tell by a man's farm whether he is a reader of the *Progressive Farmer*.

The story of Poe's life might well be a typical "success" story of an American who rises from poverty to wealth and influence. He grew up in the poorest county in North Carolina, during the darkest days of Southern agriculture, when cotton was selling for five cents a pound, and when science had brought no life or colour into the unrelieved drudgery of farm work. One of his most important books is dedicated to the memory of his father and mother, plain, hard-working farmer folk, with whom he shared "the poverty and hardships of the days before education had brought the hope of better things, or coöperation pointed out the way—the days when no equitable system of rural credits offered escape from the robbery of time prices, when outworn marketing methods left to others the handling of our products and all voice in pricing what we bought of others or others bought of us; and when the inevitable mortgage followed, menacing like a sword of Damocles, while we toiled." He went to school eleven weeks a year in a dilapidated one-room shanty that was the worst building in the community. He overcame the limitations of his education by borrowing all the books in the neighbourhood and by getting sample copies of magazines. He made enough money picking cotton to subscribe to the *Progressive Farmer,* to which he wrote an article when he was fourteen years old, pleading for better schools for boys like himself. The editor was so impressed with him that he offered him a position in his office;

in two years' time he was editor, and in four years he owned a majority of the stock. He was now able to read all the books he wanted to in the public library and all the magazines he could get his hands on. Before he was twenty-one, he had written an article for one of the leading American magazines; and then another and yet others followed. He had discovered the secret of all his later development in following the best thought of his time. His paper grew in quality, power and influence. Just the other day he celebrated the twenty-fifth anniversary of his editorship, and could well receive the congratulations of a large number of leaders who had watched his career with increasing admiration.

Poe, from the beginning, has been a follower of Matthew Arnold in desiring to know the best that is known and done in the world. He has had the best standards in his mind as he has sought to improve agricultural conditions in his native section. He has watched every successful farmer and told his story to the less successful; there is scarcely an issue of his paper that does not carry a story of what some Southern farmer has done to improve his own condition and that of his neighbours. By travel and reading he has found out what the more successful farmers of the North and West have done. If, for instance, he compares the two sections, he finds that the average Southern farmer makes $500 less than the average Western farmer, and he finds the reason in the use of better implements and of two-horse power instead of one. If he wishes to reënforce his plea for coöperation in buying and selling, he tells the story of what the community of Svea in Minnesota has done with coöperative creameries, telephones, stores, insurance, banks, live stock, consolidated schools and churches—an ideal community which makes definite his vision of what may be accomplished in any Southern community. Or he tells of what Wisconsin berry-growers, or Michigan grape-growers, or California fruit-growers, have done to improve their output and their social life.

A trip to Europe widened still further his vision. He was quick to appreciate the historic and cultural value of the Old World—its literary and artistic associations—but when he wrote to his paper he laid the emphasis on the rural conditions that surpass those at home. There is nothing of the bumptious, self-satisfied American that is revealed in the writings of Mark Twain, nothing of the American superiority complex. In all his travels in England and Scotland, he declares, he has not seen more weeds or gullies than he has sometimes seen in a single ten-acre lot at home; the fields are as carefully attended as our gardens. He compares the broken gates, gullied fields, neglected tools, shackly outhouses, unpainted and ill-kept residences of the South with the neatness and beauty of rural England. He saw more "gullied, wasted, desolated, heart-sickening land" in fifteen minutes' time between Memphis and Birmingham than he saw in a thousand-mile trip of the Old World.

He is shocked in Liverpool at the plight in which Southern cotton reaches the market, and is forced to say that it is "the most barbarously handled commercial product in the world"; the actual loss and waste in handling the ragged, dirty bales is nothing less than enormous and "a serious reflection upon the sound sense and business ability of Southern planters."

In France, he is impressed with the fact that with intelligent labour and prudent handling, the land, a thousand years in use, is still highly productive, while in his own country unintelligent labour and careless handling have ruined wide areas which have not grown crops one-twentieth as long. The kingly horses of Holland and Belgium suggest the horses' protruding ribs which so often mar the Southern landscape. More significant still is the system of public education in Germany, which has produced a population with their intelligence trained to efficient and practical work of all kinds. If German authorities had been in charge of Southern education, we should have had splendidly equipped agricultural schools in every county or district, and the elements of agriculture and domestic science would be taught in every rural school. "The whole tragic system in the South is an outgrowth of our idea that labour is degrading."

On a later trip, Poe made an intensive study of agricultural progress in Ireland and Denmark. The idea of a good Southern Anglo-Saxon—the backbone of the country, the saviour of civilization—learning anything from two such little countries! In Denmark, this alert and open-minded editor found an air of universal thrift and prosperity covering the whole kingdom like sunshine—his ideal of a nation of people, clean, industrious, healthy, alert. On account of a system of government loans, nine out of ten acres are cultivated by men who own them; the principle of coöperation is applied to every aspect of a farmer's life; and an efficient system of schools for old and young brings it about that there is nobody in Denmark over seven years of age, unless he is an idiot, who cannot read and write. The people have thus combined wisdom and work, learning and labour, education and energy. The ideal of government is to provide a broader culture for the great masses of people; to induce them to read and think and to love their country and fellows. The consequence is that their outlook on life is "social and co-operative rather than individual and competitive."

Poe's guide in Ireland was Sir Horace Plunkett, with whom he formed one of the important friend- ships of his life, and who declared that the book which Poe wrote as the result of this trip, "How Farmers Coöperate and Double Profits," was the most import- ant book that had been published on the subject on either side of the Atlantic. Ireland, like the South, had suffered long from over-attention to religion and politics; its tenant system had many similarities to that of the South. The progress made there within a comparatively short time was of special significance, and the secret of it all was coöperation in everything that affected the farmer's life and the abolition of the tenant system by the wise coöperation of the British Government. The Catholic fathers joined in the cru- sade against poverty and thus gave an interesting illus- tration of this-worldliness. Most of the credit has to be given, however, to men like George W. Russell and Sir Horace Plunkett. Of the latter, Poe says that he has all the patriotism to which Erin's poets and orators have given such vivid and eloquent expression; but "his patriotism was to take a form of constructive work rather than inflammatory eloquence"—a remark that conceals a dagger for many a Southern politician. He might have had such a man in mind when he said recently, "And if our public men had vision, they could find issues—issues as far above the petty squabbles of the ordinary campaign as the heavens are above the earth."

But Poe, however far he may travel, keeps always his eye on the immediate object—the Southern scene and situation. In "Twenty-five Years of Fighting," an editorial written on the twenty-fifth anniversary of his editorship, June, 1924, he summarizes the main causes to which he has given his attention and which may be said to have partially triumphed: the fight against the average farmer's sneer against "book larnin'," the fight for improved methods of farming and especially for the use of scientific facts and coöperative marketing, the demand for a whole-time farm demonstration agent, an intelligent and capable superintendent of schools, a health officer, a home-demonstration agent in every county, boys' corn clubs, girls' canning clubs, the organization of farm women, community clubs of all kinds, etc. In "What I Hope to See Before 1949," he outlines his vision: rich soils, green fields, and flocks and herds, the total abolition of vicious crop mortgages and time prices, making loans to landless farmers as in Denmark and Ireland, an adequate health programme in every community, old age pensions, and, above all, a richer and finer rural civilization.

One comes very near the heart of the man when he calls for leaders with initiative, courage, patience, and faith to waken their neighbours and get them together in all that constitutes a progressive community. Only in this way will they know what Doctor Eliot calls the durable satisfactions of life, or what Carlyle had in

mind when he said that man's chief glory is to make
some nook of God's creation more fruitful, better,
more worthy of Him.   The picture of a tenant's home
with its illiteracy, sickness, and poverty—seen just
after he had witnessed a glorious sunset—causes him
to exclaim against a state that will not bestir itself
against such conditions as may be found almost in the
outskirts of its capital city.   Sooner or later some
plan must be worked out by which "the stricken child
of the poor may have as good medical and hospital
attention, as fair a chance to win back life and health
and strength, as the stricken child of the rich."   Surely
some way can be found for such families to live and
work on their own lands.   A more equitable system of
taxation would enable the state to tackle some of these
difficult problems.   If such ideas be called socialism,
then make the most of it!

But Poe has never relied on political measures to
remedy the troubles of farmers.   Growing up at a
time when Tillman, Tom Watson, and a host of other
leaders were lashing the farmers into a fury against
their oppressors and organizing them into a separate
political party, and inheriting a paper that had been
actively identified with the Populist Party in North
Carolina, Poe has laid the emphasis of his work on
economic and social measures of a kind that has
already been suggested.   At the same time he has been
bold enough to write and speak for reforms that can
only be accomplished by legislation.   While independent in his ideas and spirit, he has, in the main, been connected with the Democratic Party and has used his
influence on its leaders, with whom he has had in many

cases a close friendship. A good idea of his point of view and his method of attack may be seen in an editorial entitled "Suggestions to Our Lawmakers"—a direct appeal to the last legislature of North Carolina.

He is in favour of efficiency and economy in the administration of state affairs, pointing out definite illustrations of unnecessary expense that amounts to graft and suggesting a commission of prominent business men to spend ninety days studying the business methods used in the expenditure of the people's money. But he does not favour parsimony and retrenchment in providing good roads, good schools, and effective agencies of social welfare: the state must not call a halt at these points. Because he has made it his rule to get in touch and to keep in touch with all other fighters for progress, and has been actively and often officially connected with every important organization in the state, he has the right to demand that others stand with him in demanding certain things that affect the farmer's life and conditions. Publicity of assessments and an inheritance tax would not only remove present inequalities, but would furnish additional money for needed development. The farmer is discriminated against when he is not allowed to deduct his debts from his assets while professional and business men may. The reform of county government is imperative. The usury laws of the state should be made to cover the "time prices" in which farmers pay as much as forty per cent. interest on their accounts. The encouragement of white settlers from the North and West would change a state of affairs in which North Carolina cultivates only eight million acres of land whereas Iowa cultivates twenty-eight million. These are all suggestions of a practical statesman rather than of a doctrinaire or revolutionist.

The secret of Poe's leadership is that he has a remarkable power of absorbing and using other men. Not a farmer himself, he has kept about him men who are experts, and has given them an opportunity to make their views known. Not a student of science, he has been quick to adopt the conclusions of men who have applied scientific knowledge and methods to the problems of the farm. No man has done more to give currency to the reports and investigations of men in experiment stations, state and national. He was one of the first men to appreciate the work of Doctor Knapp, whom he declared to be the greatest man that the South had produced since Henry Grady. He saw that Doctor Knapp, in his plan for showing the farmers how to farm by expert demonstration agents sent into every community, had found a new way of disseminating the treasures of truth which others had developed, and which farmers could not even read. He frequently reprints in a conspicuous place in his paper "the ten commandments of agriculture" which were born out of large experience and great wisdom. He not only read all that Knapp wrote, but he took every opportunity to hear him at Southern educational conferences, and thus came into intimate contact with him, catching something of his great zeal and consuming desire to be of service to his generation.

But Poe's interests have all the while been broader than agriculture. His paper carries into the homes of its readers suggestive ideas and stories that lead to wholesome reading, to the beautifying of yards and gardens and houses—in a word, to culture. As has already been seen, he has from the beginning been an ardent advocate of education. Denied the advantages of education himself, and making up for his deficiency by the most persistent study of the best books and magazines, he has made his paper an organ of every movement that means the training of the masses and of special experts and leaders. He early caught the real significance of the educational revival that was led in North Carolina by Edwin A. Alderman, Charles D. McIver, James Y. Joyner, and others, and he was the ardent friend and supporter of Charles B. Aycock, who on every platform in the state preached the gospel of universal education. Not a teacher himself, he has always been an interested spectator and auditor at educational conferences and assemblies. He has missed no opportunity to hear prominent men who have spoken at North Carolina colleges and has often reproduced their addresses and sayings in his paper. It is no wonder, then, that he is chairman of the Executive Committee of the North Carolina State College of Agriculture, giving to that institution his advice and support in its efforts to improve farming conditions. He is also a member of the Board of Trust of Wake Forest College, one of the progressive group that has sustained President Poteat in his fight for liberal culture and free thought. One of the ablest and most discriminating editorials on the Dayton trial appeared in the *Progressive Farmer*—all the more notable because the country people are supposed to be the backbone of Fundamentalism.

It is safe to say that there has not been an organization interested in the welfare of the state that has not found in Poe a wise counsellor and supporter. He was for many years secretary of the State Literary and Historical Society, responsible for its excellent programmes and associated thus not only with the scholars and men of letters in the state but with the most prominent men of the nation. Incidentally, he twice won the Patterson Cup given to the citizen of the state for the most notable book published each year, thus beating the scholars and writers at their own game, and he did this with his "Southerner in Europe" and "Where Half the World Is Waking Up," published first serially in the *Progressive Farmer*. He was also a prominent officer in the state Anti-Saloon League, realizing that strong drink was one of the worst menaces to rural development. He has been actively identified with the North Carolina Press Association; as president one year he made an address that produced a profound impression by reason of its appeal to his comrades to present and interpret the programmes of rural development that he had so long and so intelligently advocated.

Poe is not only an excellent writer but an earnest and forceful speaker. Without any of the characteristics of the typical Southern orator, he often awakens interest and conviction. Perhaps the most significant of all his addresses was one on the "Agricultural Revolution" delivered before the Southern Commercial Congress held in Washington in 1910—an appeal to the bankers, merchants, manufacturers, editors, and public men of the entire South to agree upon a working programme of progress for the average man. It is such a striking exposition of the real philosophy that underlies the agricultural development of the South that I quote at some length:

This is the feeling that has cost the South leadership. This is the sentiment that has kept our manufacturers, our commerce, our literature, our education—that has kept one and all of these—chained down to the unprofitable level of our unprofitable average man, our man behind the plough. Increase his earning capacity and you increase the earning capacity of every other worker in the South; free him from the chains of unprofitable because misdirected labour, and you cut the hindering shackles of every other worthy interest. . . . Ah, if our statesmen and public men these last thirty years could only have realized the fundamental truth . . . that the prosperity of every man depends upon the prosperity of the average man!

Every man whose earning power is below par, below normal, is a burden on the community; he drags down the whole level of life, and every other man in the community is poorer by reason of his inefficiency, whether he be white man, or Negro, or what not. Your untrained, inefficient man is not only a poverty-breeder for himself, but the contagion of it curses every man in the community that is guilty of leaving him untrained. The law of changeless justice decrees that you must rise or fall, decline or prosper, with your neighbour.

I do not know what we are going to do with the Negro. I do know that we must either frame a scheme of education and training that will keep him from dragging down the whole level of life, that will make him more efficient, a prosperity-maker, or else he will get out of the South and give way to the white immigrant. . . . We must either have the Negro trained, or we must not have him at all. Untrained, he is a burden on us all. Better a million acres of untilled land than a million acres of mistilled land. Our economic law knows no colour line.

He points out the fallacies—"the vampire delusions"—that have been the basis of the South's backwardness, and that have caused men of genius to go to other sections in search of larger opportunities. He concludes with his vision of what education and the co-operation of all forces will bring about:

We shall handle the land better, now more barbarously handled by us than any other civilized people. . . . We shall use improved seed and improved stock, and very nearly double our profits through this one change. . . . In a hundred other ways we shall improve the South's agricultural practice. . . . Through schools adapted to practical needs of rural people, through technical colleges, farmers' institutes, clubs, unions, etc., we shall gradually realize a comprehensive and well-rounded policy of rural development, and that is the one immediate and imperative duty of Southern statesmen and of our entire citizenship.

CHAPTER IV

LOOMS AND FURNACES

THE present industrial development of the South has been so widely heralded that I do not think it necessary to summarize or even to suggest its vast range and volume. The statistics as given in a recent mammoth edition of the *Manufacturers' Record* and the articles that accompany them fairly stagger the reader. One grows almost surfeited with constant repetition in newspapers and magazines. To some Southerners this progress has marked the definite passing of much that seemed characteristic of this section—the old charm and leisure, the old picturesqueness and romance. Those who are æsthetic or academic fear that industrialism will lead inevitably to the standardization of these Southern States until they are lost in the mediocrity and commonplaceness of contemporary American civilization. The spectre of Babbitt haunts them. Critics from the outside who have not expressed this point of view have emphasized the feudal character of the organization of the new industrial centres and the consequent degradation of labour. The opposition of some industrial leaders to modern social progress and their disposition to play the rôle of benevolent despots have met with protests from some of the most prominent social reformers of the country. Others insist that, in spite of all such criticism, the general effect is favourable to educational and social progress, and even to a larger freedom of thought. With these conflicting views, it seems wise to get a substantial basis of facts before attempting any generalizations, and especially to visualize the work of certain typical leaders who have succeeded, in the face of every sort of obstacle, in putting Southern industry upon a sound basis.

The career of the man who first expressed the philosophy of the new industrial movement in the South is worthy of special consideration. It was an important event in the history of the South, and particularly of the Piedmont section of the Carolinas, when D. A. Tompkins, in 1882, put out his sign in Charlotte, N. C., as "Engineer, Machinist, Contractor." Born in 1851 in Edgefield, S. C., he was the son of middle-class Scotch-Irish parents, who owned an estate of moderate proportions. His mother, a cousin of John C. Calhoun, was a very different type from the woman of the old régime in Virginia and South Carolina; she was noted for her thrift and management. His father said to the young boy at a time when most people were in the depths of despair just after the Civil War:

You are living in the greatest era of the world's history. You have seen the emancipation of four million slaves and the preservation of the American Union. Our age is wonderful also for scientific discoveries and inventions. Some day you will be an actor in this age; and it behooves you to keep your eyes open, mind alert, vision clear, and spirit sympathetic to all the movements of humanity, whether they happen in your neighbourhood, or far away in the distant parts of the earth.

Never did a son follow the spirit and the very words of a father more faithfully.

Unable to get the education that he wanted in his native state, he studied mechanical engineering at the Rensselaer Polytechnic Institute at Troy, New York. After his graduation he became a draughtsman in the Bethlehem Iron Works, where he had worked during his vacation to make his college expenses. He was sent to Germany to install some machinery for the company, and was later offered attractive positions at Bethlehem and in Chicago and Philadelphia. But his heart was in the South: after a year's study of South-ern industrial history and a survey of industrial con-ditions, he settled in Charlotte. As he travelled in search of business, he kept his eye open—he was able to see more with his one eye than other people with two—and was soon advocating the building of cotton mills and cotton-seed oil mills. He was an important link between Northern capital and communities that were awaking to the need of factories, he himself often building the mills. While he worked hard all the time at his business, he began to speak and to write of his vision of a new industrial order. "The year of jubilee has now come," he said, "and the time is ripe for the farmer to join hands with the manufacturer." His study of Southern history convinced him that the South was then in a position to resume the leadership in industry that it had before slavery and the monopoly of cotton became an obsession. He said repeatedly:

The development of our manufactures is a revival rather than a new development. The taste and capability exhibited by the present generation is an inheritance, and not a thing of entirely new birth. In the early days of the Republic the South was the manufacturing section of the Union. By the United States census of 1810 the manufactured products of Virginia, the Carolinas, and Georgia exceeded in value and variety those of the entire New England States and New York put together. The Henrietta Cotton Mill, near Rutherford, is on the site of old iron works. The High Shoals Mill, now being built near Lincolnton, had to be cleared of some brick stacks of old Catlin forges to make way for the new foundations. Throughout the Piedmont region there are many evidences of former extensive manufacturing plants and much prosperity. I have at home a copy of a contract in accordance with which a machinist at Lincolnton made all the machinery necessary to equip a cotton mill complete having a date of 1813. This manufacturing spirit and its success gave rise to many schemes for internal improvement. Iron and other goods were carried from Lincolnton and other Piedmont sections to Fayetteville by wagon, and thence down Cape Fear River on boats, and thence to Boston in sailing vessels.

With frankness and courage rare in those days, Tompkins denounced slavery as "the poison that ultimately destroyed this development." The cotton kingdom built upon false economic theories swept everything before it; and the Piedmont section, which ought to have paralleled Pennsylvania in its industrial development, was deflected from its true course. Wise leaders of the early days of the Republic were succeeded by men who risked all on agriculture and on the political theories that were connected with it.[1] Men like William Gregg of South Carolina and DeBow of Tennessee were prophets crying in the wilderness in the decades before the Civil War. The interrupted career of the South must be resumed; cotton must be king again—"not cotton in the fields but cotton in the mills." These general principles were reinforced

---

[1] cf. W. E. Dodd, "The Cotton Kingdom" and B. Mitchell, "Cotton Mills in the South."

with plain, practical suggestions covering every detail of cotton manufacturing, and were set forth in pamphlets, addresses, and books. As Doctor Winston says in his admirable biography of Tompkins, he had much of the shrewd sagacity of Franklin and the homely wisdom of Lincoln.[1] A national recognition of his important work came when he was appointed a member of the Industrial Commission by President McKinley.

He emphasized most of all before every kind of audience the need of technical education. Many of the pioneers in the development of cotton manufacturing were amateurs, some of them recruits from other professions. To a missionary zeal that characterized the early stages of the cotton mill campaign Tompkins added a forthright common sense and a vision of the more permanent results that would follow from expert management. He became one of the first advocates of textile schools, pleading their cause before state legislatures in all parts of the South, and becoming in many cases the most valued trustee of such institutions. He said repeatedly:

The South must move in the matter of education, and keep moving, else in time the people who are keeping up and ahead in education will own the rest of the country. As "eternal vigilance is the price of liberty," so persistent energy in keeping pace with progress is the price of being amongst the successful peoples of modern times. It is not by accident that I go from Charlotte to the North to buy water wheels, gas engines, etc. It is because of systems of education that qualify the people to be the most competent to do these things. The South should follow this lead and never rest until our people lead the world in education. If we

---

[1]George T. Winston: "A Builder of the New South," from which the extracts in this sketch are taken.

do this, we will then take a leading part in supplying the world with manufactured products. The natural resources of the South are unsurpassed. We need knowledge and skill to handle them to our own advantage, and we ought to qualify the youth of the South to handle them for our own people and not wait supinely for strangers to come and take possession of them, thus leaving the wages paid by the stranger to be the only advantage to our own people.

Realizing the need of a newspaper of a new type that would reveal and interpret these ideas to the people, he purchased the Charlotte *Observer* and secured as editor Mr. J. P. Caldwell, who was for many years one of the most brilliant and independent editors in the South. Contrasting the policy of the paper with that of the ante-bellum newspaper, Tompkins wrote:

The ante-bellum newspaper of the South was essentially a political institution. Its patrons were chiefly planters and slave-owners. The chief interest it could have for its patrons was in telling well and fully how politics were going and in exhibiting the doings of statesmen and future statesmen. Every interest in the South was entangled with the institution of slavery. Its mainte-nance depended solely upon the work of Southern statesmen at Washington and in the various state capitals.

Whoever subscribed for a paper was moved by his interest in governmental affairs and in the people who conducted them. There was no way in which a cotton planter could make money by taking a newspaper. But by keeping well posted he could help send the best men to the Legislature and to Congress to help maintain the institution of slavery in which his material interests were involved.

Newspaper men of the South are not yet freed from this heritage or habit of conducting a newspaper for politics only. Newspaper patronage in the South is also more or less constrained by this same inherited idea that a newspaper is a luxury—a sort of political luxury. But politics is no longer the one subject of public inter-est to Southern people. It is exceedingly important for the benefit of the papers and also for the benefit of the people that this fact should be appreciated and that it should have its influence in the make-up of the newspapers. Southern people are becoming more and more interested in manufactures—in diversified manufactures, and in education.

The *Observer* became in every sense of the word independent in politics.[1] Mr. Tompkins, in his addresses, announced his political principles in words that serve to show the difference between the old and the new points of view. Just as he had urged the South to resume industrial leadership, so he insisted on returning to the political ideas of creative leaders in the early days of the Republic:

Slavery circumscribed our habits of thought. It took away from us freedom of political action. It destroyed all profitable occupation for the white man who worked for wages. It made the South doubly solid; first, voluntarily solid for the protection and perpetuation of slavery; afterward necessarily solid against the disorder, violence and even anarchy that followed in the wake of the destruction of the institution. Slavery is now gone for ever. The wreck of its destruction is now about cleared away. We may now, with unhampered hands, prosecute the work of reconstructing the industrial fabric of the South which was destroyed by slavery and by an excess of zeal for agricultural interests.

We may now rebuild the working man's school, which was swept away in the interest of agriculture and slave labour. We may again, if we concur in opinion, follow the lead of George Washington, the Southern protection President. We may, if we believe with him, follow the lead of Thomas Jefferson, the Southern expansion President. We may, if we think as he did, follow the lead of Andrew Jackson, the Southern sound money President.

And why not follow these, if we believe with them? They are all Southern men.

In line with the ideas of Tompkins, practically every Southern industry is now being put upon a more sub-

[1]Cf. Chapter VI.

stantial basis as the result of better organization, expert management, or technical skill. Succeeding the era in which the resources of the South were developed, sometimes with remarkable profits even in spite of crude and wasteful methods, has come an era in which these industries are coming into the hands of trained men. Formerly it was comparatively easy to make money by the manufacture of coarse cotton goods or pig iron; men went into manufacturing from other professions and had little trouble in succeeding. Unexpected obstacles and increased competition in recent years caused these same men either to fail or to readjust themselves to new conditions. The industrial leaders are putting a new emphasis on expert superintendence and the training of employees.

What science is doing in Southern industry is well illustrated by the experiences of two men from the same county in Georgia, both of whom received an inspiration in Germany that proved to be turning points in their careers and of great service to their native sections. Professor C. H. Herty, formerly head of the department of chemistry in the University of North Carolina, while taking lectures at Charlottenberg (Berlin) under Professor O. N. Witt, one of the most celebrated industrial chemists of Europe, inquired of the professor one day what he thought of the turpentine industry of America. With a characteristic German gesture the latter threw up his hands and exclaimed: "You have no industry, you have a butchery. I speak from personal knowledge, for I have seen Florida. You are wasting your natural resources and getting nothing like an adequate return from them." The remark was a surprise to the young

American scholar, who had been born on the edge of the turpentine belt and had heard all his life of the money made from this industry.   He could make no reply at the time, having never seen the actual operation of getting resin from the pine trees.   He decided that as soon as he reached home he would see for himself and, if the criticism proved true, devote himself to finding a remedy.

When he began his investigations at Valdosta, Georgia, he saw at a glance the wastefulness of the method employed.   In addition to the necessary "wounding" of the tree to cause the resin to flow, deep holes ("boxes") were cut at the base.   These boxes weakened the trees so that they were an easy prey to winds and forest fires.   Moreover, there was a good deal of waste in dipping the resin from the boxes. Herty saw that the method pursued was not efficient in getting resin and was very destructive to the forests. Gathering all the literature on the subject, he found that in France the turpentine operators had used clay cups instead of boxes cut in the wood, and that in this way the trees had been saved for a hundred years. He found, too, that many patents had been procured at Washington by men who had worked at the problem of a substitute for the harmful box method.   The difficulty with the French method was that it called for skilled labourers that could not be commanded in the South; and the difficulty with the American patents was that none of them had been successful commercially.   So he went to work to find a substitute that would be simple enough to be used by Negro labourers, cheap enough to command the attention of operators and renters, and efficient enough to secure a maximum flow of resin.

On his first vacation—he was then adjunct professor in the University of Georgia—he went to Savannah to interest the turpentine operators in his ideas and plans. He met with almost entire indifference on the part of the men who apparently felt that it was better to leave good enough alone, especially as pine forests seemed almost inexhaustible. At the end of his second day, after almost abandoning hope, he secured the promise of some timber with which to experiment and a pledge of $150 to cover actual expenses. In the spring of 1901 he fitted up near Statesboro a sort of forest laboratory, arranged in various plots of timber to test the comparative results of the box and cup methods. He found it difficult to get labourers, the Negroes having nothing but contempt for the "flower pots" that were put upon trees, for Herty's system consisted of little metal gutters running diagonally down across the facing and emptying into a cup—an earthenware pot hung on the side of the tree. It was a very simple thing to revolutionize a great industry.

One man was not indifferent to the results of these investigations. Gifford Pinchot, then at the head of the Forestry Department at Washington, after hearing Professor Herty's story, said: "You are the man I have been looking for. What can we do? We will publish anything you write. You'd better become one of the experts of the department. This means not only increased profits for the turpentine operators but the conservation of our forests."

The result was that Doctor Herty resigned his professorship and, with the assistance of the Bureau of Forestry, conducted experiments on a much larger tract of timber at Ocilla, Georgia, the owners of the tract furnishing labour and timber and getting the profits. There, with a squad of twelve Negroes, by systematic tests, he proved still more conclusively that an increased yield over a longer period of time and a better quality of resin came from the cup method than from the old boxes. Three years later similar tests showed an increased yield of 30 per cent. in the "cuppings" of the second and the third years, while at the same time the trees were preserved from storm and fire.

The next problem was to get the cups manufactured and to secure the coöperation of the operators. The manufacturers of pottery said that they could not manufacture the cup for less than three cents, and they laughed at the professor when he said that he wanted not hundreds, but millions. One morning, in New Orleans, two years later, Doctor Herty sold one million and a half cups to two men while they were waiting for their breakfast. Meantime, a pottery plant was bought at Daisy, Tennessee, with the intention of manufacturing cups half the time and stoneware the other half. As a result of an address made at Jacksonville in 1902 before the Association of Turpentine Operators, which had been organized two years before to limit the output of turpentine in order to save the forests, Doctor Herty aroused widespread interest in the new method. The newspapers were his enthusiastic supporters. The railroads became interested to the point of giving a greatly reduced rate on the transportation of the cups, while some owners of timber lands pledged themselves to let their lands only on condition that the operators use cups.

For two years, Doctor Herty conducted demonstrations under the Bureau of Forestry, beginning with a convict camp in the swamps of Georgia in water one foot deep on a cold February day, and ending by covering the territory from South Carolina to Mississippi. While there were at first some disappointments connected with the cups, they have gradually won their way with the great majority of intelligent operators. It is estimated that the system has already added more than ten million dollars' annual value to the turpentine industry.

Not satisfied with these results, Professor Herty continued his investigations, especially in the direction of determining the results of narrow and shallow chipping of trees. Profiting by the discoveries of a Swiss professor as to the source and causes of the production of resin, he made other contributions to the improvement of the turpentine industry. For four years, near Jacksonville, Florida, the Forest Service, with his advice, conducted experiments with twenty-five thousand trees arranged in four equal crops and chipped in different ways; while in the laboratory of the University of North Carolina experiments determined the effect of shallow chipping on the quality of the product. The results when published showed that the trees which were chipped lightly yielded a greater percentage of turpentine and a better quality; that such chipping left the timber in a condition to be immediately worked again for a second four-year period; and that, by the conservative selection of trees, the same tract may be worked indefinitely and at the same time yield more turpentine than was produced by the old destructive methods. The upshot of all this patient scientific work is that we have now an intelligent treatment of one of the South's most important industries. Instead of being a self-destroying industry bound to disappear before many years, the naval stores industry, after having retreated southward and westward because its material in the old regions gave out, is now in prospect of becoming stable throughout the present Southern pine belt.[1]

The other Southerner to whom I referred as moved by the scientific spirit was Mr. George Gordon Crawford, now president of the Tennessee Coal, Iron & Railroad Company, who has, during the last eighteen years, by expert management and by the application of technical knowledge, revolutionized the iron and steel industry of the Birmingham district. The first graduate of the Georgia School of Technology in 1890, he went to Germany to spend two years in the study of technical chemistry in the Karl-Eberhard University at Tübingen with a view to supplementing his knowledge of mechanical engineering with that of metallurgy, hoping thereby to prepare himself for success in the iron and steel business. Soon after reaching Germany he heard a professor say in one of his lectures that the Southern States of America were in the matter of *kultur* at about the stage of Europeans in the

---

[1]For a full account see Professor Herty's "The Turpentine Industry in the Southern States," in the Journal of the Franklin Institute, March, 1916. This work was but the beginning of a career of increasing usefulness to the industries of the entire country. As editor of the *Journal of Industrial Engineering Chemistry,* and as president of the Synthetic Organic Chemical Foundation, he has been one of the leaders in bringing the laboratory and the business interests of the country together.

Middle Ages. Somewhat sensitive over this remark, he found upon inquiry that the professor did not refer to intellectual culture but rather to industrial efficiency. From that day he had a new sense of efficiency as a factor in industrial development. Upon his return to this country he went to Birmingham to learn the practical side of the iron and steel business, only to find that his German professor was right with regard to this industry at least; for at that time, 1892, the business was upon a crude basis, from the standpoint of both financial management and the process of manufacturing.

After three months he became an employee of the Carnegie Steel Company at Pittsburgh, first as chemist and then as draughtsman. He refused promotions at different times in order to learn every process in the manufacture of steel. His technical knowledge and practical sense soon led to his appointment as assistant superintendent and then as superintendent of the blast furnaces of the Edgar-Thompson steel mills— the largest furnaces in the world. Later, as manager of the National Tube Company at McKeesport, he not only had charge of every kind of steel mill, but directed 10,000 workmen. He completely overhauled the extensive plant of the company, putting in improvements to the extent of $13,500,000. By this time he was well known throughout the United States Steel Corporation, having successfully invented manufacturing devices and labour-saving expedients. He was serving on a half dozen of the important committees of the Corporation, some of which called for visits to the iron and steel mills of Europe. It was natural that, when the Tennessee Coal, Iron & Railroad Company was bought by the Steel Corporation in 1907, he should become its president.

The circumstances connected with the selection of Mr. Crawford have been so well told by Miss Tarbell in her recently published Life of Judge Gary that I cannot do better than quote what she says, for she writes from the standpoint of the chief officers:

The first thing was a man. One who reviews the hectic early history of the Tennessee Company cannot but feel that at last Providence was interfering in its favour, for if ever a man was found fit for a trying job it was the one that on Judge Gary's insistence the Steel Corporation now chose to direct its difficult purchase.

He at first refused. . . . The attempt to make steel in Birmingham he knew had ruined the metallurgical reputation of more than one man. . . . President Corey insisted, saying . . . "We were pushed to it by the condition of the country. The operating department feels like a man who, having had a mill-stone hung about his neck, has been thrown into a rushing current and told to swim upstream. But you are the man for the place." And Mr. Crawford took it.

In the prime of his life—he was then only thirty-eight years old—and with the knowledge of the best that was being done in the manufacture of iron and steel throughout the world, he entered upon his duties at Birmingham. Although he found that much improvement had been made since he had left there fifteen years before, there was still a condition of uncertainty, of restlessness, and even of feverishness. The company was practically bankrupt. Booms had been so often followed by panics, and periods of the wildest enthusiasm had given way so often to periods of depression, that confidence in the manufacture of steel was well-nigh gone. The Birmingham public had not forgotten what Andrew Carnegie had said when they hoped that he might be induced to put the company on a solid basis: "You have coal and iron and dolomite all here in close proximity, but you cannot make steel." This was the state of affairs that greeted Mr. Crawford in Birmingham.

He began to study the cost sheets—not only those of his company, but also those of the subsidiary companies of the United States Steel Corporation, copies of which were sent to him weekly. From his study of these cost sheets he made certain demands on superintendents and foremen; he gradually brought about more efficient management and a greater tonnage per man in every department of the company's work. Without any of the characteristics of a despot he brought the entire organization into line with the best modern business practices, and he did this without friction. Moreover, he had an eye upon every detail and every process of mining and manufacturing. He used the large sums of money appropriated by the Steel Corporation to improve trackage, to introduce labour-saving devices, to build furnaces of the best quality—in a word, to work out a complete plant characterized by permanence, economy, comfort, and safety. Overhauling the old Ensley plant by introducing new machinery, he was enabled by the duplex process of manufacturing steel to make steel rails that were used by the larger railroads of the country and of other parts of the world.

The point of view of Mr. Crawford in all these improvements may be the better understood by two characteristic sayings: "It's simply a natural development we are after. If, every month, returns are a little better than the month before, and a steady, gradual improvement shown, I am perfectly satisfied"; "Better than walking with our heads in the clouds and stumbling, is to look where we would walk, recognize obstacles, and avoid them."

He suffered from no illusions as to the superior advantages of the Birmingham district. To those optimistic citizens of Birmingham who, indulging in bombastic utterances, were bent upon get-rich-quick processes, he believed in telling the exact truth. In 1910, after three years of patient work and study and substantial progress, he analyzed the whole situation in an article that was widely published. He called attention to the fact that the production of pig iron in the South had remained almost stationary since 1902, while that of the United States had increased 45 per cent.; that the alleged low price of pig iron had been due to "skimming the cream" of the mines and bad bookkeeping; that, though the quality of steel then made in the Ensley mills was as good as any in the world, the cost of manufacturing it was too high; that, although the juxtaposition of coal, iron ore, and limestone seemed most favourable, the coal was handled less cheaply than in other sections; that the ore is so low in iron content and has so much phosphorus in it as to render its manufacture into steel a more expensive process; that a blast furnace at Ensley manufactured 10,000 tons of steel a month while those at Pittsburgh, identical in size, produced 16,000 tons; that the labour in other steel districts was more efficient because it had been better trained and better paid.

He insisted likewise that, while Birmingham, in view of its location, had the right to the iron and steel trade of 30 per cent. of the population of the United States and to a large export trade in South and Central America, it had failed to command this market. This, he said, was because of its lack of diversified finished products, its suicidal policy of selling pig iron at a low price to Northern plants, the inefficiency of transportation facilities, and the lack of steamships from Southern ports that rendered almost impossible an export trade. An export trade would be necessary in the steel business to relieve temporary depression in the home market.

With the full recognition, then, of all these obstacles, Mr. Crawford worked to remove them as fast as possible. They were to him a challenge for more aggressive work rather than a cause of depression; much had already been accomplished, but the work had just begun. He outlined plans looking to the development of diversified plants. A by-product coke-oven plant, which produces 5,500 tons of coke a day, and which, besides, conserves such by-products as gas, ammonia, and tar, was installed in 1911. At the same time the American Steel & Wire Company, another subsidiary company of the Steel Corporation, built a plant capitalized at $4,000,000 and intended for the manufacture of nails, staples, and various kinds of wire, and wire fence. A plant was built to utilize the phosphatic slag of the open-hearth furnaces as a fertilizer, another illustration of the utilization of by-products.

During the last fourteen years Mr. Crawford, with the coöperation of his officers, has steadily moved toward the remedying of the limitations suggested in his analysis, and toward the realization of the vision that first came to him as his eye swept over the valley that separates the two ranges of mountains containing the coal and iron. One can now stand on the roof of the magnificent new hospital, erected in 1919 for the 23,000 employees, and see the series of plants that manufacture many varieties of steel products to the amount of 1,100,000 tons a year—rails, heavy and light, billets of all kinds, bars, plates, sheets, tie plates, track-bolts, rivets, steel castings, and cars (steel and wood). He can see the plants that make use of the by-products of the coal and coke—sulphate of ammonia, tar, gas, benzol, naphtha—used either in the plants themselves or sold as fertilizer and road and building material. He can see, too, the 3,500,000,000 gallon reservoir, adequate for all future needs of the company. In addition to the fifty miles of trackage and a good deal more of side trackage used in the transportation of the coal and ore to the furnaces, there is now a recently completed five-mile elevated railway lifted some fifteen to fifty feet above the valley so as to prevent any delay in the transportation of material. In the villages of Westfield, Fairfield, and some twenty others live the workers in the mines and mills. All of these, within a radius of fifteen miles, give the best idea of the carefully correlated system.

In other words, many of the difficulties heretofore enumerated have been overcome until not only as good steel products of all kinds can be made in the Birmingham district as anywhere else, but they can be made as cheaply, and there is no reason why these products will not in time supply the needs of the market that rightly belongs to Birmingham. Practically all the pig iron that is made in the district is now used in the manufacture of steel or cast-iron pipe, and the additional profit that comes from the finished product stays at home. And this achievement of Mr. Crawford and his colleagues is all the more remarkable in that they have had to deal with every single problem that other companies of the Steel Corporation have had to solve separately. Some of the subsidiary companies have been concerned with the mining of coal or ore, others with transportation, others with particular kinds of steel products. Only the Illinois Steel Company and the Carnegie Steel Company manufacture the same kinds of steel products, but they have nothing to do with the mining of coal or ore or with its transportation. That all of these elements should have been fused into one gigantic problem, that they should all be correlated into one system directed by one master mind, is the most striking testimony to President Crawford's skill, ingenuity, thoughtfulness, and ability to plan and to carry into effect.

The words that I have just used to characterize Mr. Crawford are those of Judge Elbert H. Gary. Perhaps the impression made upon the Finance Committee of the Steel Corporation on a recent visit to Birmingham may best be expressed in the deliberate words of their chief counsel, Mr. Lindabury:

I had learned a good deal about that plant in connection with my service to the Steel Corporation, but I didn't realize what a vast thing it was; I didn't realize how well it was built and balanced up; I didn't realize how well it was being operated. I knew that we were paying out for wages between thirty and thirty-five million dollars a year; I knew we had twenty-two thousand employees about the works and in the mines, but I did not know that the business was going on with so much smoothness and regularity and with such promise and assurance of growth and success.

And yet, that is not the best part of the story to those who are concerned with human progress, nor is it the point of chief emphasis in Mr. Crawford's mind and heart. The same quality that has made his organization of the administrative forces involved in this undertaking so human that it seems like a big brotherhood of fellow workers is apparent in his relation to the army of his employees. He has maintained from the beginning that labour is a more important element than machinery, and that it is good business as well as good ethics to treat employees as human beings. He has no sympathy with the cave-man idea of the survival of the fittest. "The weaker members," he once said, "have something which can be given but not taken that is of far more value than what could be taken, namely, coöperation." To win that coöperation has been one of his primary aims. He inherited some convict labour which he soon discarded; but he inherited also a mass of illiterate Negroes and careless white men who had worked and lived under conditions that were destructive of all wholesome instincts. The common labourers were shiftless and often degraded and brutalized, while the skilled labourers in the plants had little to attract them as permanent workers. He once told the Governor of the state that he had to leave the ore in the earth, draw labourers from the farm, or import foreigners. His work of construction and of manufacturing was often impeded by the lack of labourers. This was a more difficult problem than the technical problems that confronted him.

One of the first steps taken to provide adequate
housing conditions for the better type of workmen was
to build a modern industrial town, but it was thought
best not to have the company build it, as had been done
at Gary, Indiana. The whole undertaking was sub-
mitted to Mr. Robert L. Jemison, Jr., a prominent
real-estate agent of Birmingham, who visited all the
model industrial towns of the United States, read all
the literature pertaining to those of England, France,
and Germany, secured the well-known landscape archi-
tect, Mr. George H. Miller, of Boston, to draw up
the plans, and with characteristic business sagacity,
proceeded to build upon 250 acres a town that would
reap the benefit and at the same time avoid the mistakes of similar experiments elsewhere. Briefly, the
fundamental features of Fairfield are the following:
all possible modern improvements for health, conven-
ience, and cleanliness; the arrangement of the town in
zones or districts—some of them for business houses,
and others for various types of residences, ranging
from a minimum of $1,250 to a maximum of $5,000;
a system of streets, sidewalks, and boulevards, artistically arranged with regard to each other, and the
elaborate planting of every street and avenue with
many varieties of trees, shrubs, and flowers; and,
crowning all, a large central portion of many acres
devoted to a plaza, a civic centre including the municipal building, school, public library, and Y. M. C. A.
building, and a large central park with provisions for
outdoor athletics of every kind and for recreation and
amusement. The Tennessee Company owns many of
the houses, but makes it possible for the employees to
buy them.

For the unskilled workmen in the coal and ore mines and quarries ample provisions have been made for substantial and even attractive homes to take the places of the former shacks, or "shotgun" houses as they were called. As early as 1908 the Company, having decided to encourage gardening by the miners on the grounds surrounding their houses, built neat wire fences around the yards. An agricultural expert from the United States Department of Agriculture was hired to supervise the work, and the result is that gardens are now being cultivated by 25 per cent. of the employees. The effects have been most gratifying to the company because labourers have been made more efficient by the increased satisfaction they have in their home surroundings, and gratifying to the employees in that their cost of living is thus reduced and that they have a pleasant occupation outside of work hours.

Not less thoroughgoing and expert is the provision for the health of the entire district with its twenty-two distinct villages. In 1913, the Department of Health was organized by the Company with its four divisions of work—Medical, Sanitary, Dental, and Base Hospital. Mr. Crawford, after correspondence with the leading medical schools and hospitals of the country, became interested in two men recommended by Colonel Phillips, second in command to General Gorgas, who was then engaged in his monumental work at Panama. To satisfy himself thoroughly, he spent two weeks in Panama and finally selected Doctor Noland, superintendent and chief surgeon at the hospital at Colon, and a native of Virginia. Colonel Phillips said that he would rather have Noland for his personal surgeon than any man in the world. That he had great power

of organization was evidenced by his work in the
Panama district.   The selection has been abundantly
justified.   The inspectors of the six sanitary districts
working under his direction guarantee the purity of
milk and water, the removal of all refuse, clean streets
and closets, the absence of mosquitoes, etc.   One
result has been that, whereas there were 6,000 cases of
malaria in 1912, last year there were less than one
hundred, and other diseases have fared accordingly.
Every precaution is taken against accidents of all
kinds.   Seventeen emergency hospitals and dispen-
saries are in the various villages, and every opportunity is given for medical and dental treatment and
clinics.   All told, 383 men and women are employed
in this department.

The central office of the whole system and its crowning glory is the General Hospital with its rooms for
318 patients, its training schools for nurses, white and
coloured, nineteen physicians, and everything in the
way of equipment and service that the most modern
city or university hospital has.   The hospital is so
good that the chairman of the Steel Corporation has
been one of its patients, and yet it is none too good for
the poorest of the labourers, who pay a nominal fee
for the privileges accorded them.

The Department of Health coöperates with the
Department of Social Science, which includes separate
divisions for education, welfare, physical education,
and school, home, and community gardens.   Mr.
Crawford employed a social expert to make a complete survey of social conditions and to secure three of
the best social workers he could recommend.   He told
them that he did not want them to follow slavishly

systems and plans which had been adopted elsewhere, but rather to work from within, to find what the whites and Negroes would like to do, and not to impose something from without. For ten years now Miss Winifred Collins has had charge of this department and has had a free hand in the solution of the delicate problems involved. Her experience and training in Chicago have been invaluable: a university graduate and later a student in the School of Civics and Philanthropy, she was an assistant to Dr. Graham Taylor, an important leader in the charity work of the Woman's City Club, a member of the General Advisory Committee of the United Charities, a regular worker with juvenile courts and courts of domestic relations, and connected with various other committees interested in philanthropic work.

There are now nine white and fourteen coloured schools with 5,494 pupils. The schools are a part of the county school system with a special assistant superintendent paid by the company and with additional salaries that guarantee a better type of teachers than those in the county at large. In addition to the regular academic teachers, the company provides for a director of welfare, domestic science teachers, kindergarten and recreation instructors for each village, and these work not only with the children but with the adults. There are community centres, instructors' homes, recreation grounds, community bathhouses, churches, and in some cases clubhouses for men and women. In coöperation with the health department every opportunity is taken to improve the health of young and old: toothbrush drills, dental clinics, safety work, and health-crusade work are regular features of

school and community life. The ingenuity of the
directors is shown in all kinds of community sings,
festivals, pageants, band concerts, athletic contests,
moving pictures, civic clubs, canning clubs, garden
clubs, etc. While the company coöperates by giving
financial aid, the communities themselves are learning
to take the initiative in supplying funds for special
purposes. Instead of the old commissaries, which
used to be run on the basis of large profits for the
company, are now found stores that sell goods at the
same prices as obtain in chain stores in Birmingham,
and they are models of cleanliness.

If this sounds like the standardized welfare work
done in many modern industrial centres, it should be
said, in all fairness, that this company has itself made
contributions to the national movement, and that the
paternalism so characteristic of such work has been
reduced to a minimum. Mr. Crawford's attitude to
those who wish to investigate conditions in the villages
and homes is revealed in what he said to a writer for
an American magazine: "There are no restrictions.
Go right ahead on your investigations. And if you
see fit, I would like to know just what you find—it may
help to improve conditions."[1] Lest I be accused of
overstating the case, I quote the words of Dr. Frederick L. Hoffman, third vice-president of the Prudential
Insurance Company of America, who made a thorough
inspection of the whole system in company with a member of the British Commission in 1918, and gave his
impressions as follows:

---

[1] An interesting human story was the result of this investigation:
Success, January, 1924.

The work of the Tennessee Company in the Birmingham district is one of the most remarkable contributions to the ultimate solution of the labour problem of which I have knowledge. That problem, as I conceive it, involves no more and no less than the whole question of contentment, or absence of friction, on the part of the employee with any and all conditions giving unnecessary occasion for irritation, discomfort, etc. Now, of all that concerns labourers, there is nothing so vital as the houses in which they live, and the surroundings that go with them, and the conditions of family life that depend upon them. The company has taken hold of this question with a thoroughness rarely met with in this country. Familiar as I am with what has been done by the Krupps at Essen, and by other large employers of labour in Germany, and by a number of large corporations in England, as, for illustration, at Port Sunlight, or at York, I am absolutely satisfied that these efforts are on a distinctly higher plane, and bound, in course of time, to produce more satisfactory and lasting results.

Captain Sand and I were particularly pleased with the high order of intelligence on the part of your welfare workers, including the teachers whom we met and their associates. They reflected a practical idealism and common-sense viewpoint, than which there is nothing of greater importance in efforts of this kind. . . . We were delighted with what is being done for the children, the admirable playgrounds provided for them, the excellent school facilities, the wholesome atmosphere surrounding the schoolhouses, the insistence upon personal hygiene, etc.

What pleased us most, however, was the fact that the Company disregards racial lines and aims in its home and housing provisions to provide the same comforts and surroundings for the Negroes as for the whites. The contribution to the so-called race problem may, in the course of years, have a more important influence, in my judgment, than what is being done by Hampton or Tuskegee. After all, there are no impressions more enduring upon the plastic minds of the young than those of early childhood spent amidst pleasing and even impressive home surroundings. Nothing has hindered the Negro as much as the deliberate policy on the part of the whites to provide him continuously with housing accommodations frequently unworthy of the name. While some progress has been made from the one-room cabin to one of two or more rooms, the company is the first, to my knowledge, which is providing a real home life on equality with the conditions under which the best white element lives for those of the coloured race.

The effect of this work on the Birmingham district and on the state in general is quite as marked as the effect of the material development already noted. Jefferson County voted a three-mill tax in order that the schools might be brought up to the standard set by the company for its employees. Nor are the other features of the programme lost on the people of the state. Here in their midst is as enlightened a piece of social work as is being done anywhere in the country. Doctor Noland is now president of the Alabama Medical Association, while his associate, Doctor Walsh, like himself, is regarded as one of the prime movers in a health programme that may extend to the backward counties. Of the taxes paid by the company to the state, $850,000 goes into the support of the state school system.

Of the effects on the state and the South of the significant development that has been here outlined, one of the most striking is the part that Mr. Crawford has taken in the development of the Warrior River and the Mobile Harbour. As already suggested, he soon saw that one of the markets of the products of the Birmingham district must be Central and South America, and one of his early triumphs was the chartering of vessels to take 73,000 tons of steel rails to South America. During the war, the Steel Corporation erected a shipbuilding plant in Mobile; naturally the burden fell on the Tennessee Company and its President. On December 29, 1919, a 9,600-ton vessel was launched from the Mobile dock, and others soon followed. The policy had to be abandoned, as the United States does not seem to foster such a policy, but the whole experience left Mr. Crawford still more impressed with the possibility of Mobile as an export place for his products and for those of a whole section.

After nine years' service on the old State Harbour Board, it was not strange that Governor Brandon should have appointed him Chairman of the new State Docks Commission on the Mobile Harbour, made possible by the appropriation of $10,000,000 by the State of Alabama. In justice to his other work, Mr. Crawford could not accept the position, but he told the Governor that he could find a better man. With the permission of the Governor and the other members of the Harbour Board, he went straight to Kentucky to see General Sibert, a friend of his since the time when General Sibert was the Captain of Engineers in charge of the Monongahela River improvements with offices at Pittsburgh. General Sibert had retired from the army to spend his last days on a blue-grass farm, but when this opportunity was presented to him by a man who has a genius for discovering and inspiring men, he said, "Well, I have been on a good many jobs; I have helped the country build the Gatun Dam in Panama; I have helped Pennsylvania and other states in connection with work on the Monongahela and Ohio rivers; I have helped several other states on the Great Lakes; I have done engineering work on the Canal, but I have never done anything for my native state, Alabama, and I would like to." The services of General Sibert, with his wide experience, can hardly be measured in dollars and cents, but he accepted the position of Chairman of the State Docks Commission,

General Manager and Chief Engineer, and the only compensation he asked was a salary about equal to his living expenses. Now he is in Mobile, undertaking what may prove to be one of the largest commercial developments of the Lower South. When the docks are finished, another one of Mr. Crawford's well-devised plans will have been realized.

It might be thought that such a busy life as Mr. Crawford has led would have absorbed all his energy and left no time for the humanities. As a matter of fact, he finds refuge from business cares in his garden and in his library. He has followed with deep interest all that Burbank has written and has applied some of his methods of work in his own garden.   His favourite prose writer is Anatole France, and his favourite poet Shelley. The "Life and Letters of Sir William Osler" and Wells's "Outline of History" are recent books that have deeply interested him. He likes to travel, especially in countries most unlike America, notably Egypt and France. Interested in the cultural development of Birmingham, he rejoices in the decision of the city to build a $700,000 public library, made possible by the industrial progress of recent years. In every way, he is far removed from the Babbitt type of commercial booster.

And that statement leads me back to the question raised in the opening paragraph of this chapter: Whither is all this industrial development tending, and what is its effect on the life of the South? Such men as Tompkins, Herty, and Crawford are not typical, but they are certainly not isolated. An increasing number of industrial leaders have the same qualities that have led to success in these instances and that make for freedom, thoughtfulness, and culture. Frank C. Rand, president of the International Shoe Company, the largest manufacturers of shoes in the world, was trained in the classics at Webb School and at Vanderbilt, and has reviewed them with his children; he reads constantly the best English literature. He is now at the head of a campaign to increase the endowment of the College of Arts and Science of his alma mater with the avowed object of combating utilitarian tendencies in education. Fairfax Harrison, a descendant of one of the most aristocratic families of Virginia, has returned to the land of his fathers to make the Southern Railway one of the most prosperous and useful railroads in the country, but he has not been too busy to align himself with the supporters of Dean West in the fight for the classics in American education. Similar instances might be multiplied.

Such men in increasing numbers are supplying the money that is necessary for education and general culture. Mammon is a terrible monster, but he is a good slave for promoting the higher needs of mankind. Southern men were for so long individualistic and poverty stricken that they have come slowly to play the rôle of philanthropists. Many institutions in the South to-day are reaping the results of a new public spirit in men of means. The establishment of a great $40,000,000 Foundation for humanitarian and educational purposes by J. B. Duke, who had developed the tobacco industry to world-wide proportions and who had later established the Southern Power Company, is an event of national significance and is prophetic of still further achievements in the South. Not less significant is the change in the attitude to taxation for public purposes, state and local.

One of the best results of material progress is the movement for city planning that leads to the develop= ment of parks and public buildings. Henry James, in his "American Scene" refers to Biltmore, the estate of George Vanderbilt, near Asheville, as "a parenthesis in a barren stretch of country." As he saw the untidy stations, dilapidated farms, unkempt yards and houses, and the sallow bent-shouldered people, he said, "No- body seems to care." Even his æsthetic soul would be delighted if he could revisit these scenes. Bilt- more, with its fine château, its forest, its good roads, and its weaving industry, has had its influence on all western North Carolina and especially on Asheville and the surrounding country. Known formerly as a health resort, this section is more and more becoming one of the most attractive places for tourists from all parts of the country—a summer capital for people of the Lower South. The historic old estates at Flat Rock, long the summer homes of aristocratic Charles- tonians, have become the models throughout the whole district.

The man most responsible for the new Asheville is George Stephens, who, with the coöperation of the Chamber of Commerce, secured the services of John Nolan of Cambridge, Massachusetts, to make a plan toward which the city is building. Stephens served his apprenticeship in Charlotte. As a business leader of far-sighted vision, he worked out with expert advice one of the most beautiful suburban districts in the South. As a banker he was closely associated with the Dukes in the establishment of the Southern Power

Company. He was associated with D. A. Tompkins in the ownership of the Charlotte *Observer* and a supporter of every movement looking to the prosperity and welfare of the city and the Piedmont section. When the village of Biltmore, at the death of Mr. Vanderbilt, was put on the market, Stephens bought it, moved to Asheville, and has been since that time the prime mover in the development of that section. Making money is the least consideration with him; he has the creative point of view, the vision of the builder. The Asheville *Citizen,* of which he is half owner, is at once an organ of material development and an exponent of liberal thought and civic welfare. He is himself a highly cultivated man, a reader of history, biography, and general literature, and a lover of beauty for himself and for others. As a trustee of the University of North Carolina, almost since his graduation, he has been one of the men most responsible for its noteworthy development.

Such men as he are found in other Southern cities—men who have used their money and their brains for the promotion of worthy causes. Looms and furnaces, factories and stores, railroads and water powers, have led to the prosperity of the few and the well-being of the many, and these in turn have been largely responsible for the symphony orchestra and the Parthenon of Nashville, the grand opera seasons of Atlanta and Chattanooga, the County Court House of Memphis, the Tennessee War Memorial Auditorium, and the increasing architectural beauty of colleges that stretch from Charlottesville to New Orleans.

CHAPTER V

THERE is no better illustration of the changes now taking place in the South than the contrast between the University of North Carolina of a quarter of a century ago and the university of to-day. Then you got off a local train at University station on the branch line of the Southern Railway from Greensboro to Raleigh, rode ten miles on a slowly creeping passenger-and-freight train to a dilapidated station a mile from the village of Chapel Hill, and were conveyed in an antediluvian hack to the worst hotel in the state. Now you alight from the "Carolina Special" at Durham, ride in an excellent autobus twelve miles over the model road of the state, and arrive at a beautiful inn that is comparable in its surroundings and service with the best of modern inns elsewhere. Formerly, the backwoods village pulled the university down to its level; the university is now lifting the village to its level; streets, stores, residences, and churches have been transformed until Chapel Hill is well-nigh a model country town. The university then consisted of a few small buildings constructed in the early years of the nineteenth century, and a few of more recent origin built (from inadequate funds) in the dark ages of American architecture; now there are a score or more of new buildings that an awakened state has erected to meet the necessities of a real university. All has changed except the natural environment—the groves of monumental oaks, the lawns, and the old-fashioned flower gardens of one of the most beautiful spots in America.

Though in former days other institutions made heavy drains on the faculty, now, thanks to the far-sighted generosity of the Kenan family in providing funds for adequate salaries of distinguished professors, men eminent in their respective fields of scholarship are quite willing to stay indefinitely at an institution that has the largest and best academic department and graduate school in the South. One strong attraction is the delightful social life and the abundant opportunities for intellectual contacts. All the faculty live within an area of not more than a half-mile square, and everybody sees everybody else in the course of the day's activities. As mail is not delivered at their homes the post office is a favourite rendezvous, and the nearby drug stores are to the villagers what the café is to the Parisians. The university has a large number of clubs and learned societies in which formal discussions and reports are heard, but the informal gatherings are even more stimulating, and they have a provincial flavour that is unique. If Louis Graves— the Ed Howe of North Carolina journalism—ever weaves into a connected story the sketches and happenings that he records in the Chapel Hill *Weekly*, there will be a distinct contribution to American literature.

I hasten to add that this provincial note in the life of the university is balanced by a national and cosmopolitan spirit. The currents of the life and thought of the world flow there. Archibald Henderson, for twenty years the Boswell of Bernard Shaw and the interpreter of other European dramatists, has become more recently the historian of the Southwest and the expositor of Einstein. With the special funds provided by the Kenan bequest professors are constantly going to Europe for travel and special research. E. C. Branson has just returned from Denmark with a book that he wrote on rural conditions there which is calculated to mar the complacency of an Anglo-Saxon state because of its thesis that they manage things better in the little kingdom. E. W. Knight is now abroad studying educational conditions with the definite end in view of throwing light on the present educational system of North Carolina. Dean J. F. Royster was this year the president of the American Association of Universities, a compliment bestowed upon the university because of its high standards of graduate work. Dr. W. B. MacNider, a pathologist of national renown, gave a week's lectures at the Harvard Medical School last spring, while Howard W. Odum as secretary of the Board of Directors of the Institute for Research in Social Science has a commanding position among the sociologists of America.

I doubt if there is any faculty in the country that, in proportion to numbers, is doing more genuinely scholarly work. Everybody has written a book or an article or a monograph, or is reading the proof of one, or collecting notes for one. One is reminded of the saying of Bret Harte when he visited Cambridge at the time of the New England renascence, "You couldn't fire a revolver without bringing down a two-volumer." Even Horace Williams, who as Professor of Philosophy has for thirty years set more North Carolina boys to thinking than any other man in the state and afforded more targets for heresy hunters, has recently published a *magnum opus* on Logic. The academic sterility of most Southern scholars struggling with inadequate libraries and laboratories and burdened with excessive hours of teaching makes all the more praiseworthy the remarkable productive scholarship of this university. I shall have more to say of the more technical research of the various departments. What is even more striking is that J. G. DeRoulhac Hamilton, Gerald Johnson, Paul Green, and others already mentioned, have written some of the most important articles in leading magazines during the past year—articles notable alike for their thoughtfulness and brilliancy of style. A still larger group have made possible the *Journal of Social Forces,* now recognized as one of the most important organs of public opinion in the entire country, and the *Reviewer,* a magazine containing fiction, poetry, and essays of high quality. The University Press, which publishes these magazines and the more technical journals of the stronger departments, has recently published a noteworthy series of volumes written or edited by university men or containing the lectures delivered by leading publicists and scholars at the university.

There are other universities in the South that have better professional schools or some particular department of work in which they excel. The University of Virginia, for instance, has a better law school and a prestige that atones somewhat for the niggardly appropriations of successive legislatures. Vanderbilt has a better selected student body in the College of Arts, and one of the best equipped and endowed medical schools in America. Peabody College for Teachers has facilities for graduate work in Education that compare favourably with similar departments in Columbia and Chicago. The University of Texas has a better library, and some of the other state universities are stronger in some respects because the states have not separated the academic and professional schools from the agricultural and technical schools. Duke University, with its recent large benefactions, is laying plans that will cause it to rank with the foremost institutions of America. But, take it all in all, the University of North Carolina has now a larger and better academic faculty and a better graduate school than any other institution in the South. Indeed, its work in certain departments compares favourably with the best done anywhere.

The departments of English, History, Chemistry, and Social Science are particularly strong, manned as they are with a large number of university professors and furnished with unusual resources for both teaching and research. No other evidence of the high rank of this institution is needed than the publications that have for several years been under the direction of these departments: *Studies in Philology,* the publications of the Historical Society and of the Elisha Mitchell Scientific Society, and the *Journal of Social Forces* are all well known in academic circles by reason of the contributions of the university faculty and of their colleagues in leading American institutions. It is little wonder that some four hundred graduate students from a wide range of colleges are enrolled as candidates for the M.A. degree, and in special cases for the Ph.D. degree. The best antidote to spurious graduate work and questionable degrees is thus being supplied.

Excellent teaching and productive scholarship have gone on *pari passu* with a well-planned scheme of university extension that has kept the university in close touch with the life of the state. Nearly all the heads of the departments, while trained in the best universities of the country and abroad, are "Tar-heel born and Tar-heel bred," or are Southerners who are thoroughly conversant with conditions as they exist. Through lectures, extension bulletins, correspondence courses, and attendance upon every variety of public meeting and associations, they interpret the best that the university has to offer, and at the same time they are bringing every year an increasing number of the people of the state in smaller and larger groups to Chapel Hill for conference and discussion. Professor Connor of the Department of History was formerly secretary of the State Historical Association and has had more to do than any other man with the excellent work that is being done by that association in preserving material and in publishing documents of value; he and his colleagues are still helping to direct its widening activities. The School of Education has a close relationship with the State Department of Education and, through the summer school, is training teachers for the state's most efficient system of schools. If North Carolina has one of the most enlightened departments of Social Welfare now existing, it is largely due to the coöperation of the departments of Sociology and Rural Economics. The

Carolina Playmakers, under the direction of Professor Koch, have not only made for themselves a national reputation, but have stimulated right standards of dramatic production in the schools and communities of the state. The long maintained tradition of inter-collegiate debating at the university has resulted in the stimulation of debating in the high schools of the state, the emphasis being laid on the discussion of contemporary problems of real moment rather than on the hifalutin oratory that has too often characterized public speaking in the South. When due discount has been made for the superficiality of much of this work —and the men who are responsible for it are under no illusions—we still have here a rare coöperation of the university and the state.

Although the university has no department of agriculture, owing to the fact that there is a separate state college in Raleigh, Dr. E. C. Branson, Professor of Rural Social-Economics, has had a marked influence throughout the state in stimulating rural community development. Aside from his own investigations in this country and in Denmark, his most potent instrument has been the North Carolina Club, organized in 1914, and made up for the most part of special and graduate students who have made investigations in the counties of the state. The Club has been exploring North Carolina, in fields economic, social, and civic. It has been busy "defining conditions, causes and consequences and equally considering remedial constructive measures. . . . It has been taking stock of what North Carolina is to-day and what she can be to-morrow. . . . The young men, believing that not to know the home state is to be crippled in culture, cherish dreams of being makers of history in their little world at home." The results of their labours have been published in successive years as follows: "North Carolina: Resources, Advantages, and Opportunities," 1915–16; "Wealth and Welfare in North Carolina," 1916–17; "County Government: County Affairs in North Carolina," 1917–18; "State Reconstruction Studies," 1919–20; "North Carolina: Industrial and Urban," 1920–21; "Home and Farm Ownership in North Carolina," 1921–22; "What Next for North Carolina?" 1922–23.

During the summer of 1925, at a time when an ex-governor of the state exclaimed, "North Carolina is the wonder state, and I am not going to tell you things we haven't got, but rather the things we have got," and other leaders were extolling the superior achievements of the state, Doctor Branson, speaking to a convention of social workers assembled in Chapel Hill, emphasized the astounding fact that 132,000 whites in thirteen counties are illiterate and that there are 1,241,000 citizens who do not own a single inch of the ground they cultivate, or a single shingle of the roof over their heads, and added, "The problem of the landless, homeless people of the state is one which must be reckoned with some day." He appealed to the preachers and lawmakers of the state to create better conditions or face the prospect of a deteriorating civilization; for it is "a dangerous situation when three fourths of all the farmers move from pillar to post, from Dan to Beersheba and back again, making a restless, roving irresponsible element of citizenship." He was called a pessimist by the boosters, but he was never a pessimist. He had spent the year before in Denmark, where he had seen almost ideal conditions in rural districts. He came home with the conviction that "life is bare and hard and uninspiring for far too many people in North Carolina," and with the faith that what he had seen in Denmark might be realized here.

Howard W. Odum, Kenan Professor of Sociology, who has the same fearlessness in finding and proclaiming facts, and the same characteristic faith in the future, came to the university from Georgia after having been trained at Columbia. He had not been in Chapel Hill long before he conceived the idea of establishing the *Journal of Social Forces*. It has now been running for four years, and has maintained the high standard set by the first number. It has made good use of material at hand in the first-hand study of social problems by faculty and students and by other Southerners, and at the same time has had contributions from scholars of the country at large. It has thus become a truly national journal of sociology and has been highly praised by experts and critics. Professor Small of the University of Chicago says: "It has set a pace which is a surprise to the whole sociological continent. We certainly feel the stimulus of your enterprise at Chicago, and recognize that we have our work cut out for us to equal your record." Professor Giddings of Columbia finds in it "a most successful combination of scientific viewpoint and practical appeal." Professor Davis of Yale and Professor Ross of Wisconsin characterize it as "the best and most useful journal of sociology in the entire country." Glenn Frank writes of his deep interest in "this stunning piece of work," while H. L. Mencken, formerly so severe in his judgment of all things Southern, calls it "the most interesting and comprehensive journal of its kind, and by long odds, in the whole United States."

It is to be noted that the expression "the best in the South" does not appear in these statements, and that in itself is a significant fact—an evidence that Professor Odum and his associates are trying to get away from merely provincial standards. And yet, in its various departments, the *Journal* has kept in mind the practical aspects of distinctively Southern social problems, and the writers have handled these with the simple desire to get at the facts and to interpret them with the utmost freedom. As might be expected, it has met with criticism. By reason of an article by Professor Barnes of Smith College a few months ago, which was not an expression of the views of the editor, it was referred to by a leading organ of industrial development as a teacher of communism and socialism. It was also vigorously attacked by several ministerial associations and by one of the leading newspapers of the state as fostering "atheism worse than that of Tom Paine and Ingersoll." One ministerial alliance called upon the Governor, the General Assembly, and the President of the university to take cognizance of "so dangerous a publication and either to discipline it or abolish it." They assumed that the article was approved by the editor or he would never have published it.

Such criticism Odum had in mind when he made an address at his alma mater, Emory University, in the spring of 1924. No more significant address has been delivered in Georgia within this generation. He certainly did not carry coals to Newcastle, for he laid down these fundamental theses, which he illustrated with apt instances very near at hand:

> We do not know enough.
> We do not think enough or well enough.
> We do not read enough or well enough.
> We do not write enough or well enough.
> We do not DO enough or well enough.
> We do not work together well enough, and
> We talk too much.

And he asks pertinently:

> Are we not tired of being ranked last in education, in literacy, in lawlessness, in prison and penal standards, in the simplicity and beauty of our homes, of our towns, of our country houses and communities, of our churches and schoolhouses, in our treatment of the under-privileged, whether of individual or race?

Odum is as bad as Matthew Arnold in asking the most uncomfortable questions without necessarily answering them himself, but leaving the intelligent reader to give his own answers.   In the introduction to "Southern Pioneers in Social Interpretation," a volume of studies of Southern leaders of the past generation, recently published by the University Press, he asks:

> Why, then, are the Southern States so barren of individual leaders who represent the highest achievement in their fields?   In education, in politics, in literature, in art, in industry, in religion, in any aspect of human endeavour, where are there to be found in the South leaders occupying the foremost place in their respective groups?   Or how many even are there who have attained more than mediocre rank?

And again:

> What recognition do they have?   What time, means, opportunity and irresistible impulses have they had since the first days of their promise? . . . Who are they, on the other hand, by

whose reputations the South is known and whose leadership the South follows and esteems? Are they not far too frequently the demagogues and the dogmatists in politics and religion?

After more of this candid and piercing criticism, he closes with an appeal to "turn this Southern potential into national power," for, he insists, the more favourable aspects of Southern progress give promise of a real awakening that shall be national in its influence.

The most vigorous and most brilliant supporter of the work and ideas of Branson and Odum and of the general policy of the university was Gerald W. Johnson, for several years associate editor of the Greensboro *News*. It was natural that, when a vacancy occurred, he should have been elected to the headship of the School of Journalism. He united with knowledge and experience in newspaper work gained on what is generally regarded as the best newspaper in the state and on prominent newspapers such as the Baltimore *Evening Sun,* alertness of mind, a singular insight into contemporary Southern problems, and a style that marks him as the most promising essayist of the present generation of Southern writers. He attributes his emancipation from traditionalism and conformity to President Poteat of Wake Forest College, whom he regarded from his student days as "an amazingly lucid and convincing teacher and a personality still more amazing—a veritable high priest of truth." He was toughened and suppled by wit combats with Earl Godbey, his chief on the *News,* who gave him the opportunity of a free hand in the discussion of political and social problems. At the university he has put into his department the ideals of free and independent journalism and has at the same time written for *Scribner's Magazine*, the *American Mercury*, the *Virginia Quarterly Review*, and other magazines a series of articles on the South that have wrung the withers of sensitive Southerners. If he seems at times to be as brilliant and as forceful as Mencken, and as destructive, the attentive reader discovers that he is far more discriminating and sympathetic, that he, like other members of the Chapel Hill group, is concerned with constructive measures, and that he has a hammer for building as well as a torch for burning. His article on the "Battling South" is a veritable trumpet-blast in the war for liberation.[1]

There is something new under the sun when a college professor in a university whose trustees are nearly all upholders of stalwart democracy writes for a Virginia magazine an article on a "Tilt with Southern Windmills," in which he says:

Naturally, we Southern Democrats prefer to blind ourselves to the real situation. Having no political principles, we set up the assertion that we are conspicuous for our extraordinary loyalty to our political principles. Do we not incessantly march through slaughterhouses to open graves behind the banner of the Democratic Party? The trouble is that the Democratic Party is hardly a more specific term now than the human race. The organization led by William J. Bryan would have meant the adoption of the same political policy that would have followed the election of John W. Davis. Neither would have been likely to put into effect the policy that was put into effect by Woodrow Wilson. Yet we voted for Wilson, too. Our sole political principle is to vote for anything bearing the Democratic label. The North and West determine the bearer of the label. The South supplies his votes. The list of candidates for whom the South has voted in the last twenty-five years, is, by its diversity, irrefutable proof

---

[1] *Scribner's Magazine*, March, 1925.

that the section is politically unprincipled. A section devoted to fixed beliefs and unswerving in its allegiance to those beliefs might vote for Parker or it might vote for Wilson, but it could not possibly vote for both. . . . Had Alfred E. Smith been the candidate, without doubt the Protestant prohibitionist vote of the Solid South would have smothered opposition to his candidacy below the Potomac. Had Beelzebub been the Democratic nominee, the clergy would have been deprived automatically of the privilege of the franchise, and no doubt many of the laity also would have laid down the ballot unused; but I have a strong belief that the stalwarts would have rallied by tens of thousands and gallantly gone to hell.[1]

Nor is Johnson's criticism confined to politics. Political decadence and the evils of the Ku Klux Klan are symptoms of a more deep-rooted tendency "to spawn prophets and martyrs, demagogues, saints, heroes, fakirs, and religious, social, and political whirling dervishes like the grasshoppers for number." It is to the better type of Southerner that he appeals in "The Battling South" to withstand the onslaughts of ignorance and passion. In his exaltation of men like Aycock and Poteat he shows the way to a better and braver type of leadership. He foresees a better future only when we have the courage to face criticism, however severe. In an address before the State Literary and Historical Association last year he reviewed a series of some dozen books in which such criticism is revealed, some of it partisan and prejudiced but, nevertheless, worthy of consideration. We should give a hearing to criticism from without and from within, even from Negroes like DuBois and White:

When we Southerners realize that in reading an important new book we do credit, not to the author, but to ourselves, we shall

[1] The *Virginia Quarterly Review*, July, 1925.

abandon the foolish policy of refusing to read a book simply because it is offensive. . . . Reading unflattering books about the South may be unpleasant, but it is worse to go on in dense ignorance of the trend of modern thought on Southern affairs. When a man declares hotly, "I will not allow that book to come into my house!" he then and there proves that he is spiritually of the ostrich tribe. He reveals his secret belief that what he doesn't see is not seen, that what he knows not is not knowledge. He strikes his own name off the list of those with whom it is profitable to reason.

Mr. Johnson sets a high premium on creative talent; he is an omnivorous reader of the best literature. "The Battling South," he believes, needs poets to help fight the battle against Philistinism.

. . . We who are frankly outside the pale of the artists would cheerfully swap all the literary lapidaries south of the Potomac for one muscular stone-mason who should build us a tower of strength, as well as beauty. We are tired of gentlemanly poets whose verse is as faultless as their manners and their dinner coats. . . .

How we need a poet! . . .

We need in Philistia no moral instructors, no tin-plate messiahs. But we do need a man who can perceive or create a pattern in our chaotic life. We do need a man who can see what is loathsome in our modern civilization and can call it loathsome in words that will blister our ears. We do need a man who can see what is fine and who is able and willing to chisel away the fraudulent and foolish until the fineness is revealed for reverence and preservation. We do need a man who can stimulate an emotional reaction against the emotional debauchery that is sapping our intellectual and moral health. . . .

That cannot happen too soon, for Philistia needs a poet—one of the old Irish type, as described by Donn Byrne: "a lithe, muscular man with a sword."

Now, there is not a poet in Chapel Hill to meet the demands of Mr. Johnson, but Paul Green, assistant professor of philosophy, is a short-story writer and an author of one-act plays of some distinction. He decided, early in 1925, with the help of some of his colleagues to take over the editorship of the *Reviewer,* which had been published for the past four years in Richmond by a group that found it difficult to secure sufficient financial backing for its continuance. An editorial in the first number sets forth his attitude to Southern literature and the points of view to be maintained. With directness and candour he comments upon the latest—the seventeenth volume—of the "Library of Southern Literature." Even the names of President Alderman, Joel Chandler Harris, Charles W. Kent, and C. Alphonso Smith, the sponsors and editors of the formidable venture, do not restrain the editor's sarcasm directed to "the thousands of pages, selections from some hundreds of authors, sent forth unashamedly to convince the world that we were a wronged people, that our literature would bear comparison with that of any time and any place." He does not agree with one of the editors that the literary barrenness of the South has been overstated and its contributions to American literature undervalued, but points to the patent fact that all the reputations of Southern authors have been made by Northern critics. In these volumes there is "no hint that times are ever out of joint, that evil is among us, that there are ultimate and absolute dramatic conflicts in which a man can lose his soul."

In this latest volume of 642 pages we still have "the loud ranting note, the usual rhetoric and spectacular hyperbole bestowed upon earth-departing spinsters, shave-tail poets, nine-day wonders, cross-roads philosophers, minute Alfred Tennysons, and nostalgic, whimpering Poes." Much of the criticism is simply social recognition or state and community pride in mediocre effort. The trouble with Southern literature is that our emotions have lacked the chastening and subduing of reflective thinking. "We have written and lauded one another, founded magazines to boost ourselves, drawn our boundaries around us and refused the caustic consolation of scholarship and criticism because it did not tickle our naïve and foolish vanity."

The editor sees the possibility of a new literature based upon the unassimilated tradition; the crude, unshaped material of art is all about us. What we need is a truer and fresher interpretation of our environment and our relations to that environment; a rejuvenation of our spiritual instincts so long dead to curiosity and wonder; "a food to feed upon different from the sweetened-wind and cotton-candy stuff dished out by our party leaders and preachers and windy gullibles." Our deliverance will not come from the opposite extreme of realism, or from an imitation of Greenwich Village or of the "Bull of Baltimore"—the South has had too many imitators already. We must record our individual emotions and ideas with their very individual expression; in a word, "enlightened sincerity" is the way of hope. It should be said that Mr. Green himself, in stories like "The Devil's Instrument" and in plays like "The No-Count Boy," gives promise of realizing something of his ideal.[1]

In the same number of the *Reviewer* Addison Hib-

---

[1]Five of his plays make up the third volume of "Carolina Plays," Henry Holt & Co.

bard, a member of the English department and the author of a weekly "literary lantern" for some score of Southern newspapers, sums up Southern literature for the year 1924. Out of all the 500 who put themselves down in the census as professional authors he is of the opinion that only fifty have more than a small-town reputation, some ten have won national recognition, and probably not more than five are gifted with a creative ability which will cause their names to live a decade beyond their own death. Romance is still the dominant note in fiction. Poetry has developed most as a form of literature, but it is "remote from to-day's actualities, still refusing, as a whole, to seize upon the life about it for its material." The weak point in the literary armour of the South is the lack of satire— the inability to laugh at itself. Romantic, interested in the pretty, the South is "suspicious of a smile and jealous of a criticism." "Ever since Cable . . . moved North, railroad companies have been selling tickets to writers who find themselves unpopular at home."

When due congratulations have been showered upon these critics and scholars for their clear and straight thinking and for their productive writing, Dr. L. R. Wilson, for many years the University Librarian, will tell you with refreshing candour that the only trouble is that they are not read by the very people who need most to heed them; that, for instance, the *Journal of Social Forces* has three times as many subscribers in the North as it has in the South, that the people of the state are indifferent or judge it by extracts printed in newspapers or brag about it as a North Carolina product that has won encomiums far

and wide; that the *Reviewer* has exactly thirty subscribers in the state that harbours it; that such books
as "Southern Pioneers in Social Interpretation," Woodrow Wilson's address on Lee, the McNair lectures by
President Poteat, and the publications of the North
Carolina Club on various problems—to mention only
a few of the publications of the University Press that
ought to be of special interest to the people of this
section—are bought by only a few libraries and a few
individuals.

For several years now Wilson has been making a
careful study of the reading habits of Southern people,
especially of North Carolina, of their private and public, school and college libraries, their bookstores, publishing houses, and publications, and has come to
certain conclusions that are none too flattering for the
boosters of Southern progress.   He has had the
temerity to raise the question as to whether North
Carolina Publisher and Reader is to rival North Carolina Road Builder, or Cotton Manufacturer, or Cig-
arette Maker, or Federal Income Tax Payer, or
Educator, or Farmer, so gloriously celebrated by the
state itself and the whole country.   In a pamphlet entitled "The Use of Books and Libraries," published
first in the *Journal of Social Forces,* he takes as his
text the saying of Walter H. Page in his famous
Greensboro address on "The Forgotten Man,"
"There are no great libraries in the state, nor do the
people yet read, nor have the publishing houses yet
reckoned them as patrons, except the publishers of
school books."

With pitiless accuracy of research he established
such facts as the following: that only 35 of the 62

towns in the state possess public libraries; that these libraries contain a total of 213,408 volumes (or one book to every 12 men, women, and children); that the incomes of these libraries are pitiably small, that the best of them have a per capita expenditure of 18 cents, whereas the standard recommended by the American Library Association is one dollar; that the circulation of public library books affects not more than 500,000 men, women, and children, leaving the remaining 2,100,000 inhabitants without library service; that one half of the common schools of the state have no libraries at all; that the grand total of all the college libraries, the state library, and the library of the Supreme Court was 444,313 volumes, and of these the university has 108,405—a pitiful showing for the whole state as compared with even single libraries of the East and West.   The showing with regard to the reading of newspapers and periodicals is no better. An average of one paper for every 13.5 inhabitants, compared with an average for the whole country of one to every 3.6 persons, causes the state to rank forty-fifth among the states of the Union.   The comparison is just as bad in the statistics of subscribers to such popular periodicals as the *Literary Digest,* the *Saturday Evening Post,* and the *Ladies' Home Journal,* and even worse for the more important magazines such as the *Atlantic Monthly,* the *World's Work,* etc.   An examination of the bookstores and news-stands confirms the statement that the publishers take no note of North Carolina as a book market, that even popular books of supposedly local interest by reason of authors or subject-matter depend upon outside sales for their income.

In an address at the University of Virginia in 1924 Doctor Wilson takes a more comprehensive view of conditions throughout the Southern States and finds substantially the same situation, or even worse. Further evidences of the South's backwardness in all that relates to reading, writing, and publishing is found in the record made by the literary journals which have followed one another in quick succession to the large graveyard of Southern magazines. Even those that have survived—notably the *Sewanee Review* and the *South Atlantic Quarterly*—have subscription lists that are deplorably small and must depend on special benefactions. At no point in the South has a review achieved even an approximate success as compared, say, with the *Yale Review,* which in a short time has built up a circulation of 18,500 and a national reputation as well. With the exception of religious and educational publishing-houses, the South has no press or publishing concern of which all of us instantly think when our attention is directed to the general field of book production. The consequence is that "if only one of us out of every ten or fifteen reads a third or a fourth of that in other sections, if general public library facilities are much more limited here than elsewhere, it is inevitable that we cannot be as well informed concerning what is taking place and what is being thought of in the world as our fellow citizens who read more." The effect on men who might be inclined to write is that their impulse is killed at the very start, and we do not have a steady contribution of pertinent, vital comment concerning the affairs of the South and nation by men who know at first hand the situations to which their comments relate. There is "no current of stimulating, regenerating criticism from within."

But Wilson is never content with revealing the unfavourable aspects of the situation. For more than a quarter of a century he has been steadily and intelligently struggling to improve conditions. Not content with building up the university library to its present high position, he has been a leader of library progress throughout the state, coöperating with state and local authorities in not only providing libraries but seeing to it that they are properly administered. He has been a prime mover in the extension department of the university. He has from the beginning been at the head of the University Press, which, by publishing the journals and magazines already referred to, and a notable series of books, has won a real place among similar presses throughout the country. All these facts, unfavourable as they may be by comparison with the ideal or actual conditions elsewhere, are heartening and prophetic of still greater progress in the immediate future. The organizations are there, the workers are ready, the appropriations have been started, and Wilson is in a position of commanding leadership. He has formulated the standard, the ideal for the future, and he looks forward confidently to the day when "the capital we invest in the making of men will more nearly equal that we invest in the making of things, when the wealth of our minds will more nearly match the wealth of our factories, and when the paths to learning and more perfect self-government and self-expression are made straight and accessible even unto the most under-privileged." None of the causes that are generally given for the condition here outlined—the Negro, the poverty of the South, the heavy illiteracy, the sparsely settled areas, the interest in conversation rather than in reading—should any longer be sustained. Let us face the facts and move forward!

None of these men could have done the work that has been so far indicated if they had not had the co-operation of a wise and courageous president, or perhaps I should say, succession of presidents. The university has not within this generation been cursed by political domination either in the choice of executives or the faculty. Presidents Battle, Winston, and Alderman played an important rôle in establishing the university after the disastrous period of Reconstruction. President Venable, a chemist of note and a teacher of signal ability, had most to do with fixing scholarship and research as a tradition. President Graham, an alumnus and a teacher who incarnated in a striking way the ideals and traditions of the university, the idol of the student body, the alumni, and faculty, was just in the full prime of his career when death came all too soon; but not before he had phrased in many an admirable address and article his conception of the relations of state and university and had worked out plans for making the walls of the institution the boundaries of the state.

It was nothing short of a miracle that the trustees should have chosen as President Graham's successor Harry W. Chase, a native of New England, who, although he had been connected with the Department of Education for several years, was unknown to the people of the state and had few of the gifts of a popular

leader. Fortunately, the faculty, fearful of outside
political influences and aware of the sterling character,
scholarship, and administrative ability of Dean Chase,
rallied to his support, and the trustees were wise
enough to take their advice. Events have more than
justified his selection. Capitalizing all that had been
done by his predecessors, he has worked out a satisfactory adjustment of the demands of the general
public, the instruction of students, and productive
scholarship by the faculty. Successive legislatures,
impressed by his clear exposition of the needs of the
university, have voted appropriations for maintenance and buildings that would have seemed impossible
even five years ago. It is stated on good authority
that, when President Alderman was offered the presi-
dency of another university, he told some political
leaders of North Carolina that he would remain at
the university if they would guarantee the institution
$50,000 a year; they were afraid to promise. Now
the university receives from the state nearly a million
dollars a year for maintenance and more than that
amount for buildings.

More important, however, than any material progress is President Chase's conception and interpretation
of the real function of a university. It is his conviction that Southern institutions, if properly manned and
given adequate resources—and that in his mind is a
very big *if*—are the best places to develop trained
specialists to deal with particular Southern problems
and conditions. Not that he agrees with the usual
apologist for Southern institutions, who is afraid that
Southern students may be indoctrinated with all sorts
of political, social, and religious heresies by going

North, but he does believe that there is a very definite
need of facilities for investigation, equal to the best in
the country, in the whole field of what might be called
human relationships.   Such training can best be given
by men who either by education or adaptation have
become familiar with Southern conditions.   This is
not provincialism, but a recognition of facts.   And
that is why he has backed to the limit the work done
by Professors Odum and Branson in the field of sociology and why he has taken advantage of the funds
appropriated by the Laura Spellman Memorial Fund
to promote the most minute research in all problems
of social life.

Other illustrations might be drawn from other departments.   During the present year the teaching of
science has been especially under the surveillance of the
public.   As if in anticipation of trouble, the President
outlined his views before the assembled faculty and
students at the beginning of the year.   He defined
the conditions under which real intellectual progress
can take place.   No institution, he insists, ought for a
moment to be allowed to excuse itself for the absence
of genuine intellectual freedom and high and honest
intellectual standards on any ground whatsoever; an
educational institution without these things is "like a
church without religion, or a government without
statesmanship."   He defines admirably two conflicting
theories of education:

The first of these theories holds that education means subduing
the mind, bringing it in obedience to authority, making it docile
rather than independent.   Such a theory restricts the activity of
the mind to the boundaries of such territories as its advocates consider safe and sane, and marks with "no thoroughfare" signs the

entrance to all others. It is this theory of education as the subjugation of the human mind to authority that was so successfully practised by the Catholic Church in the Middle Ages.

The second theory is precisely the opposite. It holds that the business of education with men's minds is not to subjugate them, but to set them free; that the essential condition of intellectual growth is the maintenance of an atmosphere of freedom of thought and of discussion; that if men are to be educated men they must learn to respect facts, to weigh evidence, to reach conclusions based on facts and evidence, not on prejudice or preference; that they must follow truth wherever it leads; that in a conflict between authority and truth the higher allegiance is always to truth. It holds to that great utterance of Thomas Jefferson, "I have sworn upon the altar of God eternal hostility to every form of tyranny over the human mind." Such a theory of education the university holds.

Referring to the attacks that are now being made upon American, and especially Southern, institutions, he continues:

It matters not whether they are directed, as once they were, against the physicist and the astronomer, or against the biologist or the economist. They are all equally fatal to the very conditions which make possible intellectual growth. They all lead inevitably in the direction of a civilization that is characterized by intellectual sterility. It is impossible to restrict the freedom of intellectual inquiry and teaching in any direction without damage to the whole intellectual structure; without creating an atmosphere of evasiveness and compromise and even downright mental dishonesty that students carry with them all the balance of their lives. It is impossible to fit men to participate effectively in a twentieth-century civilization on the basis of a mediæval theory of education.

The words were scarcely out of his mouth before an Anti-Evolution bill was introduced into the Legislature, aimed at all public institutions. He did not wait to be summoned to the committee hearing; he went to fight for his principles and for the institution. The bill was defeated.   How much was due to his opposition cannot be said, but he gave a shining example of bold public service.   On his return to Chapel Hill he received an ovation from faculty and students when he made a public statement of his action, and later from the alumni and trustees gathered at the annual dinner at Commencement.   He does not propose to let matters rest with the temporary victory, and he is ready for any other fight that may come.   He will not sidestep the main issue for any temporary material gain.   At the same time, he does not let the extreme position of the exponents of science and freedom affect his own religious faith, or his desire that the university shall minister to the strengthening of religious faith in the minds of students.   It is his belief that "scientific truth has never, in the long run, done the slightest harm to religious faith, but has, on the contrary, widened and deepened that faith.   North Carolina is a deeply and genuinely religious state.   It is in no denial, rather in a positive affirmation of its faith, that it has taken the stand that faith in God and the free pursuit of knowledge are handmaidens each to each, that the priesthood of science can be at the same time the priesthood of the living God."

What the student body really thinks of all this would be hard to determine; whether its support of the President is simply a conventional form of college loyalty in the face of an attack, or whether it is a deep-seated acceptance of the progressive point of view. But there is one student at the university—in many ways the most unique and distinguished student in an American college—who has left no doubt of his position.   Robert W. Winston was one of the first students to enter the University in 1875 when its doors were opened after the Reconstruction period. He became a distinguished lawyer, appearing in some of the most famous cases in the history of the state; he was for a time judge of the Superior Court, and might have continued on the bench to an honourable old age. Long ago he formed the idea of going back to spend his last days in retirement at Chapel Hill, but nobody ever believed that he would unless it was when he could no longer do anything else. At sixty he proceeded to keep his vow by matriculating as a freshman, and for three years he has been taking courses in a great variety of subjects with all the gusto and curiosity of youth and the ripeness of mature life. More than that, he has caught the Chapel Hill habit of writing. In *Scribner's Magazine* he recently told of his experiences as "A Freshman at Sixty" in one of the most charming of contemporary essays.

He has taken the best courses in the departments in which he is most interested. With the scientist and the philosopher he has talked about religion and science and then published in the *Journal of Social Forces* a striking article, "The Noose of Darwin and the Neck of Orthodoxy." In the field of history he has just published in *Current History* an article on the "Rebirth of the Southern States," in which he shatters the illusions of the Old South with a recklessness that reminds one of the radicals of the younger generation. Courses in the short story with Hibbard, in æsthetics with Paul Green, and in the one-act play with Koch have awakened his creative faculty so that he is now writing a story and a play. All in all, he is one of the most interesting and significant psychological phenomena that we have in America to-day. Here is a man who ten years ago would have been picked out by many as a Southern Bourbon, though those who saw him in his library or sat with him by the fireside knew that he was cherishing underneath a veil of conventional opinion and standards many suppressed desires and thoughts. He had to make money, he had to have clients, he had to make a speech now and then that had the characteristic fustian and orthodoxy. And now, when he is independent in fortune and freed of family responsibilities and no longer ambitious of honour in his profession, he is born again in the atmosphere of his alma mater.

Robert Winston could tell better than anybody else the difference between the university of the late 'seventies and of the present, how things are happening there now that make those buried in the little cemetery turn in their graves, what ghosts walk there in the night time. He belonged to a generation of students that included Alderman, Aycock, McIver, Josephus Daniels, and other leaders in every field of human endeavour. But he is very much enamoured of the present. He said the other day: "I would not give twenty minutes of the Chapel Hill of 1925 for a hundred years of 'befo' de war.' Great but narrow was 1875; 1925 is broad and universal." In his own student days the university community was emotional, personal in its criticism, full of taboos and obsessions —in a word, proud, sensitive, belligerent. Now men take all sides of questions and discuss them with fairness and moderation: "the spirit of the place is freer and finer and more democratic."

The only doubt in his mind, and in the minds of

many others, is as to whether the state that has made such remarkable progress is going to meet the test of building an even greater university. If it is not willing to increase its appropriations and thus enable the university to build on its present foundations, or if it is not willing to grant the administration and the Faculty the fullest freedom in the search for truth, then North Carolina will remain a "militant mediocrity."

CHAPTER VI

NO STRONGER statement of the principles involved in academic freedom has been made in recent years than the address on "Liberty and Slavery in Universities" by Professor W. M. Thornton of the University of Virginia before the Phi Beta Kappa Society of that institution in June, 1924. Expressing his joy that "the child of Thomas Jefferson" has been remarkably free from the blighting effects of "the tyrannies which have too often abased scholarship and throttled scholars," he pleads with his audience not to forget "the fates of the graduates who went to labour in the far-flung fields of American scholarship," and to strengthen the influence of public opinion which will best defend "the sanctities of science and learning." With a long array of historic instances in which states and churches have tried to stop the advance of truth, he concentrates attention upon incidents nearer home that illustrate the tendency to control by legislation the truths of science and upon efforts of the Church to stay the hand of critical scholarship. He does not hesitate to denounce a certain state university for "its ignoble treason as a public guardian of American scholarship" in dismissing without a hearing, and on "pretexts too flimsy to be even a decent veil," one of the graduates of the University of Virginia. He takes pride in the fate of another alumnus who was "demoted from slavery in a secluded seminary of denominational theology to the large freedom of modern scholarship in the oldest and greatest university in America." Should the University of Virginia, he asks, keep silence when one of her own graduates is the victim of gross wrong? The publications of every American university should recite the flaming story of its own alumni; and through the columns of the public press such offenses should be "exposed by college men to reprobation as not only a private evil but a public wrong."

In words that remind one of Emerson's address on "The American Scholar," before the Phi Beta Kappa Society of Harvard in 1837, Thornton asks:

What mission could be nobler, what more useful, what more fitting for a group of picked men, drawn from the graduates of so many famous universities, filled with the scientific temper, self-dedicated to the belief that this temper is the only safe guide of life, than to take for your aim the conservation of university freedom and dedicate your society to the abolition of slavery and the maintenance of intellectual liberty in the universities of America? . . . You would have powerful fighters to face sometimes: prejudiced prelates intrenched behind their mystic creeds; ignorant politicians with their popular slogans, such as "Back to the Rock of Ages and forget the ages of rocks!"; selfish plutocrats with their unscrupulous propaganda. But the strength and the truth and the uprightness and the far vision would be yours. For you would be lifted above selfishness; professors even the most distinguished are handicapped by their calling in this conflict; from you, men would hear the ringing note of a trumpet of no uncertain sound.

Not even this appeal, nor the more powerful words of Virginia's patron saint, Thomas Jefferson, have been able to stem the tide of public clamour that now and then sweeps over Southern colleges. There has been scarcely a year during the past quarter of a century when some institution of higher learning has not had to face the question of academic freedom. Unfortunately, the cases that receive the most public attention are those in which some professor is ousted from his position. The dismissal of Professor Winchell from Vanderbilt University in the late 'seventies and of Professor Woodrow from the Presbyterian Seminary at Columbia in 1888 have lingered long in the public mind by reason of the accounts given in Andrew D. White's "Warfare of Science and Theology." But they are not isolated cases. Professor Andrew Sledd was dismissed from Emory College because of an article in the *Atlantic Monthly* on the Negro problem, but he is now a member of the same faculty. Professor Enoch Banks met a similar fate at the University of Florida because of his interpretation of the issues that led to the Civil War. Professor Robert Kerlin, moved to protest against the treatment of Negroes in Arkansas, found his usefulness at the Virginia Military Institute so impaired that the trustees could dispense with his further services. When Professor John A. Rice wrote a book on the Old Testament which drew the fire of the Fundamentalists of Texas because of its expression of opinions that are shared by liberal preachers of all denominations, the trustees of Southern Methodist University, moved by resolutions of church conferences, asked for his resignation. The efforts of the Southern Baptist Convention to set up an inquisition in its colleges by submitting questionnaires to all professors led to the dismissal of Professor Fox at Mercer University and to the withdrawal of several teachers from Baylor. And the end is not yet.

I am quite aware that in all these cases, as in all other cases of academic freedom, there are extenuating circumstances. It is not a question of absolute right or wrong, white or black. Some defects in a man's temperament, some limitation that affects his usefulness, some failure to do his job, some eccentricity of manner or folly of speech—these become involved in the issue. Trustees are sometimes their own worst enemies in not meeting the issue long before any question of opinion arises. It is often true also that men remain in the institution who hold substantially the same opinions but have tact and wisdom enough, and the confidence of the community and the public enough, to ward off any attack or criticism. And there is always the argument of the good of the institution that must be considered beyond the welfare of any individual.

But when all is said, it remains true that presidents and boards of trust often use these excuses as a pretext for their cowardice. They are too often time-servers, thinking only of patronage or material progress. For immediate expediency they sacrifice a principle that is the very glory of an institution. Nor do they seem to realize that the dismissal of a man for opinion's sake is a form of the direst persecution; in essence, it is taking away a man's means of livelihood, the support of his family; nor is this point obviated by the fact that men do get positions elsewhere.

I prefer, however, to lay the emphasis in this chapter on the victories rather than on the defeats of academic freedom, and to concentrate especially on two cases that have come within my personal experience. In one case, Trinity College—now Duke University—retained Professor John Spencer Bassett in the face of an almost hysterical clamour that he be dismissed because of an article on the Negro question. In the other, Vanderbilt University successfully resisted a lawsuit brought by the Southern Methodist Church to secure an unprecedented ecclesiastical control over its Board of Trust. In both cases, all the reactionary forces of public opinion were turned against the institutions, each of which emerged from the crisis more powerful and influential than before.

I

In October, 1903, Dr. John Spencer Bassett, at that time Professor of History in Trinity College, published an article in the *South Atlantic Quarterly* on "Stirring Up the Fires of Race Antipathy"—a frank, rather extreme, but not revolutionary, article on some phases of the Negro problem. A native of North Carolina and a graduate of the college, he had spent several years as a graduate student at Johns Hopkins in history and had been for ten years one of the most successful and most admired teachers at Trinity. He had been a good faculty officer, especially successful in building up an adequate college library. He had inspired some of the strongest students to do special work in history and had himself done research work of a high order. Through local and state historical societies he had stimulated the people of the state to preserve much rich historical matter. In 1902, he had taken the initiative in establishing the *South Atlantic*

Quarterly, which from the start was recognized as an important organ of liberal thought in the South.   Few men of his age stood out more prominent in academic circles or looked more promising to the general public.

So much needs to be said in order to have a setting for the article that aroused so much criticism and led to a crisis in the life of Trinity College.   The primary object of the author of the article was to call attention to the great danger of passion and prejudice in dealing with the race question, and especially to the harm caused in the South by the continual interjection of politics into any discussion of so delicate a problem. In distinguishing between the upper and lower classes among the Negroes, he condemned pessimists for generalizing from the latter and optimists for pointing to Booker T. Washington as a typical product of the Negro race, and then added this sentence which, more than any other, awakened passionate indignation: "Now Washington is a great and good man, a Christian statesman, and, take him all in all, the greatest man, save General Lee, born in the South in a hundred years; but he is not a typical Negro."   Unfortunately, the comparison with other Southern leaders was unnecessary and unwise, and was calculated to draw attention away from the more important points in the article.

Two weeks after the publication of the article, the editor of the Raleigh *News and Observer*—at that time the most influential paper in North Carolina— printed the entire article, and wrote a long editorial in which he distorted passages and made sensational appeals to the prejudice and passion of the people. If he had been as eager for the welfare of the people and for the suppression of everything calculated to make the race question more serious, as he had claimed to be, he would never have given wider circulation to an article, which, according to his judgment, was of the most inflammatory character. To give a definite idea of the views of the editor the following passages will suffice; they are taken from the issues of November 1st, 10th, and 20th, respectively:

Of late years the pulpit and the chair of the college professor has too often become the fomenter of strife and the forum of absurdity. Chicago University is the head centre for educated freaks and the chief institution where men are taught that it is wiser to put their trust in Standard Oil than in the Water of Life. But that is not the only institution that harbours freaks who rush into print with absurd statements and dangerous doctrines—statements, which, if true, damn the State of North Carolina, and doctrines, which, if carried out, would destroy the civilization of the South.

Such a freak is John Spencer Bassett, of Trinity College. He is a student and writes well. Somebody once asked Senator Joe Brown, of Georgia, what he thought of Senator Ingalls. His reply was: "Ingalls is a right smart fellow, but he 'hain't' got no sense." That will be the estimate of Professor Bassett by those who judge him solely by the article that he prints as the first contribution in the October number of the *South Atlantic Quarterly*.

The truth is that Professor Bassett moves and lives in an atmosphere that is as far removed from the things which nine tenths of the North Carolinians hold dear as if he resided on another continent. The spirit of measuring everything by the standard of the dollar, of looking up to the trust as beneficent institutions, of regarding political questions from the standpoint of Hannaism, and regarding hostility to and contempt of the things that are dear to the North Carolinians as the only evidence of breadth and liberality, has long dominated Doctor Bassett and some of his associates. Step by step he and others have gone

away from every Southern ideal and every Southern tradition
and every Southern conviction, until he and they think they are
right only when their opinions conflict with Southern thought. It
was, therefore, not a long way for Mr. Bassett to go to reach the
conclusion that the Negro is the equal of the white man, that
Booker Washington is the greatest man, except one, born in the
South in a hundred years, and to declare that the only way to
solve the race question was to repudiate the idea of Negro inferiority.

. . . When a Southern educator proclaims that the Negro
is the equal of the white man, that the public men of the South
have been guided by base motives in their advocacy of white government, that one bright mulatto is greater than Stonewall Jackson, Jefferson Davis, Ben Hill, Zebulon B. Vance, Henry Grady,
and every other Southern man born in the South within a hundred
years except Lee, and when he declares that the race conflict will
grow worse as long as one race is regarded as inferior to the other
—when a Southern educator proclaims such views, abhorrent to
Southern thought and destructive of Southern civilization, he ought
not to desire to teach Southern youths. If he holds views utterly
antagonistic to what the South believes and knows to be true, he
should not retain a position in a Southern college. . . .
. . . The trouble with Mr. Bassett is that he has been
feeding upon husks of trust contempt for the rights of the people,
political hatred of the dominant party in the South, hostility to
the old-time creeds and traditions that have made North Carolina
folk a sturdy, manly, independent, and just people.

In these contentions Mr. Daniels was joined by a
large proportion of the newspapers of the state, which
indulged in vituperation, invective, and scurrility not
surpassed since the days of Reconstruction. The columns of the paper were filled for weeks with appeals
to sectionalism, partisanship, religious bigotry, and
personal enmities. Extracts from the most ignorant
country editors were displayed in bold-face type. As
the discussion waxed in passion it took a wider range

and included attacks on the president of the college, the benefactors, and other members of the faculty. The general policy of the institution was said to be out of harmony with "old-fashioned North Carolina Methodism" and opposed to everything that was best in Southern life. The very men who had insisted that the elimination of the Negro from politics would permit greater freedom of discussion led the cry for Doctor Bassett's expulsion—the men who live on stirring up race hatred whenever it serves their purpose.

A boycott of the college was proposed. Parents were urged to take their sons away. Then it was demanded that Doctor Bassett, and perhaps others, should be summarily dismissed from the faculty. Against both these suggestions a few notable protests were made. The editor of the Charlotte *Observer*, in an editorial of much dignity and poise, while regretting the "radical statements" of Professor Bassett, called attention to his noteworthy services in behalf of the college and the state, and made a plea with the public not to allow the usefulness of a worthy institution to be impaired by the blunder of one man. The editors of the *Biblical Recorder*, the Baptist paper, and of the *Progressive Farmer*, an influential rural paper, argued with equal earnestness against the dismissal of Doctor Bassett as a menace to the cause of free thought and free speech. But these appeals were not heard in the general clamour of the multitude. Besides the extremely prejudiced writers on the subject, there were some honest men—loyal but mistaken friends of the college and even of Doctor Bassett— who believed that the best interests of the institution demanded his unconditional resignation. They argued

with sincerity that any other policy would bring immediate ruin upon the college and a division in the
Methodist Church. There were others who held to
the theory that a teacher in a Southern college ought
to teach only those things that are in harmony with
"Southern public opinion," and that as soon as a college teacher found himself out of agreement with that
opinion he should immediately retire, or the college
should dispense with his services. To very few did
the principle of academic freedom even suggest itself.

In view of this widespread agitation and almost universal demand for his resignation, Bassett offered to
resign in case the trustees thought it best for the institution. As soon as this announcement was made and
a meeting of the Board of Trustees was called, pressure was brought to bear on every one of the trustees
—pressure through political and ecclesiastical leaders.
Up to the time the Board met, no statement had been
given out from the college. There were rumours that
President Kilgo, the faculty, and students would stand
by Bassett, but no public statement had been made.
When the Board met, the general impression was that
the resignation would undoubtedly be accepted.

But the public had left out of their reckoning the
most vital factor in the situation—the spirit of a
young, progressive, unhampered, free institution, which
for ten years had been steadily growing in endowment, in influence, and in the spirit of freedom and
nationalism. Its constitution had stated as one of its
primary aims: "to advance learning in all lines of
truth; to defend scholarship against all false notions
and ideals; to develop a Christian love of freedom and
truth; to promote a sincere spirit of tolerance."

President Kilgo, in a strong address to the Board, gave his views of the situation. He made a plea for a spirit of tolerance in the case of one who had done such valuable service for the institution. Passing from the consideration of an individual, he presented the principle of academic freedom as it affected the life and destiny of Trinity College and all other institutions of learning. "I am ready to declare," he said, "that coercion of opinion in all times has been a miserable failure; that truth and reason and life have never been advanced by force and physical pain. . . . Tolerance is a virtue which has been well established in all modern civilization, and is the foundation virtue upon which American civilization has been built and developed."

In answer to those friends of the college who maintained that the retention of Bassett would seriously impair the usefulness of the institution, he said:

You cannot hurt this institution more fatally, you cannot deal it a severer blow, you cannot bring upon it more fully the suspicions of just and honourable men than by enthroning coercion and intolerance. Bury liberty here, and with it the college is buried. . . . It were better that Trinity College should work with ten students than that it should repudiate and violate every principle of the Christian religion, the high virtues of the commonwealth, and the foundation spirit of this nation. . . . Personally, I should prefer to see a hurricane sweep from the face of the earth every brick and piece of timber here than to see the college committed to policies of the Inquisition.

To the same effect spoke the faculty in a formal statement of their position—a statement signed by every member, and accompanied, as only they and the President knew, by their resignations in case the Board

accepted their colleague's resignation.   They did not
defend or approve of some of the expressions in Bassett's article, but they declared that the spirit of the
college must be preserved from violation.   They
stated the problem in the light of their own work and
that of other institutions of learning:

> We should be recreant to the principle and false to our brothers
> in other colleges if we did not now urge upon your body the
> gravity of the crisis.   If American colleges are to be the homes
> of seekers after truth, their atmosphere must be favourable to the
> free expression of opinion.   This college has now the opportunity
> to show that its campus is undeniably one spot on Southern soil
> where men's minds are free, and to maintain that the social order
> of the South need not be shielded from criticism, because it has no
> reason to fear it, because it is not too weak to bear it.   .   .   .
> Money, students, friends are not for one moment to be weighed
> in the balance with tolerance, with fairness, and with freedom.

In a final appeal to the Board they said:

> We urge you to say of Trinity College what Thomas Jefferson,
> the founder of American democracy, said of the institution he
> founded: "This institution will be based upon the illimitable free-
> dom of the human mind.   For here we are not afraid to follow
> truth wherever it may lead, nor to tolerate error so long as rea-
> son is left free to combat it."

The students were not less loyal to the ideals of
their institution.   Their admiration for their teacher,
and their demand that the ideals that they had been
taught to reverence should be strictly maintained, were
made manifest to the Board.   No more gratifying
thing ever happened in the Southern States than the
unanimity of this student body in the crisis through
which the college was passing.   In spite of all attempts
to bring about a boycott, not one student left the col-

lege. Letters were read to the Board also from many alumni of the college—especially those of recent years —pleading that the spirit of the college might be preserved. And besides all these counter influences was the active sympathy of the Duke family, the generous benefactors of the institution, with the principle of tolerance and freedom.

And yet, against all these contentions, a strong element in the Board made a determined fight. It was led by the most successful politician of the state, who demanded that the voice of the people should be heard. He said that expediency was the only idea involved. He appealed strongly to race prejudice, saying that he was making a fight for "white supremacy." He was aided by the editor of the official organ of the Methodist Church in North Carolina. After a seven-hours' session the Board voted—eighteen to seven—not to accept the resignation of Professor Bassett, and it adopted the following strong statement of the reasons for its action:

1. Any form of coercion of thought and private judgment is contrary to one of the constitutional aims of Trinity College, which is "to cherish a sincere spirit of tolerance." We prefer to exemplify this virtue rather than hastily to set it aside and thus do violence to a principle greatly esteemed by all men of noble feeling.

2. We are particularly unwilling to lend ourselves to any tendency to destroy or limit academic liberty, a tendency which has, within recent years, manifested itself in some conspicuous instances, and which has created a feeling of uneasiness for the welfare of American colleges. Whatever encourages such a tendency endangers the growth of higher education by intimidating intellectual activity and causing high-minded men to look with suspicion upon this noble profession. We cannot lend countenance to the degrad-

ing notion that professors in American colleges have not an equal liberty of thought and speech with all other Americans.

3. We believe that society in the end will find a surer benefit by exercising patience than it can secure by yielding to its resentments. The search for truth should be unhampered and in an atmosphere that is free. Liberty may sometimes lead to folly; yet it is better that some should be tolerated than that all should think and speak under the deadening influence of repression. A reasonable freedom of opinion is to a college the very breath of life; and any official throttling of the private judgment of its teachers would destroy their influence, and place upon the college an enduring stigma.   .   .   .   The same broad principle holds both in the college and the state. While it is idle to deny that the free expression of wrong opinions sometimes works harm, our country and our race stand for the views that the evils of intolerance and suppression are infinitely worse than those of folly.

When the decision of the Board was announced, at three o'clock in the morning, the students, who had waited eagerly for the outcome, rang the college bell and lighted bonfires. To them it seemed, as to the entire community, that the college had resisted one of the strongest attacks ever made by forces of intolerance, bigotry, and mistaken friendship.

None of the dire calamities that had been predicted for Trinity College materialized. There were more students the next fall than ever before, and the affirmation of the right and duty of the college to express freely its matured conviction on political and other debatable questions was accepted as final. President Roosevelt expressed the point of view of the entire country when he said in an address at the college the following year:

I know of no other college which has so nobly set forth as the object of its being the principles to which every college should be devoted, in whatever portion of this union it may be placed. You stand for all those things for which the scholar must stand if he is to render real and lasting service to the state.   You stand for academic freedom, for the right of private judgment, for the duty more incumbent upon the scholar than upon any other man, to tell the truth as he sees it, to claim for himself and to give to others the largest liberty in seeking after the truth.

The continued growth of the college in standards and endowment reached a sudden climax when in 1925 Mr. J. B. Duke, long time a friend and benefactor, announced his establishment of a $40,000,000 foundation, a third of which was to go to the establishment of Duke University with Trinity College as the nucleus. At his death a few weeks ago it was found that he had made still further provision for building and endowment.   While the full plans have not been matured, it may now be taken for granted that within a few years Duke University will take its place among the great institutions of the world—great in its architectural beauty, in its resources for the most advanced graduate and professional work, and great in its maintenance of the spirit that triumphed in the struggle of 1903.

II

The Semi-Centennial Celebration of the founding of Vanderbilt University, combined with the inauguration of its eight million dollar Medical School,[1] served to emphasize the national significance of the growth of this Southern institution to its present position of power and influence.   Of the many addresses made by distinguished leaders of America and foreign countries, none caused more favourable comment at the

_____
[1] October 15–18, 1925.

time and since than those of Chancellor Kirkland and Whitefoord R. Cole, president of the Vanderbilt Board of Trust. The Chancellor, in reviewing the history and the policies of the university, said:

The answer to the episode at Dayton is the building of new laboratories on the Vanderbilt campus for the teaching of science. . . . The remedy for a narrow sectarianism and a belligerent Fundamentalism is the establishment on this campus of a school of religion, illustrating in its methods and in its organization the strength of a common faith and the glory of a universal worship.

It may be doubted if Americans generally, or even the large number of prominent speakers and delegates who attended the impressive exercises, realized just what lay back of the occasion. The liberalism that was manifest throughout the four days' programme was not a sudden flare-up. As the long and colourful academic procession made its way from the State Capitol to the Tennessee War Memorial Auditorium, some were doubtless thinking of what had taken place at the meeting of the last Legislature, and others of a day in March, 1914, when many of the trustees, faculty and alumni of Vanderbilt walked down from the same capitol with joy in their hearts over the unanimous decision of the State Supreme Court that had decreed the independence of the Board of Trust from an extreme form of ecclesiastical control. The celebration of fifty years of steady progress would have been impossible but for this decision, which came at the end of a decade of conflict between the forces of progress and reaction. Reactionary forces met an utter defeat in their attempt to bind a growing and progressive institution with the chains of a narrow and sectarian policy.

The crisis through which the university passed from 1905 to 1914 was one of the most serious that ever confronted a university. The victory it won over the attempt of the Southern Methodist Church to control the Board of Trust should be heartening to all who are interested in the maintenance of academic freedom. The General Conference of that church through its bishops brought a lawsuit to establish two contentions or claims: first, that the Conference had the right to elect the trustees of the university, and, second, that the bishops had the right of visitation, which amounted to a veto over any action of the Board. Such rights had never been exercised or claimed during the forty years of Vanderbilt's history, or over any other institution, or board, or organization of the Church. When the Supreme Court of Tennessee, despite the overwhelming sentiment of the general mass of the people, held by a unanimous decision that the Conference had no such rights, but that it was entitled to continue the relations with the university that it had held since the foundation of the university— namely, the right to confirm or reject the trustees selected by the Board of Trust and otherwise to co-operate with the Board—then the Conference withdrew from all connection with the university and proceeded to establish two other institutions of higher learning in its place. Many in the Church at that time and later saw that the propaganda and lawsuit amounted to an exaggerated case of ecclesiastical "rule or ruin."

The whole affair is worth looking into, as it throws

light both on one of the most important institutions in the South and on one of the most significant aspects of Southern opinion and leadership.

The efforts of the leaders of the Church to strengthen their control over the university were made in the face of the broad and liberal policy that had been laid down by Commodore Vanderbilt, Bishop McTyeire, and Chancellor Garland, and that had been continued since 1893 by Chancellor Kirkland. Bishop McTyeire, who had been the prime mover in the plans looking to the establishment of a university in the Southwest under the general auspices of the Southern Methodist Church, realized that the whole scheme was a failure on account of the exhausted condition of the South. At that crisis Cornelius Vanderbilt, desiring to help a struggling people and to "strengthen the ties between the two sections," and with confidence in the broad-minded leadership of Bishop McTyeire, gave what was then the large sum of one million dollars. As Chauncey Depew, one of his intimate friends, said later: "It never entered the mind of the Commodore or his sons that he was to found a purely denominational college. . . . He never could have been induced to give a dollar for a purely sectarian institution." Bishop McTyeire, as if anticipating the later contentions of the church leaders, said of the method of selecting members of the Board of Trust:

The constituency, the fitness and the safety of the Board having this vast and growing interest in trust will be very uncertain if, by popular election, on hasty and perhaps ill-considered grounds of choice, its future members are to be supplied. Whereas, the Board knows its own wants, is familiar with the nature of the work to be done, has the university and its interests in mind and heart, and is ever watchful of its welfare and on the lookout for suitable agents and instruments to promote it. . . . This course is not only demanded by provident wisdom, but is in analogy with other and the oldest institutions of learning under the care of the Church. The Board elects or nominates, and the Annual Conference confirms.

A resolution to this effect prepared by Chancellor Garland became a by-law, which declared that "the charter of Vanderbilt University confers upon its Board of Trust the exclusive right and power to fill vacancies that may occur in its own body, and that this power cannot be delegated to any other body of persons whatsoever. . . ."

Both Bishop McTyeire and Chancellor Garland agreed that the faculty should not be limited by denominational affiliations, but determined by attainments in scholarship.   In the early 'eighties, under the leadership of a faculty, notable alike for their scholarship and their knowledge of the best educational practice in this country and abroad, the university raised its standards of admission and graduation to a point not then reached by other institutions in the South, fostered by this policy the development of the best secondary schools, private and public, and thus created its own constituency outside of purely denominational lines.

The leader of this faculty, Dr. James H. Kirkland, who was elected Chancellor in 1893, said in his inaugural address:

No spirit of narrowness or prejudice controls us here. . . . We are engaged in the broad work of Christian education. We have no peculiar tests for professors and students, no concern for denominational preferences.

And again, at the twenty-fifth anniversary of the founding of the university in 1900, he said at the end of a comprehensive survey of the university's history and prospects:

We stand committed to a high educational policy, and from this policy we do not propose to swerve. . . . We propose therefore to be for ever true to our position as a Christian institution. We shall follow this high ideal in the same spirit that has controlled us in the past—a spirit of enlightened patriotism and broad Christianity.

Meanwhile, there were leaders in the Church who were nursing their wrath and waiting only for a favourable opportunity to call a halt to the growing liberalism of the university. As early as 1895, the editor of the central organ of the Church, Dr. E. E. Hoss, sounded a note of warning that Vanderbilt should be more "Methodistic." Speaking of the faculty, which, under the administration of Chancellor Kirkland, had maintained the same proportion of Methodists and non-Methodists as the first faculty selected by Bishop McTyeire, he said, "If we had our way, they should also be zealous and active Methodists. If this be sectarian bigotry, then any one who wills may make the most of it." Later on, he said with unmistakable candour and undeniable force:

Other denominations are never guilty of the false liberality of proclaiming that they do not look for discrimination in their own favour in the schools which they have established. Why should they be? What do they establish schools for? It has been left to the Methodists to show the extreme folly of spending their time and money and influence to rear colleges that make a boast of their indifference between the different churches. We have had enough of this. *Denominational colleges are set up for the same reason as denominational newspapers and publishing houses—to advance the interests of denominations.* Is this sectarianism? Is it bigotry? It is nothing of the kind. It is only common sense applied to the sphere of ecclesiastical life. We say to all concerned with the utmost frankness that they will find it to their advantage to adjust their plans to the views which we have expressed.

On October 4, 1900, he returned to the attack:

What is here said in reference to preachers and editors applies also to teachers in our church schools, particularly to presidents and principal professors. They should be men or women of solid piety, who both know and love Methodist doctrine and discipline. School men who have an eye to the main chance as well as to the interests of the Church do not always observe this precaution. . . . As we see the matter, it is neither uncharitable nor evidence of bigotry to demand that the faculties of Methodist schools should be filled with Methodist teachers. This would be far better than to show the secular spirit of employing mixed faculties solely to draw patronage. Our schools should stand on their merit and be what their names indicate, Methodist institutions.

In accordance with the editor's prophecy that the Methodist Church would "tighten her grip on every brick of the buildings, on every foot of land on the campus, and on every dollar of endowment," one of the bishops offered in the Board of Trust a resolution to the effect that the faculties be so constituted as eventually to draw a majority of their members from the Church.

We feel [said he] that the time has come to make a distinct record of the purpose and policy of the university in this particular to the end that our people may be reassured of the intention of the institution to serve them as a church in the most unfalteringly loyal fashion, and that they may be moved to sustain the institution by their patronage and their gifts.

This resolution precipitated a controversy within the Board that led Chancellor Kirkland to proffer his resignation. The question arose as to whether Dr. F. W. Moore should be appointed Dean of the Academic Department. There was no criticism of his scholarship, or of his fitness for the position, but solely as to his membership in the Baptist Church. The same criticism had been made against Dr. H. C. Tolman, one of the foremost Sanskrit and Greek scholars in America, and against Dr. W. L. Dudley, who had had more to do with the purification of athletics in Southern colleges than any man of his generation, solely because they were Episcopalians. At a called meeting of the Board, the Chancellor defined his position as to the qualifications for members of the faculty and called for a definite expression of the future policy of the Board. He said that he had inherited the policy he had sought to maintain; that the university was "a great trust, committed to the Methodist Church, not for selfish ends, but for the good of society and the upbuilding of Christ's Kingdom." Fortunately, broad-minded leaders like Bishops Hendrix and Galloway led the Board by a unanimous vote to give the unwritten policy of the university the authority of a statute and to decree that in the future, as in the past, they would "secure the most competent scholars of the highest attainments in their respective departments." Whereupon the Chancellor withdrew his proffered resignation, and a crisis was averted in the Board.

Another point of attack throughout the Church was the alleged heresy of the professors in the Biblical department. It was claimed that the very citadel for the training of preachers had been captured by the higher critics and evolutionists.   Not only regular professors in their classrooms, but in the preachers' institutes men like George Adam Smith, Shailer Matthews, and E. D. Burton were sowing the seeds of heresy, and in the Cole lectures the most eminent Biblical scholars and preachers were destroying the faith of the fathers. Twenty years ago, the lines were thus drawn between the Fundamentalists and the Progressives.

The storm that had been brewing for years broke when the Board of Trust in 1905 passed an amendment to the by-laws to the effect that hereafter, instead of all the bishops being *ex officio* members, five in the order of seniority should act as trustees.   It was heartily approved by all the bishops present, who saw, as the Chancellor pointed out, that very few came to the meetings, that most of them were more interested in their own local institutions and really preferred to be relieved of that responsibility, and that they filled up places on the Board that ought to be held by alumni, who were demanding a larger part in the management of the institution.   It was as sensible a proposition as was ever made, and met with the unanimous approval of the Board.

It so happened that this amendment of the by-laws served to exclude from membership on the Board the man who had been for a decade leading the attack on the university and who had recently been elected bishop.   He construed the action of the Board in his absence as a direct thrust at him, wrote a vigorous protest to the Chancellor and to Bishop Galloway, the president of the Board, charging the latter with a deliberate affront to a colleague in the episcopacy.

When his protest and threats had no effect upon the parties concerned, he began a persistent and ruthless propaganda throughout the Church to overthrow the administration then in power and to tighten the hold of the Church in every possible way. The delegates to the next General Conference were in most cases elected upon this issue, with the result that when it met in Asheville in 1910, the Conference, after failing to get the Chancellor and trustees to call a special meeting of the Board, proceeded, in defiance of forty years' practice and of the expressed opinions of those who had had most to do with establishing the university, to elect three trustees. They, furthermore, ordered the bishops, in case the trustees refused to accept those who were elected, to institute a lawsuit to establish the rights of the Conference and furthermore to assert the rights of visitation and veto by the bishops over the action of the Board.

As might have been expected, the Board denied all these contentions and proceeded to elect other trustees. Then the battle in the courts began. The Church won the decision in the lower court. But in the Supreme Court, after long and careful deliberation, all the essential contentions of the Board of Trust were upheld by a unanimous decision.

The writer has never witnessed a more dramatic scene than the one in the Tennessee capitol the morning of March 21, 1914. Not only the two groups of eminent lawyers who for four years had been engaged in the lawsuit, but high dignitaries of the Church on the one side and the representatives of the university on the other, crowded the Supreme Court room and waited anxiously the reading of the decision. It was soon apparent that the Court had overruled the major contentions of the plaintiffs, but for a while it looked as if the basis for an indeterminate war between the two forces concerned was being laid. The Court, however, said at the conclusion of the decision that "if the Church should at any time voluntarily surrender, or renounce, this relation, or contumaciously refuse to confirm members elected, and cease to cooperate with the university, its rights to representation in the Board of Trust and in its management would as a consequence cease"; and that, in that event, "the Board of Trust could proceed, independently of the General Conference, to the election of members to fill vacancies in its own body." The university authorities and constituency went down from the Hill with an ill-concealed joy over the result. The newsboys were by that time shouting extras on the streets, and Nashville awoke to the realization that the university had been saved a great disaster.

But for the sentence in the Court's decision regarding the possible action of the General Conference, the university might have been forced to go to the Courts again to determine its legal status. There was not much doubt as to what the Conference would do. Smarting over the decisive overthrow of all the major contentions and stung by the Court's use of the word "contumaciously," the reactionary leaders swayed the Conference, though not without a very stiff opposition from men who saw that the Church had made a mistake in bringing the lawsuit upon such extreme and revolutionary points, and that there was still a basis of relationship guaranteed by the decision and by the practice of forty years. If the minority had won, and it came very near doing so, the fight might have been continued to this day between the Board of Trust and the Church over the control of the administration.

The vote of the Conference to withdraw from all connection with the university was final, and the university was free to work out its destiny along independent lines. The question all along had been as to whether the fact that the university had become in its patronage, its policies, and its constituency an independent institution could be harmonized with the laws of the state. When the Court, after a review of all the evidence, found that the Church had paid only $18,000 of the original subscriptions and that that amount had been used as a sustentation fund for theological students, that with all the machinery of the Church behind it the campaign for special funds for the Biblical department in 1906 had netted only $25,000 to be expended for new ventures and not to be used at all to relieve the financial burdens already existing, it held that in no sense had the Church "maintained and patronized" the university. That the university was not dependent upon the Church for its student body was evidenced quite strikingly when there were as many Methodist students after the decision as before.

Since that time, the student body has steadily increased in all departments, except in the School of Religion, despite the constantly increasing standards of admission and the fact that Vanderbilt has always deliberately held down its student body to one of quality rather than of quantity. In fact, none of the disastrous results foretold by the opposition leaders have materialized. The alumni, who had almost unanimously supported the Chancellor throughout the controversy, have rallied as never before, and have added substance to their loyalty by giving the largest sums ever given by the alumni of a Southern institution. The Vanderbilt family, and especially the late William K. Vanderbilt, showed their confidence in the administration by giving more money after the lawsuit than before. The General Education Board and the Carnegie Corporation, recognizing Vanderbilt's high standards of work, its strategic position in the Southwest, and the national spirit that has characterized the institution since its foundation, have been most liberal in their support. The total assets of the university are now, approximately, $14,000,000. Of its high standing in the educational world, there could be no better evidence than the Semi-Centennial celebration already alluded to.

The story of this long-drawn-out struggle serves to define one of the main obstructive forces in the South and at the same time to show what may be done by a wise, courageous leader and by an institution to combat popular prejudice and passion. Aside from the issues involved, it was a dramatic struggle between two personalities as wide apart as the poles in temperament and point of view. The man who temporarily wielded such a dominating influence over his church was highly emotional and belligerent, honestly resolved to accomplish his purpose at any cost. If he had shown the slightest moderation, restraint, and patience, the cards might have been dealt to better advantage.

Chancellor Kirkland was exactly the opposite type. With a naturally calm temperament disciplined by years of training in scholarship, rational rather than emotional, so reserved as to give the impression of secretiveness, a master of clear exposition, with business ability that would have made him a leader in industry, arriving at his conclusions by clear and straight thinking, so fearless of public opinion as to be almost indifferent to it when conscious of his own integrity, and with a deep sense of responsibility for the university that spares no labour to promote its interests, he met wisely and bravely the onslaught. These qualities of mind and heart explain why all the bishops who had ever come in close contact with him —and especially Bishops Hargrove, Galloway, and Hendrix—and all the faculty, student body, and alumni of the university were in sympathy with him when the attacks on his administration began. He fretted his chief opponent because he would not talk back, and he at times worried his friends for the same reason. But he bided his time. His long testimony in the lawsuit is as accurate and as comprehensive as a doctor's thesis, so balanced, so fair, so honest that it was doubtless the chief basis of the Court's decision. It anticipates the verdict of history.

Any man less resourceful, less patient, less courageous would have yielded to a compromise that settled nothing, or would have taken positions in other institutions that were offered him. To the burden of this long agitation and trial was added that of his inability to meet the growing financial needs of the university. Everything that has ever beaten down Southern leaders was raised to the extreme degree in his case— limited resources, ignorance, prejudice, mob psychology expressing itself in the most inflammatory way. That he stood firm in this crisis was due to fortitude and faith, well expressed in a passage quoted by him on three occasions that marked milestones in his career:

> In this faith
> I shall not count the chances—sure that all
> A prudent foresight asks we shall not want.
> And all that bold and patient hearts can do
> We shall not leave undone. The rest is God's.

It is little wonder that the three hundred delegates from all parts of the country and from abroad and leading citizens of Nashville should have given him a spontaneous ovation when he arose to deliver his address on "Vanderbilt in Retrospect and Prospect" at the recent celebration.   It was to him an hour of triumph, but still more of dedication.   It was characteristic of the man that he should have quickly turned from the achievements of a half century in which he had played so conspicuous a part to a clear and bold outline of the future progress of the university.   After thirty-two years of arduous service he has just projected a campaign for the still further expansion of the university.   He still has the vigour and the confidence of youth.

CHAPTER VII

PENS THAT ARE SWORDS

NO SEVERER rebuke was ever given by a President of the United States to a member of his cabinet, nor was there ever a severer condemnation of the point of view that would make the South solid for ever, than a letter written in 1896 by Grover Cleveland to Hoke Smith, then Secretary of the Interior and publisher of the Atlanta *Journal*. Secretary Smith had done all in his power to hold the Democratic Party to an endorsement of the second Cleveland administration and to the support of sound money. He had in press an elaborate edition of the *Journal* which was to present the necessity of a gold standard to the people of the South. When Bryan was nominated at Chicago and a free-silver platform was adopted condemning in unmeasured terms the administration of Cleveland, Mr. Smith decided suddenly to swing his paper to the support of Bryan, and wrote to his chief, giving as his reason for his decision the fear of the Negro in the South:

> I consider the protection of person and property involved in the local Democratic success which can only continue through Democratic organization. I would strike my own people a severe blow if I repudiated a nominee of a regular convention, thereby setting a precedent for disorganization. While I shall not accept the platform, I must support the nominee of the Chicago Convention.

Later he added:

> I hope I am sufficiently devoted to the nation, but in 1860 I should have gone with my state, and now I must stand by it.

In President Cleveland's answer it is difficult to tell whether he is more surprised at personal disloyalty, all the more significant because all the rest of his cabinet stood by him, or at a man's sacrificing his convictions on a matter of prime importance, or at the thought that the issues of 1860 had anything to do with the present crisis.   It indicates so clearly the attitude of one of the greatest friends that the South ever had, and states so strongly what many have felt with regard to the solid South, that I quote it in full[1]:

> I have determined to say to you frankly that I was astonished and much disappointed by your course and that I am by no means relieved by the reasons you present in justification of it.
>
> When you addressed the citizens of your state so nobly and patriotically, you were discussing the silver question alone; and when you assured them that you intended to support the nominee of the National Convention you could certainly have intended no more than to pledge yourself that in case you were overruled by the Convention *in the question under discussion* you would accept your defeat and support the platform and candidates which represented that defeat. This—considering your strong expressions on the silver question, your earnest advocacy of sound money, and your belief in its transcendent importance—was going very far.
>
> You surely could not have intended to promise support to a platform directly opposed not only to sound money but to every other safe and conservative doctrine or policy, and framed in every line and word in condemnation of all the acts and policies of an administration of which you have been from the first a loyal, useful, and honourable member. You could not have intended a

---

[1]McElroy: "Grover Cleveland: Man and Statesman," p. 227.

promise to uphold candidates, not only pledged to the support and advancement of this destructive and undemocratic platform, but whose selection largely depended upon the depth and virulence of their hatred to our administration. I say "our" administration because I have constantly in mind the work we have done . . . the good we have accomplished and the evil we have averted in the face of the opposition of the vicious forces that have temporarily succeeded in their revolt against everything good and glorious in Democratic faith and achievement.

It is due to our countrymen and to the safety of the nation that such an administration should not be discredited or stricken down. It belongs to them and should be protected and defended. . . . None can defend it better than those who constitute it, and know the singleness of purpose and absolute patriotism that have inspired it. You say, "While I shall not accept the platform, I must support the nominees of the Chicago Convention." I cannot see how this is to be done. It seems to me like straining at a gnat and swallowing a camel.

The vital importance of the issues involved in the national campaign, and my failure to appreciate the inseparable relation between it and a state contest, prevent me from realizing the force of your reference to the "local situation." I suppose much was said about the "local situation" in 1860.

. . . I cannot believe that I will do my duty to my countrymen or party—either as President or citizen, by giving the least aid and comfort to the nominees of the Chicago Convention or the ideas they represent.

The great majority of Southern politicians and newspapers followed the lead of Mr. Smith. The man who had done much to bring the South back into the house of the fathers by appointing a large proportion of his cabinet and many diplomats from the South, who had brought the party to two great victories on principles of the soundest kind, was deserted by the South and made the object of vicious attacks. He was even called "a political leper." "Nothing in all his public life," says George F. Parker, in his "Recollec-

tions of Grover Cleveland," "gave him so much grief."
The one consoling fact to Mr. Cleveland was that
so many Gold Democrats rallied to the support of
Palmer and Buckner—many of them Southerners who
had never scratched a ticket in their lives. The bolt
from the regular party by men like John G. Carlisle
and Hilary A. Herbert was a noteworthy act of political independence. Among the newspapers that
supported the cause of sound money was the Charlotte (N. C.) *Observer*, whose valuable service was
recognized by President Cleveland in a letter to Kope
Elias, June 29, 1895:

> Such able presentation of the arguments against the dangerous
> and delusive notion of free and unlimited silver coinage cannot
> fail to arrest the attention of men as intelligent as those in North
> Carolina. I look upon those who take such an active and earnest
> part as the editor of the *Observer* in clearing up the fallacies and
> correcting the misapprehensions so prevalent . . . as true
> patriots.

The stand taken by the editor of the *Observer*,
J. P. Caldwell, in the election of 1900 was the beginning of the independence of the press in the Carolinas.
Well do I remember reading his "declaration of independence" written just after the party had nominated
Bryan for the second time. It was like the sound of
a trumpet to many of the younger men of the state,
for it seemed to usher in the day of which they had
dreamed. The announcement was received with
amazement and indignation by the party papers of that
section. Personal attacks were combined with charges
that the paper had gone over to the enemy and had
sold out to Wall Street. Despite the storm of hate

and vindictiveness he encountered simply because he refused to go further contrary to his honest convictions, the editor won out for three reasons: he was a man of unquestioned integrity and honour, a high-souled gentleman of the old school; he had made a newspaper so good in all its departments that people could not do without it—they simply ignored the editorial page; and he had the backing of the principal owner of the *Observer,* D. A. Tompkins, who, more than any other man, had been responsible for the industrial development of the Piedmont section. The editor and the publisher might well have dodged the issue, voted according to their conscience, paid lip service to the Grand Old Democratic Party, and raised the flag of White Supremacy. Instead, they made, for a few years at least, one of the great newspapers of the South.

The growth in number and influence of such papers is one of the encouraging facts of the present time. The Nashville *Banner,* for instance, has for an even longer time gone so far as to support the Republican national and even state tickets and is primarily responsible for the fact that Tennessee is to-day a doubtful state. Besides the papers that are to be specifically commented on in this chapter, the Columbia *State,* the Macon *Telegraph,* the Chattanooga *Times,* the Asheville *Citizen,* and the Montgomery *Advertiser,* have given repeated evidence of independent thought and leadership.

The Committee charged with the responsibility of awarding the Pulitzer prizes each year has recently given signal recognition to two such Southern newspapers. In 1923, it awarded the prize for the greatest public service rendered by an American newspaper during the preceding year to the Memphis *Commercial Appeal* for its continued exposure of the Ku Klux Klan in the very capital of the Black Belt. In 1925, it awarded the prize for the best editorial of the year to Robert Lathan of the Charleston *News and Courier* for an editorial on the "Isolation of the South."

In the first case, there was no specific editorial or article but rather the aggressive policy of the paper as revealed over a period of time in numerous articles and editorials. Mr. C. P. J. Mooney, the manager and editor, is one of the most intelligent, resourceful, and truly patriotic editors and publishers that the South has ever produced. The perfectly natural reaction of many who read the news of this award was that Mr. Mooney is himself a Catholic, or that a Northern committee would naturally be impressed with the opposition to the Ku Klux Klan, but neither remark would be just; for when the facts are all known, it is apparent that Mr. Mooney's efforts rose far above any consideration of denominational lines, and that the Committee had deliberately estimated the nature of the service as of commanding significance in the life of the nation. It was a striking illustration of what a newspaper may do to withstand fearlessly the tide of public opinion and even to direct it. Nor is this the only instance of its service; to the three states that look upon Memphis as a capital, Mr. Mooney has been a wise counsellor and friend—a steadfast champion of good roads, improved agriculture, and good schools.

On the day of the last national election the editor of the *News and Courier,* in a mood of serious thoughtfulness and even sadness, and not at all in any spirit of hypercriticism or smartness, wrote in a few incisive words his interpretation of the political plight of the South as revealed in the campaign and in the undoubted result of the election. Mr. Lathan has for several years brought fresh vitality to one of the historic papers of the South. His alert mind, his following of the best thought of his time, and his wide acquaintance with men and books, give an additional significance to this interpretation of political conditions. The editorial is worth quoting as a whole, so accurately does it phrase what has been in the minds of many Southerners in recent years:

This article is being written on Election Day but before the result of the voting can possibly be known. No matter. The suggestion it contains will still be pertinent whatever the story told by the first page this morning. It makes very little difference what any of us thinks about the outcome of yesterday's balloting. It makes a considerable difference whether or not the people of the South realize the precarious situation which the section has come to occupy politically.

As yet we doubt if very many of them do realize this; and yet it is, we think, the outstanding political development of the time so far as we are concerned. Look at the facts. They are not pleasant to contemplate but they cannot be ignored longer. We are in a sad fix politically in this part of the country and if we are to find a remedy for our troubles we must first of all determine what they are. That will take considerable discussion and all we can hope to do now is to help start the ball of this discussion rolling. If that can be accomplished we may achieve this new programme and the new leadership which we so much need.

For at the root of the South's present plight lies the fact that it has to-day virtually no national programme and virtually no national leadership. Is it strange that it should be treated by the rest of the country as such a negligible factor? What is it contributing to-day in the way of political thought? What political leaders has it who possess weight and authority beyond their own states? What constructive policies are its people ready to fight for with the brains and zeal that made them a power in the old days?

The plight of the South in these respects would be perilous at any time; in a period when political currents are deeper and swifter than ever before, with more violent whirlpools, more dangerous rocks and shoals, ours is truly a perilous position. Changes which used to be decades in the making now sweep over us almost before we know they are in contemplation. It is true everywhere. In all the countries of Europe the pendulum is swinging, now far to the left, now far to the right. Centre parties have lost their power. They are in a very bad way.

And the South has belonged to the school politically which sought as a rule the middle of the road, eschewing ultraconservatism on the one hand and radicalism on the other. With labour organized and militant, with radicalism organized and in deadly earnest, with conservatism organized and drawing the lines sharply, what is the South to do, what course shall she take, where do her interests lie, what is due to happen to her?

These are the questions which already begin to press for answer. Who is to speak for the South? How many of her citizens are prepared to help formulate her replies?

Rather typical reactions to the editorial came almost immediately. Senator Heflin of Alabama, who was at that time lecturing in North Carolina, in a characteristic speech, construed it as an attack on the Solid South, whose traditions, ideals, and virtues he proceeded to laud in extravagant fashion. He spoke of the wisdom of Southern statesmen and of the valour of Southern soldiers. He rehearsed the issues of the Civil War, maintaining that the South had a right to secede and that the North was the aggressor. He was proud of the land of his birth. The editorial was unworthy of a Southerner and unjust to his people. The article was adjudged best by Northerners so that they might have a pretext to give it wide currency. And the audience applauded wildly. A colleague of

Mr. Lathan's, the editor of the Columbia *Record,* made the perfectly obvious retort:

> The Senator is a good illustration of Lathan's point. Of all the nonentities in the U. S. Senate, he is conspicuous for his vapidity. He seeks to beguile and flatter the people, to dope them with the same old bunk, to grease them with the same old soft soap they have grown used to. And he is wily enough to know that they like it.

The Savannah *Morning News,* instead of speaking directly to the editorial, answered the New York *World's* analysis and comments. Such phrases as "unusual piece to come out of the South," "preoccupied with a race issue," "petty religious and moral disputes," "provincial narrowness," "no contacts with large currents of thought" move the editor to hurl back at the *World* the greatness of Woodrow Wilson and taunts about the Harlem district in New York. He calls the roll of the Southern States to show the material progress of each, as, for instance, the astounding fact that, a few days before, Henry Ford had bought 10,000 acres of Georgia soil within shouting distance of Savannah! He then turns upon "Brother Lathan" with these words:

> So, where's all this plight stuff? The *News and Courier,* instead of having a lot of roses pinned on it for talking about the alleged plight of the South, should have been awarded the famous leather medal. . . . Now is no time, and there is no occasion, for lamentations in the South.
>
> Let's quit writing about the plight of the South, and while we may not attract much attention thereby, we can at least not give occasion for other sections to say, "See! The South admits it is no good, has no intellect, and amounts to nothing in the nation."

Just at this time Mr. Theodore H. Price, editor of *Commerce and Finance,* was the guest of honour and principal orator of the Atlantic Cotton Association meeting in Savannah. He turned aside from his intended address to reply to the Lathan editorial, which he read in full, and then dubbed it political pessimism and the author a Jeremiah. "I dissent," he said, "from the statement that the South has no leadership. Most Southerners eat, drink, and breathe politics from the time they are born." A shining example to answer the jeremiad with is Woodrow Wilson, "the greatest man of modern times." Mr. Price, of course, like many another Northerner speaking in the South, was carrying coals to Newcastle, and he received the usual ovation. Before closing he uttered one sentence that might have brought comfort to the object of his animadversions: "What the South wants now is executive and business ability rather than forensic distinction and legislative skill."

The Greensboro (N. C.) *News,* which for a decade or more has been, perhaps, the outstanding independent newspaper in the Carolinas, without waiting for Northern comment, wrote the most sensible editorial when the prize editorial was first published, and then, after the criticisms had appeared, wrote as follows:

Neither Heflin nor Price has overthrown the palpable truth. The charge that the South has no national programme and virtually no national leadership remains unanswered; for Mr. Price misses the point entirely in emphasizing material progress.

So ends the story of one editorial.

In July of the same year Senator Underwood of Alabama announced in a letter addressed to Mr. Vic-

tor H. Hanson of the Birmingham *News* that he would
not seek a renomination to the Senate in the next election, but would retire to an old Virginia estate near
Mount Vernon. The Senator had been for many
years an outstanding statesman of the South, a man
worthy of the best traditions of Southern statesmanship, a thoughtful student of political affairs, a man
of unyielding convictions. He had antagonized the
American Legion by his opposition to the bonus, the
Anti-Saloon League by voting against the Eighteenth
Amendment, the various women's organizations by his
opposition to woman's suffrage, the Labour unions by
his resistance to their demands, and, above all, the
Ku Klux Klan by his vigorous denunciation of their
methods and policies at the late national Democratic
convention. He had barely escaped defeat in his last
campaign by a mediocre man, and seemingly did not
wish to risk another hard-fought contest. His closest
political friend, Mr. Hanson, while believing that he
might have won the contest, made in his paper the following significant comment:

The day was when the Southern States sent to Washington the
real brains and courage and intellectual honesty of their manhood.
The spirits of those giants of old still stalk about the Capitol, and
their ghostly voices can almost be heard at times in protest against
the lesser ones who sit in the chairs they once occupied and sound
feeble messages to a new generation. The voice of Alabama was
heard in the land, and men gave ear to that voice. With the
passing of Underwood, that day also passes. The day of high
tradition is over for the present, awaiting the quickening finger of
some renascence, far or near, that shall touch it and cause it to
spring to life again.

There were similar comments in other Southern
newspapers, and, as might have been expected, by

Northern editors.   W. W. Jermane, Washington correspondent of the Seattle *Daily Times,* said practically the same thing as the Birmingham *News* about the decline in the quality of Southern statesmen, but took the opportunity to make some characteristic remarks about the Southern people in general.   After paying tribute to Mr. Underwood as the strongest and ablest man now in either house of Congress from the South, and a superlative tribute to the Southern statesmen of the past, and especially to the great Virginians of the early period of our history, and admitting that the ablest men in the section do not go into politics but into business and the professions, he said:

The South is ignorant, and is glad of it. It doesn't intentionally give important offices to anybody who knows too much, or who has capacity to think and a desire to be controlled by high motives looking to the common good. . . .   Class consciousness turned against its leading members of Congress, for there is obviously nothing in common between ignorance and enlightenment. . . . Their places were filled by men who understood the grunting of the herd. . . .   We may easily imagine what kind of a country this would be if there were forty-eight states of the Alabama type, and many of those who do so will doubtless pray that no such punishment be inflicted upon the American people. . . .

Whereupon the Atlanta *Constitution,* in its issue of July 19th, made the article the basis of a characteristic attack upon Northern prejudice and a defence of the South.   Ignoring some of the admissions and contentions of the Seattle editor and the point of view expressed by Mr. Lathan and Mr. Hanson, the editor comments on "the ignorance and malice that provoke and feed upon sectional prejudice," and invokes "the stalwart, dependable, forward-looking Anglo-Saxon citizenry of the South" to arise and rebuke such criticism. So far, so good. But the editor proceeds then to sing the glories of the South in superlative fashion, establishing to his own satisfaction that the South, since Reconstruction days, has "made more agricultural, industrial, commercial, financial, educational, and cultural progress combined than any other section of the United States—or of the world in a similar period under similar conditions." Becoming more specific as to educational conditions, he says:

There is not a Southern state that is not rich in educational institutions of nation-wide prominence and usefulness. What institution is there in all of the states of the Northwest combined, with the possible exception of the University of Wisconsin, that compares with the University of Virginia, the University of North Carolina, the Georgia School of Technology—the second of the polytechnic class in all of America—or with the University of Louisiana, or with Tulane or Emory or Mercer or Duke University, or with any of a dozen or more equally as outstanding institutions in the South?

What city in the Northwest compares, as an educational centre, with Atlanta, or with Nashville, or with Richmond?

Now, aside from the editor's failure to realize the essential point in all this discussion of Mr. Underwood's retirement or in the points raised by Southern critics themselves, is the optimistic comparison of the South's educational institutions with those of the Northwest and the Middle West, and by implication with those of the entire country. Why single out the University of Wisconsin when he might just as well have cited the universities of Iowa, Minnesota, Michigan, Colorado, Washington, and of many a smaller state, any one of which receives a larger appropriation each year than the incomes of all the colleges of Georgia combined.   It is a notorious fact that the University of Georgia and the Georgia School of Technology have been altogether inadequately supported by the state and that the conductors of special campaigns and the advocates of larger appropriations have repeatedly drawn a very different contrast between Georgia and almost any Northern state in the support of such institutions.   To say that the South is to-day "unsurpassed in educational advantages" and that there is not a Southern state that is "not rich in educational institutions of nation-wide prominence and usefulness," and to suggest that a score of colleges are beyond comparison ahead of any institution in the Northwest with the possible exception of the University of Wisconsin— all of this is an illustration of the boastfulness that has been one of the main obstacles to Southern progress. The Georgian who read that editorial immediately patted the editor and himself on the back and became proudly impervious to all appeals of colleges for funds.   If we already have as good as anybody else, why should we worry!

How much braver and wiser is the point of view of the editor of the Columbus (Georgia) *Enquirer-Sun* in an editorial entitled "The Empire State of Illiteracy" in the issue of June 7, 1925!   Taking as a basis of his contention a recent monograph by a professor in the State University and an expert survey of the present status of the educational system of the state by T. J. Woofter, Jr., Julian Harris, the editor and owner of the paper, drives home ruthlessly the facts that Georgia "holds the first place among her sister states for the number of native-born illiterates and the last place in her per capita expenditure for education," that she pays the lowest average salary for teachers except Arkansas, and that she is at the bottom of the list in appropriations to the higher institutions of learning. He does not propose to permit himself to be deafened to the fact of "the disgraceful neglect of the University of Georgia and the dull complacency of most Georgians in the face of our state's shameful illiteracy by the din of Empire State shouts, or to be lulled into inaction by the monotonous repetition of such phrases as 'It's great to be a Georgian.'" In other editorials of recent years he has battled manfully for the idea that politics should not be allowed to interfere with the freedom or usefulness of the university, and more especially that the selection of a Chancellor should be determined only by the desire to secure an educational expert rather than a political or ecclesiastical leader. Otherwise, it will fall into the third or fourth rank of colleges.

Nor is this the only instance of the editor's fearless and intelligent discussion of public questions. Julian Harris, the son of Joel Chandler Harris, after a varied experience as reporter, advertising and managing editor, and special correspondent on the Atlanta *Constitution, Uncle Remus' Magazine*, the New York *Herald* and the *Telegram* at home and abroad, bought the *Enquirer-Sun* five years ago with the avowed purpose of fighting intolerance and bigotry of all kinds. With a wide knowledge gained from experience and reading, and with a brilliant style and absolute fearlessness, he has championed every progressive movement in the state and has thrown his influence against

every reactionary tendency. He has realized his
father's ideal of an editor:

> I shudder when I think of the opportunities the editors in
> Georgia are allowing to slip by. It grieves me to see them harp-
> ing steadily on the same old prejudices and moving in the worn
> ruts of a period that was soul-destroying in its narrowness. What
> a legacy for one's conscience to know that one had been instru-
> mental in mowing down the old prejudices that rattle in the wind
> like weeds.

Independent in politics he has not hesitated to flay
the political corruption of men in high places and has
especially criticized the present Governor and his ap-
pointees and fellow officers for their alleged connection
with the Ku Klux Klan.

This is but one illustration of his persistent attack
upon the order which he conceives to be the greatest
menace in the history of the state. Soon after taking
charge of the paper, he published in full the *exposé*
of the Klan by the New York *World* when no other
paper in Georgia would touch it. Whereupon he lost
20 per cent. of his subscribers and was threatened in
every conceivable way by anonymous letters and by a
parade of the Klan in front of his office. In defiance
of the masks of hooded faces he appealed to his colleagues of the press to remove their mask of silence
and join him in the crusade against intolerance and
lawlessness. His condemnation of lynching under any
and all circumstances reached its climax in an editorial
of September 24, 1925, protesting against "a lawless,
cowardly mob of Georgians" lynching a lunatic in the
state asylum who had killed a nurse—"a helpless,

crazed human being." "We first explain to the world that the Negro is a child, and then, when he commits a heinous crime, we lynch him as if he were a Harvard professor," is one of his oft-repeated statements.

And this is but a sample of his consistent attitude to the treatment of the Negro race. Students of eugenics may find it significant that the creator of Uncle Remus should have a son who has fought for fairness and justice to the descendants of that kindly, genial humorist. In a series of editorials written at the time of the Negro exodus in 1923 he said repeatedly that the principal reason for the exodus was that the Negro is not treated fairly in the courts and that he is not given adequate protection. He has been one of the ardent supporters of the Interracial Commission in its efforts to bring about better conditions of living and educational facilities.

A valuable ally in his work has been his wife, Julia Collier Harris, a woman of rare intelligence and culture, author of the "Life and Letters" of Joel Chandler Harris. She writes editorials and a weekly article entitled "Here and There with Books and People," in which she reveals a literary taste and critical intelligence quite as noteworthy as the political and social editorials of her husband. She writes, for instance, enlightened articles on Anatole France, Sherwood Anderson, and H. L. Mencken, and reviews with keenest interest and sympathy the most liberal Southern magazines and books. Significant of the spirit of the paper and of the attitude of the editors was the fact that both of them went to the Dayton trial and wrote daily articles and editorials expressing the utmost sympathy for the defendant and his attorneys.

For all their pains, they lost 400 subscribers, so enraged were the Fundamentalists at the criticism of Bryan and his cohorts. But they had the satisfaction of believing that they helped to kill an anti-Evolution bill in 1924 and again in 1925. All of their positions on public questions have been taken regardless of the effect on advertising or subscriptions, and they have lost money in their uphill fight—lost a good deal of money; just now they are on the credit side of the ledger. It would be a calamity if this citadel of enlightenment and freedom should be silenced. The main appeal of the paper has been for the Southern people to "shake off the throttling grip of the Lilliputs, rid ourselves of our intellectual lethargy, purge our soul of all narrowing prejudices, and take up again a leadership which we should never have lost."

A more important newspaper from the standpoint of circulation, place of publication, and influence is the Richmond *News-Leader,* owned and edited by John Stewart Bryan and Douglas Freeman. The trouble with many Southern newspapers, as indeed with American papers generally, is that the owners and managing editors hamper the free expression of opinion by the editors; many an editor and his staff, ready to speak their minds on public questions, are held in check by those who are concerned with advertising receipts, or subscription lists, or political affiliations. In the case of the *News-Leader* the editor is not only part owner of the paper, but is loyally supported by Mr. Bryan in his efforts to mould public opinion; they are one in spirit and united in their purpose to make the paper the organ of the liberal movement in Virginia and to create a wholesome dissent with the established order.

They have the great advantage of being identified by birth, education, and social connections with the best traditions of Virginia.   Mr. Bryan, the son of one of the most prominent citizens that Richmond ever had, publisher for many years of the Richmond *Times-Dispatch,* is a graduate of the University of Virginia and was for a while the rector or chairman of the Board of Visitors of that institution.   In 1921, he was one of the outstanding figures of the university's centennial celebration.   Doctor Freeman is a graduate of Richmond College and Fellow and Ph.D. graduate of Johns Hopkins, an expert student of history and economics, and member of the Alumni Council of all the colleges of Virginia.   Both of these men are prominent in their respective churches and are identified with the best business interests of the state.   These associations and attachments make all the more noteworthy their progressive spirit and at the same time give assurance of the success of a large, independent, liberal newspaper.

At a time when the editorial page has so often been sacrificed to other departments of a paper, Doctor Freeman has made his page a thing of power, worthy of the best traditions of editorial writing.   He is a real personality who adds to the influence of the written word that of the spoken word.   No man in the state is more sought after by the colleges and universities for academic occasions or by the general public for historical and community addresses. Trained as a research student in history and devoting all his leisure hours to that work, he is director of the Confederate Museum, president of the Southern Historical Society, and an important member of the Virginia Historical Society. He has published the "Calendar of Confederate Papers" and "Lee's Despatches," and is now preparing a Life of Lee based upon hitherto unpublished material that he has found among hidden treasures. That is enough to make any man a typical Virginia conservative gentleman; and yet he combines with his study of the past a liberal and progressive mind. He has insisted that much of our history deadens while it should inspire, and that we cannot say unto ourselves, "We have Abraham for a father." He insists, in his brilliant chapter on Virginia in "These United States," that Virginia's past history should be read for inspiration rather than for contemplation.

He writes editorials on a wide range of subjects that show his extensive knowledge and culture as well as a clear, forceful, and distinguished style. No editor, for instance, understands better the relation of science and religion or has written wiser comments on the controversy between the Fundamentalists and the Modernists. He has given special attention, however, to political questions. In a large number of editorials written during the past year he has come nearer than any other editor of whom I am aware to a full consideration of the problem suggested in Mr. Lathan's editorial already referred to. One of the greatest causes in the decline of political life in Virginia he finds to be the apathy of the people as revealed in the constantly decreasing number of votes in both national and state elections. Analyzing the vote of the last gubernatorial primary, he says that if Virginia Democrats, male and female, had voted for the two candidates as they voted for Grover Cleveland, the poll of 174,896 would have been about 430,000. He finds that in the last national election, even with the nation-wide campaign to get out a larger proportion of voters, there was a decline of 63,000 in Virginia's vote, or, to put it another way, only 13.4 per cent. of the potential vote was brought to the polls. "Think of it," he exclaims, "only one voter in the oldest of the states for four elsewhere! . . . North Carolina casting more than two and a half times as large a vote as the Old Dominion! It is enough to break the long sleep of George Mason, to raise the ghost of Thomas Jefferson, and to fire again with exhortation, even from the tomb, the voice of Patrick Henry!" And he writes again:

The tragic truth, once more brought home, is that the people of Virginia have lost their old interest in politics. Occasionally they may stir from their apathy, if they are called loudly and often enough. At other times they are indifferent. Many have actually lost touch with politics, and have ceased to be politically-minded. . . . They put aside their political duty when they thought the Constitution of 1902 removed the obligation of discharging it. They will never be awakened again until organized intelligent political dissent is revived in Virginia. That dissent, to be effective, will not be Republican in name, in association, or in point of view. It will not be radical or proletarian. But it must come from some quarter, in some form of honest, alert liberalism, if Virginia is to be saved from political stagnation. *The man who serves Virginia best to-day is he who keeps his spirit free from the thraldom of political names,* and studies, questions, challenges, participates in the public life of the state and *courageously dissents from the mandate of mediocrity.*

One reason for the small vote is found in the provisions of the Constitution that were made to keep the Negro from voting, but which are so cumbersome and so complicated that thousands of white people are discouraged or deterred from voting. "It is the negation of democracy. It mocks the pretensions of the bill of rights. It stultifies Virginia." Why continue it when there is no longer any danger of Negro domination, with the decreasing Negro population and the Republican Party no longer catering to his vote? This is but one illustration of the need for a new constitution: "Instead of this sunset constitution Virginia needs a sunrise document, written by *men* who are not afraid of the day." The Governor ought to be given more power so that he may be the responsible head of his party, and the Legislature ought all to be elected at the same time under definite party pledges and platforms. The newly elected governor announced no policy or state programme and made no appeal except to "party regularity." No wonder that Virginia is "politically sterile." Democrats who rejoice in party concord forget that there is such a thing as "too much peace politically." The price of concord, in a state under the control of one party, is nothing less than stagnation. What Doctor Freeman would like to see is a clear-cut fight between liberals and conservatives—a renewal of bi-partisan political contest; for every party grows careless if it is not put on its mettle. He says:

Everybody knows that no political party that has been in power for years ever goes forward unless it is prodded. There is no progress without opposition and no opposition without dissent. Virginia has long been in danger of political stagnation. After the domination of her government by Negroes, carpet-baggers and scalawags, the veterans of the war between the states buried all their differences in an effort to redeem Virginia. Insurgency was close to treason. It meant outlawry or affiliation with the

party that had despoiled the commonwealth. This state of mind
continued long after the threat of Negro rule had passed. *Forced
to think alike, politically, many ceased to think at all.*

Why, it may be asked, does he not favour building
up the Republican Party, especially when there is the
worthy movement led by Fairfax Harrison and other
prominent men to elevate that party. Because the
liberal Democrats have nothing in common with the
Republican machine, and they are not in sympathy
with the conservative policy of the present national
administration. If the liberals will unite, two parties
can be built up corresponding to the ante-bellum Whigs
and Democrats. Each will watch the other, each
will be equipped to take over the administration.
Virginia will be saved from "the blight of political
one-mindedness and from the plague of sectional narrowness." What is needed is a new opposition party,
"free from old names, old labels, old prejudices"—a
party that will stand for a real state programme of
progress. Such a programme would call for good
roads built by a bond issue, tax reform, agricultural
development and coöperative marketing, and, above
all, education that will give equality of opportunity to
all and that will produce leaders in the higher institutions. As might be expected, Freeman is a special
champion of education, believing that Virginia will
be great again only when she makes "her superb history dynamic through the new educational movement
that is the hope of every progressive Virginian." To
this programme the *News–Leader* has been calling
men for several years. It has been fighting the office-
holders whose power is in the vicious fee system and
who have become an oligarchy so strong as almost to

defy opposition.   Political dissent is increasing again.
Says Doctor Freeman in a vein of cheering optimism:

Not in fifty years has the tone of the daily press of the commonwealth been comparably as close to political independence as
it is to-day.   The spirit of public utterance, except by politicians
and office-seekers, is far bolder.   Men are cheered to-day where
they would have been hissed twenty years ago for saying Virginia
needs political dissent and a vigorous, intelligent opposition group.
Some are acclaimed as political prophets who would have been
denounced as potential traitors as recently as 1900.

What, then, should be the attitude of such liberals
to the problems of the nation?   Or, as Mr. Lathan
put it in his inquiry, how is the South, through the
Democratic Party, to make a real contribution to the
nation?   In editorials written December 17 and 19,
1924, Doctor Freeman addresses himself to this delicate problem:

Shall the South associate itself with the conservative East or
the West that tends always to become liberal?   .   .   .   If the
South goes with the West, Democrats will form the left-wing
party.   If the South votes with the Eastern Democrats, the party
wheels to the right.

He believes with Mr. Lathan that the South may stand
for the middle course, be the centre party that may
rally the country to a higher plane of political action.
The liberals, not the conservatives, in the South must
bring this about.

The conclusion of the whole matter may be thus
stated:

The South, as every close observer knows, has two distinct
types and many minor gradations of Democrats.   Some Southern
Democrats are so fundamentally and unchangeably conservative
that if they were living in the North they would be Republicans.

But in every Southern state there is an element, usually a minority, distinctly liberal in its point of view and quite sympathetic with some of the policies of the Western Democrats. If a precise distinction had to be made between the views of this second type of Southern Democrat and the Westerner, one probably would be accurate in saying that they advocate much the same ends, but seek in the one instance to act through the states and in the other through the states and the central government as well.

The immediate prospect is for the continuance of the rule of the conservative in the South. Nowhere is there promise that rebellion means successful revolution, this year or next. Yet if the Democratic Party is to become a left-wing party—and most of those who have contributed to the debate consider this is its destiny —how else is this reorganization to be brought about than through affiliation between the South and the West? *The hope of the party may prove the hope of the country, and it may depend on liberal, independent political thought in the South. And that, the* News-Leader *must confess, is its prescription, its one prescription, for the present ills of the party.*

To bring men to that liberal independent thought is the task of the papers about which I have been writing. Even yet there may come out of the South a group of statesmen who will cease to consider always party expediency and party concord, unite in a programme of national idealism and draw the other sections to them. Such men will fight for a cause even though it is lost temporarily; they will become national in their vision, passionate in their devotion to progressive democracy and steadfast in their opposition to unsound ideas. Then the South may regain something of the leadership that the great Virginians had when they laid the foundations of the Republic.

CHAPTER VIII

FROM ROMANCE TO REALISM

SCARCELY had the public recovered from Mr. Mencken's severe indictment of the South in his "Sahara of the Bozart" before he was recording the appearance of certain new Southern writers who belied his sweeping generalizations. In a recent number of the *American Mercury* he noted with much satisfaction, as if he were partly responsible for the fact, that for the first two years of the magazine's existence the South had supplied twenty-three contributors and fifty-five contributions, while New England had supplied only twenty-four contributors and forty-one contributions. This "good showing of the South" was to the editor the best evidence of a growing critical intelligence. Verily, there are some oases in the desert.

Scribner's Magazine, which played such an important part in the growth of Southern literature in the 'eighties and 'nineties, announces in a current advertisement that the South is "at the beginning of an inspiring renaissance." It cites as the basis of its prophecy the fact that a recent number of the magazine carried nine contributions from Southern writers, and that for several months there has been in its table of contents abundant contradiction of "the false notion that the South is producing no writers and is dead, culturally speaking." Dubose Heyward, one of the most prominent of the younger Southern writers, in the *Bookman* (April, 1925), summarizes this recent development, while Frances Newman[1] presents a similar but more brilliant résumé of "The Status of Literature in the Late Confederacy," in *Books* (August 16, 1925).

To these witnesses—and other magazines might tell something of the same story—should be added the quite recent establishment of new magazines in the South, such as the *Virginia Quarterly Review* at the University of Virginia, the *Southwest Review* at Dallas, the *Double Dealer* at New Orleans, the *Reviewer* and the *Journal of Social Forces* at the University of North Carolina,[2] and the *Fugitive,* a magazine of poetry edited and published at Nashville by a group of instructors and alumni of Vanderbilt University. While these magazines have had contributions from writers in all parts of the country, they have been mainly filled with those from Southern writers. Back of every one of them is an interesting group of intellectuals and progressives.

When due discount has been made for the partiality of Northern editors happy in their discovery of new talent and for the optimism of Southern groups all too ready to lose sight of that graveyard of Southern magazines that looms so large in the history of Southern literature, it remains true that more men and women are writing fiction, poetry, plays, and literary criticism than at any time in the past quarter of a century, and that they are displaying a critical intelligence, a sense of literary values, and a reaction against

---

[1] For an interpretation of Miss Newman's writings see Chapter VII.
[2] For a fuller treatment of the Chapel Hill group see Chapter V.

sentimentalism and romance which have not been hitherto regarded as characteristic of Southern writing.

Because I have had the opportunity to know intimately the Nashville group of poets, generally recognized as one of the most significant groups now writing poetry in this country, I shall use them as an illustration of what is being done by the younger writers.[1] Sidney Lanier once wrote to Bayard Taylor that he suffered from being totally unacquainted with other literary men; the *Fugitive* group is an illustration of coöperation and has some of the characteristics of Oliver Wendell Holmes's Mutual Admiration Society. In 1921 John Crowe Ransom, Donald Davidson, Allen Tate, Stanley Johnson, W. C. Curry, and others began to meet in the home of Sidney Hirsch and James Frank, the latter a Nashville business man, to talk about a wide range of subjects and to exchange poems for criticism.   They formed the habit of bringing carbon copies of their poems so that every one could criticize intelligently a poem as it was read.   These fortnightly meetings, generally extended into the late hours of the night, altogether informal in their nature, became increasingly beneficial to all the members of the group; there was real criticism from men who had high standards of literary taste.   By the spring of 1922, they discovered that they had accumulated a good deal of material; and the suggestion was made that they start a modest poetry magazine.   The result was that the first number of the *Fugitive* appeared in April, the

[1]Another interesting group is the South Carolina Poetry Society, with Dubose Heyward as its leader.   His volumes, "Carolina Chansons" (written in collaboration with Hervy Allen) and "Skylines and Horizons" are volumes of real distinction and are noteworthy for their local colour.

poems being printed without the names of the authors. They themselves did all the work of mailing and correspondence and paid the deficit at the end of the first year.

In time there were added to the group two Rhodes scholars, William Frierson and William Elliott, at home on their vacations; three brilliant undergraduates of the University, Merrill Moore, Ridley Wills, and R. P. Warren, and two young Nashville business men, A. B. Stevenson and Jesse Wills, who had been writing poetry since their college days. Letters of appreciation from the English poet, Robert Graves, and from leading American poets and critics stimulated their efforts. Prominent American poets became contributors to the magazine, the increasing material warranting the publishing of six numbers a year rather than four. Strangely enough, some of the expenses of the publication have been paid by the Nashville Retailers' Association and by the man who put Maxwell House Coffee on the American market. In spite of much ridicule from the general public, who contended that they could not understand the poems, the *Fugitive* has been praised almost extravagantly by critics like Louis Untermeyer, William Rose Benét, and W. S. Braithwaite. The latter selected twenty-three of the *Fugitive* poems for his "Anthology of American Verse" (1923), and singled them out for special praise in his review of American poetry for the year.

As a result of this activity two volumes of poetry appeared in 1924, John Crowe Ransom's "Chills and Fever" and Donald Davidson's "An Outland Piper," published, respectively, by Knopf and the Houghton,

Mifflin Company. Another volume of Ransom's, "Grace Before Meat," was published at the same time by the Hogarth Press in England under the critical patronage of Robert Graves. Ransom may never be popular; but for a combination of intellectual subtlety, refined sentiment, originality, boldness of poetic diction, and withal a certain whimsical imagination, his poetry is destined to increasing recognition. He, like the other poets of the group, has little or no local colour, and is not consciously Southern except in an indirect protest against a sentimentalized South and a commercialized South. Davidson has a lyrical quality that is rare in contemporary poetry; he has used the old forms of verse with a certain freedom and infused into them something of the modern spirit and technique. Even though the *Fugitive* has recently suffered the fate of most ventures of the same kind, it has justified itself in giving an opportunity for expression to this group of writers.

The contrast between the poems of Timrod and Hayne on the one hand and those of Dubose Heyward, Davidson, and Ransom on the other is suggestive of the change in Southern literature. There is a similar contrast between the memoirs and histories of the post-bellum period and the histories of a rather large group of Southern scholars who have applied critical and scientific standards to the writing of Southern history. The essays of Gerald W. Johnson and Frances Newman, noteworthy for courage, insight, and style, are prophetic of a new criticism applied to Southern life and problems. But the change is most evident in the contrast between the stories and novels of the school that flourished a generation ago and those of, say, Ellen Glasgow, Corra Harris, James Boyd, Laurence Stallings, and T. S. Stribling, more realistic in their method and more searching in their portrayal of Southern life.

The passing in quick succession of Thomas Nelson Page, George W. Cable, Charles Egbert Craddock, and James Lane Allen serves to mark the closing of an era in Southern fiction. Long before they died they had ceased to produce anything that added to their fame or their influence. The reaction was as inevitable as has been the reaction against Victorianism and Puritanism in other sections. The general reader must have felt long ago that he would never again like to hear of the picturesque and romantic civilization of the Old South, of the Southern colonel and his lady, of the old-time coloured gentleman living in the glamour of the good old days, of the creole, the mountaineer, or the "poor white trash." And with this reaction against the outworn types, manners, and scenes came a reaction also against the conventionality of the style and the *genre* of the provincial story. When the cult of the plantation had degenerated into the farce of the vaudeville and the comic opera, time had come for the falling of the curtain on the mode and the fashion.

As in every such swinging of the pendulum, some injustice has been done by younger writers to men whose writings had given evidence now and then of the critical attitude toward the life they were portraying. Joel Chandler Harris wrote the Uncle Remus stories, but he wrote also "Free Joe," in which he showed the pathos and tragedy of the free Negro under the old régime. James Lane Allen wrote "The Kentucky Cardinal" and "The Choir Invisible," but he wrote also "King Solomon of Kentucky" and "The Reign of Law," the latter a representation and a prophecy of the intellectual and religious situation that now prevails in the South. Cable wrote "Old Creole Days," but he wrote also the novels and essays that show his complete detachment from the social philosophy of the Southern people. Mary Johnston turned aside from her romantic stories of colonial days to write in "Hagar" a realistic story of the reaction of a Southern girl against current standards and taboos. And in all of them there was a critical point of view that was markedly differentiated from provincial or parochial standards of literary judgment. Joel Chandler Harris said, with characteristic frankness:

What does it matter whether I am Northerner or Southerner if I am true to truth, and true to that larger truth, my own self? My idea is that truth is more important than sectionalism, and that literature that can be labelled Northern, Southern, Western, or Eastern, is not worth labelling at all. . . . The writer in the South must be Southern and yet cosmopolitan; he must be intensely local in feeling, but utterly unprejudiced and unpartisan as to opinions, traditions and sentiment. Whenever we have a genuine Southern literature, it will be American and cosmopolitan as well. Only let it be the work of genius, and it will take all sections by storm.

But the school as a whole has been adjudged as failing to meet the standards set up by the present generation and by the followers of modern fashions in literature. Miss Glasgow's "Barren Ground" has been heralded by the publishers and by numerous reviewers as a portentous event, signalling the fact that "realism has at last crossed the Potomac." Such critics overlook the fact that Miss Glasgow has for a quarter of a century been consciously reacting from the sentimentality and the romance of her predecessors in the field of Southern fiction, that she had tried from the beginning to write truthfully and sincerely and to interpret life as she had known it and had found it to be. And not only Miss Glasgow, but Corra Harris, who wrote "The Circuit Rider's Wife" and "The Recording Angel," realistic stories of typical Georgia communities, long before Sinclair Lewis set all the nation talking about Main Street. She has in all her stories and in "My Book and Heart" given evidence of a critical mind and brilliant humour applied to many a Southern idol.

Mrs. Harris in violating the tradition of what a Southern woman ought to be, what she ought to think, and how she ought to write, has done much to destroy an illusion that is as sacred to Southerners of a certain temperament as that of the old-time Southern gentleman or lady is to another. She was born with a tendency to see the other side of things, and a twist of humour which, she says, was never converted in any of the revivals through which she passed. She soon got the bridle off her mind. Reared as an Episcopalian and with the healthy instincts of a somewhat worldly young woman, she was plunged, by her marriage to a Methodist circuit rider, into the religious life that reigns in the rural districts of the South, and especially into the excitement of great revivals that annually sweep through such districts. A sentimentalist would have seen only the better side of this emotional religion and would have put haloes around the heads of those who made up the Church militant, but with much of the realism that characterizes Longstreet's "Georgia Scenes," she has written about people as they are and about the conditions that still prevail in wide stretches of the country.

In "The Recording Angel," Mrs. Harris represents a stagnant, sentimental, reactionary community suddenly made aware of a new life by the return of one of its own prodigals from the active West—"a human bomb that drops down into a somnambulent community with his fuse burning." As he looked down on the town in its arrested development, with its established customs and torpid ideas, he "undid his mouth, stretched it at the corners, and snickered." In his clear eyes and purposeful activity we see "the back of reality turned upon the sweet, old-whiskered face of romanticism."

Some people in Ruckersville—in other words, Gopher Prairie or Spoon River—had a certain literary ambition to indulge in reminiscences of the war and in sentimental poetry—"the kind of literature suited to monuments and tablets, and to the shining headboards of maidens' graves." In the midst of this torpid intellectual existence lives a blind woman who conceives the project of writing a little Book of Life.

"I have been wondering [she says in a passage that might be taken as the keynote of the new realism in American fiction] if there is not beginning to be a demand for just the truth. Suppose someone wrote about the men and women in Ruckersville as they are, and put in all the mitigating circumstances which the Recording Angel leaves out. Long after we are dead posterity might be as much interested in facts about us as it is in the fiction

we have written and laid away. Maybe it would read like the
best fiction then."

I would not leave the impression that Mrs. Harris
is altogether critical and cynical in her ideas or in her
delineation of types. There are real saints scattered
throughout her books, only they are very human, and
some of them are sinners outside the pale. The Circuit Rider himself often breaks through the shell of
his hard and stern Gospel. Another preacher, the
hero of the sequel, is veritably like the "Servant in the
House" in his emphasis on the religion of Jesus as
contrasted with ecclesiasticism and dogmatism.

Just as Mrs. Harris delineates the old-time revival
and the people who participated in it without the traditional glamour, so does Mary Johnston in "The
Long Roll" and "Cease Firing" present the Civil War
shorn of much of its romance and glory. She is at
times as realistic as Barbusse in his "Under Fire."
She actually presents "Stonewall" Jackson as he appeared to his officers in the early period of the war, and
she undoubtedly had the documents to justify her.
One general exclaims: "I think that he is really mad,"
and another: "The individual at the head of this army
is not a general; he is a schoolmaster. Napoleon or
Cæsar, or Marlborough, or Cromwell wouldn't turn
their heads to look at him as they passed. He's a
pedagogue. Let him go back to Lexington and teach
the rule of three, for, by God, he'll never demonstrate
the rule of one." And yet another: "Stiff, fanatic,
inhuman, callous, cold, half-mad, and wholly rash,
ambitious as Lucifer, and absurd as Hudibras·—a

crazy Barebones masquerading as a Cromwell." The author speaks of him as "an awkward, inarticulate and peculiar man"; there was about him no breath of grace, romance, or pomp of war. He was ungenial and ungainly. He was even eccentric.

The Daughters and Veterans of the Confederacy were quick to protest against such a sacrilege, failing to realize that the author's tribute to Jackson is all the greater because he does overcome all these limitations. What they wanted was a demigod, a superman, combining both Cavalier and Puritan in his personality. They failed to see that, as the story develops, Jackson fulfils the prophecy of a captain who said: "I predict there'll come a day when we'll all cheer like mad—our friend from Georgia, too—when General Jackson goes by leading us to victory." In his great victories all say with Richard Cleave: "It's strange to see how the heart of the army has turned to him. 'Old Jack' can do no wrong; he may stand like a stone wall, but, by the Lord, he moves like a thunderbolt." That's enough glory for any man, but the author has never been forgiven for the realism of her portrait.

Although the late O. Henry cannot be claimed as a distinctively Southern writer—for the background of most of his stories is either New York or the Far West—yet he was born and lived for a good part of his life in the South, and he wrote stories—notably "The Rose of Dixie," "A Municipal Report," and "Hostages to Momus"—which reveal certain glimpses of the South. It may be interesting therefore to note just how some of the Southern types strike him. Nashville has never forgiven him for his realistic description of its peculiar quality of air and atmosphere, nor his portrayal of a typical Southern major:

> Major Caswell banged the bar with his fist, and the first gun at Fort Sumter reëchoed. When he fired the last one at Appomattox, I began to hope. But then he began family trees, and demonstrated that Adam was only a third cousin of a collateral branch of the Caswell family.

Perhaps his most acute analysis of the oratorical, sentimental Southern temperament is "The Rose of Dixie," the hero of which is Colonel Telfair, the foreordained, fit and logical editor of a new Southern magazine. "In a forty-minute speech of acceptance, Colonel Telfair gave an outline of English literature from Chaucer to Macaulay, refought the battle of Chancellorsville, and said that, God helping him, he would so conduct *The Rose of Dixie* that its fragrance and beauty would permeate the entire world." His library contained 10,000 volumes, "some of which had been published as late as 1861."

> The first assistant editor, Tolliver Lee Fairfax, had had a father killed during Pickett's charge, the second assistant, Keats Unwin, was a nephew of one of Morgan's Raiders, the book-reviewer, Jackson Rockingham, had been the youngest soldier in the Confederate Army, having appeared on the field of battle with a sword in one hand and a milk bottle in the other. The art editor, Rancesvalles Sykes, was a third cousin to a nephew of Jefferson Davis. . . . The head office boy got his job by having recited Father Ryan's poems complete, at the commencement exercises of the Toombs City High School. The girls who wrapped and addressed the magazine were members of old Southern families in Reduced Circumstances.

The editor's conception of his magazine is that it should be devoted to the fostering and voicing of

Southern genius; its watchword—displayed on the
cover—is "Of, For, and By the South."

The Rose of Dixie blossomed five times before anybody heard of it, except the people who buy their
hooks and eyes in Toombs City.

To save the magazine the directors, much to the
annoyance of the editor, call in an enterprising Yan-
kee who announces a new policy in characteristic
sentences:

> "You got to buy stuff according to its quality, without any re-
> gard to the pedigree of the author." "It's a magazine we're trying
> to make go off—not the first gun at Fort Sumter"; "Give the
> readers some change from goobers, governors, and Gettysburg."

The editor is prevailed upon to accept an article by
Theodore Roosevelt (who was then President of the
United States) when assured that his mother was a
member of a distinguished family in Georgia!

But, the undiscriminating advocate of realism insists, all these writers are realistic and satirical only in
spots. In style and in temperament they belong with
the romanticists and the sentimentalists of the older
Southern group. They may suggest the foibles of the
saints, but they still cling to religion as a fundamental
fact in life; the moderns will have none of it. They
may laugh at the limitations of the Old South, but true
realism discovers that there was nothing in ante-bellum
life that was worth while, that there never lived a lady
or a gentleman who approximated the ideal. They
may suggest that war is not altogether romantic, and
that generals were not demi-gods, but to the moderns

war is altogether what the authors of "What Price Glory?" make of it. The only true delineators of life are the unmitigated cynics and naturalists.

By some such process of ratiocination many of the younger generation have arrived at the conclusion that the only supreme man of genius in the South to-day, a sort of demi-god of Art, is James Branch Cabell, and that Mencken is his prophet. He is the only thoroughgoing shatterer of illusions, the supreme master of irony who looks upon all life as a comedy and even a farce. The first illusion that he shattered on his long journey to Poictesme was the romantic world of the Virginia aristocracy as revealed in the gallantry of Robert Townsend and in the chivalry of Rudolph Musgrave, and the next was that of the New South with its cant about democracy and its deification of material progress. Poictesme is as remote in space and time as Poe's Eldorado and Ultima Thule, but Fairhaven and Lichfield can be located by any Virginian as not far from Richmond.

Carl Van Doren in a recent monograph on Mr. Cabell refers to the "miracle" of his emergence from the world in which he grew up—a remark that reminds one of a similar remark of a biographer of George Washington that the miracle of history was the appearance of the group of great Virginians in a society so lacking in the elements that make for great leadership. I should not undertake to refute the remark about Mr. Cabell with as much assurance as I should the other remark, but it is not difficult to see how the situation in Virginia, and more specifically in Richmond and its environs, caused just the reaction against life as it is that is characteristic of all his stories. The biography and bibliography of Rudolph Musgrave in "The Rivet in Grandfather's Neck" sound strikingly like those of the author as given in "the most trust-worthy of contemporary authorities." Is not Mr. Cabell, too, secretary of all sorts of historical societies organized to do justice to ancestors, and did he not get his love of the antique by studying genealogies in Vir-ginia, Ireland, France, and England? Is not he the lineal descendant of the best F. F. V.'s, and were not his earliest memories of mullioned windows and beau-tiful lawns and gardens and portraits; and did he not go to college in "a hamlet of hamlets, whose actual tragedy isn't that their fathers were badly treated, but that they themselves were constitutionally unable to do anything except talk about how badly their fathers were treated"?

What will a man of keen insight and sardonic humour born and reared under these circumstances actually do with himself? Join the crowd of bustling fellows who go to the outside world and make huge successes as engineers or captains of industry, or be-come a booster of the New South whose glories are celebrated in many an orator's words? One who was destined "to write perfectly of beautiful things" could find no material there.

In his first story, "The Eagle's Shadow," Cabell wrote a satire on this New South. Frederick R. Woods, who started from nothing and made himself a power in the world of finance, who "had sent more men into bankruptcy and more missionaries into Africa than any other philanthropist in the country," became a country gentleman by tracing his pedigree back through the seventeenth century to Woden the Scandinavian god, building a handsome Tudor manor, and adopting the eagle as his coat-of-arms. This eagle, carved in woodwork, set in mosaics, chased in tableware, woven in napery, glazed in china, casts its shadow over a group of money-loving people gathered in a typical Cabellian house party.

The chorus of the story is Felix Kenaston, a dilettante and cynic, the idle singer of an empty day, who exclaims that he is out of place in this company—"a mere drone in this hive of philanthropic bees." In his whimsical way, he shatters the most pompous platitudes and the most arrant nonsense of this group, "lost in the weltering seas of advanced thought." He concludes that "Life is a trivial farce played in a stately temple."

Cabell, like Kenaston, like Charteris, escapes, therefore, from the contemporary life and scene, but when he does he finds in the old aristocratic society of Virginia another form of the comedy of limitations and appearances. "The Rivet in Grandfather's Neck" is the first stage of his journey to Poictesme, and illusion meets him, as in all other stages. Colonel Rudolph Musgrave of Metacton is the social triumph of his generation. His military title was won by four years of arduous receptions and parades while on the staff of a former governor; he is flattered when the ladies tell him that he is indispensable in leading cotillions and in the prevention of "unpleasant pauses among incongruous dinner parties." His *bon mots* are cherished as traditions of the village:

"Ignore almost any crime that is just a matter of common knowledge and has not got in the newspapers." "The very best people are sometimes respectable." "It is not becoming in a Musgrave to speak of woman in any tone other than the most honeyed accents of chivalry."

He believes that one "must conform to the customs of yesterday under the comfortable delusion that this is the only way to uphold yesterday's ideals." He handles all situations with a beautiful gesture. The skeletons in the closet of his family he frankly admits, and he has as many adventures in love as his lineal ancestor, the incomparable Jurgen. Dressed up in amiable heroics he is a Southern gentleman "comically perceived and rendered." In this novel, we have, then, "all the follies and affectations and absurdities of the traditional South."

On examination, then, "those glorious days of chivalry, of fair women and brave men, of gentle breeding, of splendid culture" turn out to be full of unscrupulousness, vanity, deceit, rapacity, and lust. In that world over which the last of the Musgraves presides with such *éclat,* in which we have amours of every type under circumstances just as picturesque and idyllic as any in Poictesme, there are two figures that suggest the hypocrisy and the corruption better than any others. Leander Pilkins, the coloured butler for a long while now to the Musgraves, was

the handsomest man whom Lichfield had produced; for this quadroon's skin was like old ivory, and his profile would have done credit to an emperor. . . . Indeed, he was generally known to be a by-blow of Captain Beverley Musgrave, who in his day was Lichfield's arbiter as touched the social graces.

Not as garrulous or as romantic as Page's old-time darkeys, he looks on the elaborate dinners and seems to judge the house party with a certain Olympian calm and humour. Not so another mulatto, the

housewoman of many years' standing; in her mind
rages the resentment of an ancient wrong when she was
the mistress of a great Southern orator.

"That coloured boy," says the wife of Musgrave, half patrician
and half plebeian, "was your own first cousin. He was killed for
doing exactly what his father had done. Only they sent his father
to the Senate and gave him columns of flubdub and laid him out in
state when he died and they poured kerosene upon the son and
burned him alive. And I believe Virginia thinks that wasn't fair.
She is only a Negro, but she was a mother once."

Here is a blot on the morality of Southern society
scarcely hinted at in the old romances. Now, Miss
Glasgow is aware of this dark spot in Southern society
and of many other limitations of the old order and
the new. She has as critical a mind as Mr. Cabell;
she is even possessed of irony and other forms of
humour in dealing with sentimentalism and false romance. They were brought up in the same environment in Virginia, and they have gone a long way from
inherited traditions and standards. But the essential
difference is that Mr. Cabell escapes reality in order to
find romance, if indeed he ever finds it; his beautiful
happenings are all in a world of legend and myth, and
even these vanish into illusion, so potent is the world
from which he has escaped. Miss Glasgow sees the
world as it is without any of the glamour of romance
or the veil of what she often calls evasive idealism,
but she finds a romance that springs from reality and
an idealism that glows even on the surface of the
baldest and barest fact. Mr. Cabell runs away from
life, or to use his own figure, loiters in the alcoves
instead of walking boldly through the main corridor.
Miss Glasgow, like so many of her heroines, runs to

meet life, wrestles with it ever so grimly, and sometimes sees the vision of Jacob's Ladder.   Through disillusionment and disenchantment her strongest characters pass to a faith that is creative and vital because it is based upon knowledge of life as it is and not as it appears to be to those who wilfully evade facts and changing conditions.   If the former's stories are infinitely diverting by reason of their humour and their artistic beauty, the latter's are inspiring to those in the South who are working at the task of redeeming the impoverished soil, or cleansing politics, or saturating society with thought.   The one is like an opiate, the other is like a tonic.

Miss Glasgow is not only a great writer; she is also one of the wisest thinkers of our time, and more particularly in all that relates to Southern life, past and present.   No one has written with more penetration and discrimination about the forces of reaction and progress that have been for a half century contending for supremacy in the South.   She has written, artistically to be sure, about social life and customs, politics, science, religion, education, material progress, and all other major concerns.   There is not a single progressive movement in the South to-day that may not find enlightenment and inspiration in some one of her novels.

She has written a series of novels that now approach a certain epic proportion by reason of their presentation of a well-defined period of history that reaches from the Civil War to the World War.   While her books may seem at first glance to deal with the same types and many of the same situations, a more careful reading shows that she has so discriminated between periods and types as to reveal a gallery of diverse personalities all the more interesting from the fact that they shade into each other, and a variety of scenes and situations that enable one to visualize the Virginia of yesterday and to-day.

Her first important novel, "The Battleground," seems at first like a conventional Southern story of the Civil War: there are majors, colonels and governors, old-time uncles and mammies, and typical women and girls. But there is a difference between the novel and the short stories of Thomas Nelson Page dealing with the same material. The author's mind is at work on her material. Side by side with the Negroes of the conventional type is the free Negro—a tragic figure on the outskirts of life—"an honest-eyed, grizzled old Negro, who wrung his meagre living from a blacksmith's trade, bearing alike the scornful pity of his white neighbours and the withering contempt of his black ones." Major Ambler is far removed from the conventional Southern gentleman.

What is more important than any one character is that the novel suggests the dissolution of the whole ante-bellum social system. The seeds of its own destruction had already been sown. The Lightfoot family is decaying by reason of gambling, improvidence, and a fiery passion that breaks out in fury with any infringement of the ancient code. Betty Ambler has the individuality, the wit, the spirit of adventure that take her from childhood clean beyond the confines of conventional standards and ideals; she finds paths on the mountains that other people have not found, and these are symbolic of her revolt against the limitations of her life. Dan Lightfoot, after a violent scene with his grandfather, goes forth into the world to find a job, which turns out to be that of a stage-driver for an innkeeper who belongs to a lower order. He rejoices in his freedom. He violates all the traditions of a Virginia gentleman by remaining a private throughout the war. His most cherished companion in the camps is Pinetop, who came down out of the mountains to fight for "he knew not what." Near the end Dan finds his comrade studying the first reader in his tent by the light of a pine knot. For the first time in his life he was brought face to face with "the tragedy of hopeless ignorance for an inquiring mind, and the shock stunned him, at the moment, past the power of speech." Until he knew Pinetop he had, in the lofty isolation of his class, regarded the plebeian in the light of an alien to the soil, "not as a victim to the kindly society in which he himself had moved—a society produced by that free labour which had degraded the white workman to the level of the serf." Even the spectre of slavery, against which he had rebelled in his boyhood days, faded abruptly before the very majesty of the problem that faced him now—the undeveloped life of the common people.

Afterward Dan becomes his teacher on many evenings, and is the forerunner of those who for a generation have been teaching the Pinetops of the South. The new era has already started in the South with Dan as stage-driver, Levi a free man, Pinetop on his way to an education, and Betty, now the wife of Dan, the forerunner of a self-reliant, radiant line of women. The author recognizes the inevitable result of the war and, unlike the conventional historians of the Lost Cause, rejoices in it.

Here, then, as in all her later novels, she portrays the struggle between conservative and progressive forces, and there is never any doubt as to where her sympathy lies. When one reads Page's "In Ole Virginia," he sees the curtain fall at the end of the story as if the end of the world had come; there is no outlook, no promise of a life that is superior to that of the Old South, or even equal to it. In Miss Glasgow's novels we witness the transition to something different, and, despite the crudeness and the confusion, to something better. She is a realist in the sense that she shows us life as it is, life shorn of its romance and illusions, but she has also the hope, the courage, the patience, and the faith of the chastened romantic and the tempered idealist.

Her greatest heroes are those who find in politics, in agriculture, in business, a challenge to what is largest in their natures, a call to expend themselves to the uttermost to break through the shell of tradition. Such men have the courage to defy social prejudice, faith in democracy despite its crudities, and the vision that was characteristic of an earlier period in the history of Virginia. Some who oppose them are comic in their ignorance and prejudice, and some are as tragic as any of those protagonists of drama who have fought against the stars in their courses.

This conflict between progress and reaction is essentially the conflict between democracy and aristocracy. Miss Glasgow has a faith in democracy as real and as vital as was that of Thomas Jefferson or Walter Page. She knows its crudities, its imperfections, but it is like life, not something already finished.

It is raw stuff.   It isn't a word or a phrase out of a book, or a formula.   It is warm and fluid, and it is teeming with living forms.   It is as much alive as the earth or air or water, and it can be used to develop as many varying energies.

Democracy, restless, disorderly, and strewn with the wreckage of finer things, has in it vast possibilities. The very paradoxes of democracy make it interesting —and helpful:

Ugly facts and fine ideals, crooked deeds and straight feeling, little codes and large adventures, puny lives and heroic deaths, the smoky present and the clear future.

To the making of a more democratic state of society in the South, both the descendants of the best families and certain elemental men who spring directly from the soil make their contributions.   It is the aristocratic Tucker Blake in "The Deliverance" who has through suffering and in the light of his humour and common sense come to see that "Love is worth more than big titles or fine clothes, or even than dead grandfathers," and that "our levels aren't any bigger than chalk lines in the eyes of God Almighty."   Judge Page in "One Man in His Time," who played a conspicuous part in the Virginia of the past and who attained a certain wide outlook by travel abroad, says:

"If we are going to exist at all outside the archæological museum, we must learn to accept men like Vetch; we must let in new blood; Vetch may be the vital element we need.   We must live up to our epitaphs."

Stephen Culpepper in the same novel, inheritor of all that is best in the wealth and culture of the old order, is torn by a conflict between inherited traditions and standards and the impulses of new forces. The struggle is between his love for Margaret Blair, the distilled essence of all that was fine in breeding and culture, and a growing love for Patty Vetch, who sprang from unknown parents and from the crudest circumstances and is yet groping for something in the way of culture and beauty. At the same time he is influenced, now by Benham, a typical, successful politician who has emotions but no convictions and who indulges in "sonorous rhetoric and gorgeous purple periods of classic oratory," and now by Vetch, an elemental man like Lincoln, who is an embodiment of the liberal spirit in politics, and who dreams of a fairer social order and a practical system of coöperation in industry. In the conflict between tradition and adventure, philosophy and experience, age and youth, he craves something larger, something wider, something deeper than the world in which his fathers lived. Rich veins of feeling buried beneath his conventional surface yield their treasures, and his inarticulate longing for heroic and splendid deeds seems, at the end, to be at the point of realization.

The same struggle with the caste feeling is the basis of "The Deliverance," in which the scene is transferred from Richmond to an old-time plantation, which has passed from its original owners, the aristocratic Blakes, to the overseer. The latter's colossal vulgarity of soul and brutishness of manner awaken in Christopher Blake a loathing and contempt that lead him to passionate revenge. Trying to preserve for his blind mother, seated in a massive Elizabethan chair and dressed in rich black brocade, the illusion that she is still the mistress of the ancestral estate, he becomes a slave of the soil, debased by ignorance and passion to the level of the beasts. Predestined by his forbears to read Horace in the library and to maintain the traditions of a Virginia gentleman, he has the odour of tobacco fields and the stain of the soil on his clothes. Strangely enough, he is attracted by the granddaughter of the overseer who has grown into a woman of refinement and culture. He had denied the possibility of such development in the common people. His passionate love is in conflict with an equally passionate hatred for her grandfather, the murder of whom by his grandson is due to Blake's influence over the boy. Accepting responsibility for the deed, Blake spends several years in the penitentiary to atone for his sin. The conclusion of this tragic story is that he and Maria Fletcher learn through much suffering that "the fulness of life does not come from the things outside of ourselves and they must create the beauty in which they live." They both have a vision of "the kindly earth with its untold miracles, the sky with its infinity of space." Together they stand expectant of a new life and a new order in which all men shall be delivered for ever from the spirit of caste.

The hero of "The Voice of the People," Nicholas Burr, likewise sprang from a shiftless father of the poor white class and from a mother who was "one of those sallow, over-driven drudges who stare like helpless effigies from the tumble-down cabins along a country roadside." The aristocratic Dudley says of him that he is common—"common as dirt"—while an old-time Negro interprets his rise to political power in a bit of social philosophy which still dominates the minds of some people:

"De niggers, dey is gwine plum outer dey head, en de po' white
trash, dey's gwine plum outer dey places. . . . In ole Miss'
time dere wa'n't no traipsin' roun' er niggers en intermixin' up de
quality en de trash. Ole Miss, she des pint out der place en dey
stay dar. . . . She know whar she b'long en she know whar
dey b'long. . . . Dese here new come folks hev des' sprouted
outer de dut."

Burr is frustrated in his love for Eugenia Webb
because of the gulf between the classes, but he makes
his way to a commanding position in politics by his
ability and sheer honesty. He seemed like one of the
great Virginians come to life again.

"I'll fight the ring [he says], and, if need be, I'll fight the party.
So long as the right and the people are with me, the party may go
hang."

In this spirit he brings about important reforms as
Governor of the state and is well on his way to the
United States Senate when he returns to his old home
only to die at the hands of a mob bent upon lynching
a Negro. He had taken pride in the fact that there
had not been a lynching during his administration, and
he is willing to risk his life for the sake of the law.
The masked mob finds too late that it is the Governor
himself and one of them exclaims, "By God, it's Nick
Burr, and he died for a d——n brute!"

Such courage and martyrdom may be necessary even
yet to awaken the people of the South to the evil that
is the darkest blot on great commonwealths. Nowhere does Miss Glasgow better show the critical intelligence that is so characteristic of her than in her
analysis of political conditions that call for men of
independence, of initiative, and of vision such as Nich-

olas Burr and Gideon Vetch. The Solid South will never be broken and the section will never play a part in national affairs until such leaders become the rule and not the exception.

Significant as are Miss Glasgow's portrayal of such men and her interpretation of social and political problems, the most important contribution that she has made to social philosophy is her artistic representation of the problems of woman's work and development. Not since George Eliot has any one entered more profoundly into the souls of women characters or drawn with greater skill and detail their deterioration or growth. She has little to say of the political rights of women, but of their right to live their own lives with a certain individuality and fulness, of the necessity to find expression for their inmost souls outside the relation of sex or marriage, of their ability to profit by the advance of modern life and thought, she has given abundant evidence in her novels. Women finding useful and inspiring careers in agriculture, in business, in art, as well as in intelligent marriages, loom large in her later stories.[1] How wisely she has written of woman's work and ideals will be apparent in the following chapter.

[1]For an interpretation of "Barren Ground" see page 50-51.

CHAPTER IX

THE REVOLT AGAINST CHIVALRY

M R. DOOLEY once remarked that in his youth he
wrote a book about Woman, but that, when in
maturer life he came to publish it, he added at the end
what the scientists call *Errata,* in which he requested
his readers, wherever they found "is," to substitute
"is not," and wherever they found "is not" to substitute "maybe," "perhaps," or "God knows." With
due recognition of the danger of writing about the
eternal woman question, and especially about the
Southern woman, I shall use Southern fiction as a
revelation of types and social ideals, and then let certain women speak for themselves. All are agreed
that something has happened to change the status of
women; some are very happy over the change, and
others are very sad, tragically sad.

Long after Burke had lamented the passing of the
age of chivalry in Europe, the South maintained the
outward form and inward spirit of chivalry in the
whole structure of ante-bellum social life; and when
that was shattered, the chivalric attitude toward the
gentler sex was maintained as a precious survival. In
the stories of Thomas Nelson Page, as we have already seen, the aristocratic women of the old régime
were idealized and glorified. Owen Wister was clearly

under the spell of the great tradition of the women of Charleston when he said in "Lady Baltimore" that their charm was like that of some sweet old melody— "a reflection of the old serene candlelight we once talked and danced in." "If they seem to me," he adds, "as narrow as those streets, they also seem to me as lovely as those serene gardens; and if I had smiled at their prejudices, I had loved their innocence, their deep innocence, of the poisoned age which had succeeded their own."

In striking contrast with these women were those of what we should call to-day the middle class. Far more than has been sometimes thought, there was a democratic element in the ante-bellum South. Small plantations and villages constituted the background of a distinctly different type of civilization from that of Virginia or South Carolina. Plain, pious, energetic, and resourceful, the Methodist, Baptist, and Presbyterian women of somewhat primitive days took part in what Corra Harris has designated in her "Circuit Rider's Wife" "the candle-lit drama of salvation." Except in this novel, this type of woman has not found adequate expression in written words. Her face comes to us not in splendid portraits, but in faded daguerrotypes or crude photographs. Her interests were centred in the home and in the church; she read but one book, the Bible, or perchance "Mother, Home and Heaven"; she had but little education, but she was a familiar figure at camp meetings or in the small churches, which were like beacon lights in pioneer communities. Her daughters and granddaughters are to-day the strength of the evangelical churches, though it is only recently that they have won recognition in the councils of these churches.   The Pauline conception of woman has died hard.

Neither the romancer nor the haze through which we see the past should cause us to idealize the charm of the one or the piety of the other type.   The ante bellum South was not the golden age.   Side by side with these two types should be placed two who were, in a sense, the victims of the old order.   Walter H. Page pointed out what he called "The Forgotten Woman" of the South when he said in a well-known address:

Both the aristocratic and the ecclesiastical systems made provision for the women of special classes—the fortunately born and the religious well-to-do.   But all the other women were forgotten.   Let any man whose mind is not hardened by some worn-out theory of politics or of ecclesiasticism go to the country in almost any part of the state and make a study of the life of the women.   He will see them thin and wrinkled in youth from ill-prepared food, clad without warmth or grace, living in untidy houses, working from daylight till bedtime at the dull round of weary duties, the slaves of men of equal slovenliness, the mothers of joyless children—all uneducated if not illiterate.   Yet even this condition were endurable if there were any hope, but this type of woman is encrusted in a shell of dull content with her lot; she knows no better and can never learn better, nor point her children to a higher life.   Some men who are born under these conditions escape from them; a man may go away, go where life offers opportunities, but the women are for ever helpless.

Ellen Glasgow, in her "A Voice of the People," portrays such a type in the mother of Nick Burr, "worn by hardness, crippled by poverty, embittered by sorrow."   In a moment of bitterness at the sordid tragedy of her life she says:

"It's goin' on ten years since I have stopped to drow breath, and I am clean wore out. 'Taint no better than a dog's life, nohow—a woman and a dog air about the only creatures as would put up with it, and they're the biggest pair of fools the Lord ever made. I have had a hard life and it warn't fair."

Such a figure is the sad commentary upon a vanished social order in the light of present democratic ideals, and by its contrast is the prophecy of a new day in which all classes are being brought within the range of education and culture. The same author has portrayed in "The Deliverance" the daughter of an overseer who rises from the soil with all its coarseness to unexpected heights of culture and refinement, fitted in every way to become the wife of a descendant of the old cavaliers.

There is another type, scarcely less poignant in its tragedy than this of the forgotten woman. She was found even in the most aristocratic circles—one who never realized herself by reason of the limitations of the social life by which she was surrounded. Again we have recourse to Miss Glasgow. In "The Miller of Old Church" she portrays an old maid who in her youth had had a yearning for art and a desire to study abroad, but whose ambition had been thwarted by the ideals of womanhood that prevailed in her family.

Generations of ancestry had bred in her the belief that woman existed only to win love or to bestow it. Since in the eyes of her generation any self-expression from a woman, which was not associated with sex, was an affront to convention, that single gift of hers was doomed to wither away in the hot-house air that surrounded her. She had pulled in vain at the obstinate tendrils that held her to the spot in which she had grown. Why on earth should a girl want to go streaking across the water to study art, when she had a home she could stay in and men folks who could look after her?

Here again, then, we have an indictment of the old order from another standpoint. Writers have often spoken of the democracy of the New South from the standpoint of men and races, but they have not yet seen, with some intelligent women, that it is also a most vital question in the life of women. How some women have struggled against traditions, crystallized in definite formulæ and conventions, is thoughtfully, though not always artistically, presented in Miss Mary Johnston's "Hagar." The heroine is a brilliant and somewhat eccentric young woman struggling against the society in which she moves. She is told by everyone that woman's place is the home; "we can surely trust everything to the chivalry of our Southern men." Her irritable and obstinate grandfather—a somewhat typical Southern colonel—exclaims in passionate indignation at the new women and at modern society in general:

"People defying their betters, women deserting their natural sphere, atheists denying hell and saying that the world wasn't made in six days, young girls talking about independence and their own lives! Their own lives! Ha!"

When Hagar reads Darwin and Shelley and Ibsen, her grandmother says:

"I don't pretend to be 'literary' or to understand literary talk. What Moses and St. Paul said and the way we've always done in Virginia is good enough for me. You are perverse and rebellious. It is against the Bible."

Unable to subdue the mind of the young rebel, her guardians turn her over to an old-fashioned boarding school for girls.   To its presiding genius is committed the guardianship of the young female mind in the safe and elegant paths into which she guided it, for she "has the gift for preserving dew and bloom and ignorance of evil in her interesting charges."   This teacher is horrified that one of her pupils is to be a nurse, another a journalist, and exclaims:

"One of those girls has a brother and the other a father quite able to support them.   Women working for their living!"

To a passionate lover who insists that she must just be her beautiful self and keep on loving him, Hagar replies:

"Well, I am real too.   I am as real as you are."

At the end of the story when she has at last found opportunity for complete self-realization, she sums up her struggle with all the forces about her in these words:

"I had to think away from concepts with which the atmosphere in which I was raised was saturated.   I had to think away from creeds and dogmas and affirmations made for me by my ancestors . . . the idea of a sacrosanct Past and the virtue of Immobility. . . . I had to think away from Sanctions and Authorities and Taboos and Divine Rights."

A more attractive heroine is drawn by Mr. Harrison in "Queed."   "Sharlee" Weyland, the descendant of one of the best families of Virginia, has to act as stenographer, clerk, and "office boy" because of the reduced circumstances of her family, and becomes in

time the assistant secretary of the state department of
charities.   She has all the charm of one of Thomas
Nelson Page's heroines—the sort that "old ladies
stop and watch."   There is nothing in the least
businesslike, officious, or stenographic in her manner.
If her head bulged with facts about the treatment of
deficient classes, no hint of that appeared in her talk
at parties, where she was the queen of dancers and the
cynosure of all eyes.   But she has something that the
typical girl does not have—she has ideas, a certain
business-like sagacity, and a high social purpose.   To
her aunt who, though keeping a boarding house, will
not dun her boarders, she says:

"I am not well bred.   I am bold, blunt, brazen, I am forward.
I am resolute and grim.   In short I belong to the younger generation which you despise so."

To her mother, who resents her association with
those who have not the distinction of birth and breeding, she says, "I am a democrat."   And her mother
replies, "That's what no lady ought to be." In her official position and as a woman of conviction, she gives
herself to the work of establishing a reformatory for
girls, and has visions of many other public institutions
of which her native state has need.   In the end she
marries Queed, but her life of quickened social interest
has not been in vain; she will make a good wife and
mother but also a good citizen.   To her eccentric
lover she speaks words that characterize happily the
present era in the South:

"Heigho!   We are living in an interesting time, you and I.   It
isn't every generation that can watch its old town change into a
metropolis right under its eyes.   You say that you are an evolu-

tionary sociologist. Yet a wonderful demonstration in social evolution is going on all around you, and you don't even know it. On the one side there are Colonel Cowes and my grandmother. On the other there are our splendid young men, men who, with conditions of leisure and cultured idleness in their blood, have pitched in with their hands and heads to make this state hum. On the one side there is the old slave-holding aristocracy; on the other the finest democracy in the world. A real sociologist would be absorbed in watching this marvellous process—social evolution actually surprised in our workshop. *A tremendous social drama is being acted out under your very window and you yawn and pull down the blinds.''*

Very important figures in this social drama, or social evolution, are certain new types of women who are finding themselves in opportunities that are opening up to them. Hagar and "Sharlee" and Miss Glasgow's Dorinda and Gabriella have their counterparts in many Southern communities. I do not refer now to those who have been driven by economic necessity to find employment in stores, factories, or business offices; they frequently are rather hopeless drudges waiting for some turn of the wheel of fortune that may bring them the opportunity of marriage. Almost any city has some widow who, left with an estate, has increased her holdings by wise management and has become a leader in civic life—the natural successor of those remarkable women who met the disasters of the Civil War with a calm temperament and executive ability that enabled them to manage large plantations. In Nashville, for instance, one such woman has been the prime force in establishing the Centennial Club, which has been an influence for culture and social welfare in the community, and another has stimulated the love of art to such an extent that the Parthenon, an exact and complete reproduction of the original in Athens, is a chief source of pride to the city. I know a married woman in Georgia who grew tired of social life and has developed two large orchards which are among the best in the state. Occasionally a younger woman finds an outlet for her executive ability as a private secretary and gradually works into a position of great responsibility, but the opportunities for a higher grade of business activity are still too limited.

Teaching has for a long time been the refuge of those who looked upon it as a temporary resource, as "the only nice and respectable occupation which required neither preparation of mind nor considerable outlay of money." What is new is that an increasing number of women are becoming principals, supervisors, and even superintendents, of public schools, and are finding a creative joy in lifting whole communities and counties and even states to new levels. A few years ago Miss Charl Williams, the county superintendent of Shelby County, Tennessee, was elected president of the National Educational Association because of the excellent system of schools that she established in her county. I have heard stories of such intelligent and consecrated teachers that might be included in a book of golden legends. Mrs. Cora Stewart's moonlight schools in Kentucky and her warfare against adult illiteracy have attracted world-wide attention.

Sometimes one who does not teach becomes, like Mrs. Beverly Munford of Richmond, a powerful agency for promoting educational progress throughout a state. No history of education in that state would fail to emphasize what she has done for a quarter of a century through the Coöperative Society of Virginia; she has given every institution the right to claim her as a friend. And yet, when she and others had worked out a plan for a coördinate woman's college at the University of Virginia, they were met by the determined opposition of students and alumni.

How would the chivalric younger South answer her appeal for the higher education of women? I know of no utterance more typical of conservative opinion in the South than an editorial that appeared at that time in *College Topics,* the weekly paper of the University of Virginia. The students could not see the difference between this plan and co-education, to which they, like the students in nearly all other Southern colleges and universities, are steadfastly opposed. The editor in this case is sure that he voices the opinion of every other student, for there is "not a man who does not speak of the proposition with bitterness and believes that its fulfilment would destroy all of the traditions and higher ideals for which the University of Virginia has always stood." He is shocked by the thought that, though the women might have a separate campus, they would use the same lecture rooms, study under the same professors, and "rub elbows with the men students going to and from lectures." They would exercise "a demoralizing influence by their presence alone, for it is not believed for an instant that anything but female riff-raff would take advantage of the opportunity offered." Virginia students would have their opinion of the woman "with such a lack of modesty as to put herself on an equal footing with men, free from all restrictions, unsexed into a depreciation of womanhood by the allurement of women's rights." They would not live side by side with "this dismal brood." The editor concludes by suggesting a mass meeting for the preservation of Virginia traditions similar to one held four years before when President Alderman was accused of destroying other traditions of long standing, and he goes so far as to cite what happened at the University of Washington when co-eds were roughly handled as a prophecy of what may happen at the university. And this is Southern chivalry!

How much the attitude of the students and alumni as thus expressed influenced the Legislature I do not know; but the coördinate college was not established. Gradually, however, women students have been admitted, first into the summer school attended by a goodly number of regular men students, and then into the department of education under certain restrictions as to age and previous training. No disastrous results have as yet been reported, and it is quite probable that other women will be admitted. It is against such prejudice that women seeking for the best education have had to struggle. With a few notable exceptions the attitude of men students in institutions where co-education exists is that of the editorial cited. Why, it is asked, cannot the girls be satisfied with their own colleges? Well, they might reply, there are less than a half-dozen colleges in the South that have standards equal to those of the best men's colleges, and these are far below a score or more of men's colleges in endowment and equipment. The typical girls' college does not appeal to the more intelligent and ambitious, and these often cannot go to the more expensive colleges of the East. The fact is, that the South as a whole, including women themselves, has had a false idea of woman's education. It is well expressed by Miss Glasgow in "Virginia," where she analyzes the aims of the Lady Principal of the Dinwiddie Academy for Young Ladies and the results in the heroine's training:

> Her great hope with regard to her girls was that she would not leave a single unprotected breach in a girl's mind through which an unauthorized idea might enter, and her conception of a perfect pupil was one who deferentially submitted her opinions to her superiors; to go through life perpetually submitting her opinions was, in the eyes of her parents and her teacher, the divinely appointed task of woman. Her education was founded upon the simple theory that the less a girl knew about life, the better prepared she would be to contend with it. . . . Knowledge . . . . was kept from her as rigorously as if it contained the germs of a contagious disease. She was taught that a natural curiosity about the universe was the beginning of infidelity. . . . The whole tradition of woman's education was to paralyze her reasoning faculties so completely that all danger of mental "unsettling" or even movement was eliminated from her future. . . . To solidify the forces of mind into the inherited mould of fixed beliefs was to achieve the definite end of education.

In spite of all these obstacles, more and more young women are going to the Southern universities that admit them, however grudgingly, and to the larger universities of the East and Middle West. They are becoming specialists in various fields of knowledge and are, as professors, deans, and in a few cases presidents, of the various colleges, exerting an ever widening influence. Miss Martha Berry's establishment and maintenance of a school for mountain boys and girls in Georgia has won national recognition. Those who do not teach find in organizations and clubs of all kinds opportunities for leadership. When due discount has been made for the superficiality of women's clubs, for their tendency "to discuss everything from Homer to Kipling between two spoonfuls of ice cream," it yet remains true that they are profoundly affecting the culture, the health, the civic progress of communities. That Southern women rank in effectiveness as well as in charm with the leading women of the country is evidenced by the distinguished career of Mrs. Percy V. Pennybacker of Austin, Texas, who for two years was president of the American Federation of Women's Clubs and has remained ever since one of the formative influences in directing its plans and policies. As a presiding officer, an effective speaker on social and even political questions, and as an executive, she has few equals.

She and others not so well known may be said to be playing the rôle of reformers—the very type that the conservative Southerners used to despise. The prejudice against the type has a historic basis in the contempt for the abolitionists and the temperance and suffrage advocates of New England. Southern women are now vitally interested in social problems; they have their hobbies; they are sometimes called busybodies meddling with things with which they have no right to be concerned. Their loose-leaf notebooks and shiny black bags, as Miss Haardt has suggested recently, may detract from their manner, but they are intelligent and earnest. Two of the best educated and most attractive young women I have ever taught are now, after having been trained for social service in a large university, special agents of the North Carolina Board of Charities and Public Welfare, and as such have to deal with some of the most difficult social problems. Another graduate of a Southern university taught several years at Hampton Institute and is now training students in Scarritt College for every form of home mission work, and especially for work in social settlements for Negroes.   Such women have careers fully as useful as, and sometimes more significant than, those of women who have found themselves in the home and in society.   They have made homes for the delinquent and the unfortunate; they have lighted fires on the altars of human souls; they have caused the light to shine in the dark corners.   Their children have been incarnate ideas in the lives of others.   They have done for the state and for communities what others have done in the home.   They do not lose their womanhood, nor their sense of motherhood.

Such workers found long ago that their most cherished dreams for the betterment of social conditions could not be approximately realized without effective legislation and political influence.   Charitable institutions that used to be under the control of private boards are now under local or state control.   The need for suffrage and for real civic interest became apparent.   The consequent struggle for the ballot by Southern women before and during the passage of the Nineteenth Amendment is one of the most dramatic and significant in Southern history.

If Tennessee has loomed somewhat large—or small —in the imagination of the country by reason of the Anti-Evolution law and the Dayton trial, it should be recalled, in all fairness, that in 1920 she withstood the last desperate charge of the Old Guard of the Southern Confederacy in adopting the Nineteenth Amendment, which gave the women of the South and the nation the right of suffrage. The vote of the Legislature was the dramatic climax of a long-drawn-out struggle that had begun in other sections of the country in the mid-years of the last century. Nine Southern states had already rejected the amendment and remained true to the traditions and ideals of the past. The cohorts of the "Antis" assembled in full mass to stay the national tide, or at least to save from the invaders the fair land in which chivalry still reigned.

No one who attended the session of the Legislature can ever forget the crowded halls and corridors in which the embattled hosts waged their warfare. The Battle of Nashville in 1864 was a five o'clock tea in comparison with this one. The Governor of the state, an avowed champion of the amendment, was opposed by some of the most astute politicians of the state, one of them the Speaker of the House, who threatened the device of breaking the quorum by having the opponents of the amendment leave the state. A mammoth mass meeting was held in the largest auditorium of the city, at which impassioned orators repeated the old, old arguments: the fear of Negro domination by giving suffrage to Negro women; the chivalry of the South which demanded that white women live within their divinely appointed sphere of the home; the theory of state rights, which had been temporarily defeated in 1865 but which must be preserved to save the Republic. Nor did they overlook the presence of national leaders of suffrage in the lobbies and hotels as a confirmation that the whole movement was fostered by reformers and busybodies from the North. And to all of these arguments and conten-

tions was added the presence of many of the fairest
daughters of the city and of the South, who pleaded
with lips more eloquent than men's for the maintenance of the tradition that had ennobled and sanctified
womanhood.

But none of these things could daunt the local and
national leaders who, with intelligence, courage, and
political good sense, finally won, albeit by a slight
majority. Some of them were descendants of families as aristocratic as those of any of their opponents.
They were fighting for the stars in their courses, and
the inevitable happened. As Miss Nell Battle Lewis
of Raleigh, N. C., viewing the battle from afar, wrote,
in a vein of delightful sarcasm:

> By the irony that so often enters into human fate, humiliation
> awaited the defenders of the ancient faith, and Tennessee, the
> renegade, forsook the fatherland in its hour of need, knocked the
> bright halo from the head of Southern grace and beauty . . .
> and made the women of the United States a present of the
> suffrage. . . . Time and tide do not wait for Southern chiv-
> alry, nor freedom halt its progress at its word. . . . The
> world will move, be the Confederacy ever so gallant. Tennessee,
> the renegade, has broken the idol!

Miss Lewis, in a series of articles on the woman
movement, written for the Raleigh *News and Observer*
in May, 1925, analyzes with rare penetration and
frankness the status of woman in the South. After
showing the steadfast resistance to woman suffrage
that was broken only by Tennessee's adoption of the
suffrage amendment, she considers all aspects of the
feminist movement, of which the struggle for political
rights was only one. The idea of chivalry, she insists,
threw about woman "an artificial glamour that she did

not and could not possess." It disregarded a large proportion of women in its devotion to the superior class. When full tribute has been paid to the graciousness and charm, the courage and *esprit,* and the high moral excellence, of the more favoured women, it must be confessed that there was a denial of "something infinitely more precious than any distinction or grace, the right to full personal development and individual freedom." Politically, economically, educationally, and socially, women were "tightly corseted," "tragically incomplete." To the qualities of beauty and grace, modesty and purity, goodness and love, there needed to be added those of intelligence, courage, and freedom. Woman was an idol, an object of ostentatious reverence, but "like all idols, to be jealously guarded and carefully protected from the wind and weather of the world." A more serious criticism of the old order was that beneath the form of chivalry were "those waters of deep agony through which passed many a spotless Southern woman" as she became slowly and unwillingly aware of the loose morals of her men in their relations with women of another race.

The fundamental trouble was that these women, and even more those who did not become wives and mothers and those who lay outside the pale, were not properly educated. As domestic and social accomplishments were considered of first importance, any education aimed at any other object was considered unnecessary and undesirable. Education was left to governesses or to poorly equipped colleges that taught the conventional subjects of music, china-painting, elocution, and *belles-lettres.* Slavery put the badge of inferiority on work of all kinds.   What became then of the unmarried women "who had no slaves and household to supervise and who were denied any other opportunity for the exercise of their gifts and powers?"   Economic independence had to be won by a struggle.   When the struggle for political rights came, "the South's chivalric sword was drawn to defend the ancient *mores*."

Now a new day has come, exclaims Miss Lewis:

The idol, thank God, is broken beyond repair.   For, graceful though it may have been, romantic though it certainly was, it was only an image after all.   And whatever its artificial beauty, it lacked the beauty of life.   In its place is a woman of flesh and blood, not a queen nor a saint nor a symbol, but a human being with human faults and human virtues, a woman still only slowly rising to full stature, but with the sun of freedom on her face.

Those last words might have been written of Miss Lewis herself, so accurately do they portray her own temperament and her successful struggle to find expression for her brilliant and unbridled mind.   It cost her something to write so critically of the old order, for she is by heredity and association related to that past; she has repeatedly paid tribute to the men and women it produced; she is enamoured of the old houses, the "old towns, dreaming through a brisker, cruder day," and she is repelled by some of the signs of the new order.   In writing the article she felt as if she "had stuck a knife in a friend's back," but she could not "sacrifice either to sentiment or to false patriotism" an estimate of the old régime as it related to women which she had reached after careful thought and honest investigation.

And she herself is one of the best illustrations that can be cited of a woman's mind playing freely about all sorts of subjects. She publishes every Sunday in the Raleigh *News and Observer* a column—or double column—entitled "Incidentally," in which she writes about politics, literature, social life, religion, or what‐ ever else may attract her attention in the passing show of men and women and events. There are more fa‐ mous columnists in America, but none that surpass her in delicate literary allusions, the free play of the mind about a variety of happenings and ideas, and withal a certain poise of mind and serenity of wisdom. If she ever publishes a book containing the best of her writ‐ ings, it will be a human document and a real contribu‐ tion to literature. She has shocked her sisters at times with what seems to some of the more sheltered ones blasphemy in dealing with sacred subjects. A striking illustration of her point of view is seen in what she wrote not long ago about Eve as one of the "mothers of science":

But to get back to Eve. She has never received her due. Though she has been held up as execrable because she "brought the curse upon mankind," Eve is really one of the most attractive of all allegorical figures. The "curse" she brought was the in‐ quiring mind, always brightly dangerous. Adam was a clod beside her. The beautiful, tempting apples on the tree of life might have rotted before Adam would have picked them. Like Ruth, Adam was a conformist. Eve was an adventuress, the first great gam‐ bler with life. "Sink or swim, live or die, I give my heart and hand to my vote," said Eve, reaching for the apple. "You call this 'paradise' with the fruit of that tree untasted?" perhaps she said. "Frankly, since we have nothing to amuse us but each other, Eden is getting a trifle on my nerves. How do we know but that the taste of those apples may bring a paradise compared to which Eden is nothing? Anyway, I'm going to investigate." And so

saying, she ate, and the lethargic peace of Eden was dispelled for
ever, and the mind of the race was born. "The curse," they call
it! The curse of inquiry and courage, the curse of LIFE!

And then she indulges in a bit of theology:

> The God in Eve's heart who whispered to her that the freedom
> of the mind is more precious than any paradise was a much more
> worshipful deity than the jealous Jehovah.

She has used something of Eve's inquiring mind and
critical spirit in the consideration of a variety of problems and interests. She resents the way in which
North Carolinians ignore disagreeable facts about the
state. Not in vain did she graduate at Smith College
and then devote two years to work in her native state's
Department of Charities and Public Welfare. There
came to her a quickened sense of social conditions in
which women are particularly interested: the status,
for instance, of the feeble-minded as revealed by a
survey of the inmates of seven typical "homes."
"If in North Carolina we wish to encourage illegiti-
macy," she concludes, "if we wish to foster miscegena-
tion, if we wish to bring about a speedy and extensive
increase of the mentally defective, already one of the
state's gravest social problems, heaviest burdens, and
sorest cankers, then we shall continue to put the mentally defective in the existing county homes." The
wise policy, she insists, would be to confine them in a
state institution of their own, adequately financed,
adapted to their peculiar needs and equipped with a
staff of specialists who understand those needs and
how to treat them, and some day, when we have
waked up to the importance of eugenics, to have a

workable sterilization law to supplement institutional care.

At another time she speaks out boldly in condemnation of the prison system, which was recently revealed in its worst plight by the murder of a Negro prisoner in one of the state camps by one of the state guards. She attributes the murder of one who was confessedly a mental defective to the fact that "the people do not care a hoot what happens in prison camps," that they make no distinction between the insane or mentally defective and those who are morally responsible, that the average prison camp is operated as an economic enterprise rather than handled as a sociological problem, that those who have in charge such camps are unacquainted with the principles of penology. "The surprise is that with all these facts a prisoner is not sent to his heavenly home every week or two."

What does the emancipation of women mean if it does not lead to the solution of problems in which they have every right to be vitally interested? The result of the efforts of the women of the state to improve certain social conditions is suggested in the following remarks:

I don't know whether the General Assembly of 1925 set out with the definite intention of insulting The Good Wimmin, but I can say that my information is that it succeeded in doing just that, at least those of The Good Wimmin who care what the Legislature does. The N. C. Legislative Council of Women representing seven state-wide women's organizations had a programme that included the Australian ballot, an eight-hour child-labour law, publication of marriage banns, a reformatory for Negro girls, and a separate prison for women. Not one of these measures passed the General Assembly. The best showing was made by the Australian ballot tabled in the House by one vote. . . . The women's bill that made the most disgraceful showing was the eight-hour child-labour law, which received only one vote in committee. It was probably very presumptuous of the women to think that any manufacturer should be inconvenienced for the sake of the welfare of children. The gross and blatant materialism of the defeat of that bill sickens me.

At another time she protests strongly against the plea of the "unwritten law," which has been often urged as one of the chief glories of the South and has so often defeated justice:

As a matter of fact, from a woman's standpoint, it is entirely inexcusable. The unwritten law has its basis in the centuries-old idea of woman as personal property, an idea which is still the foundation of many customs relating to women. As, under the written law, a man may kill to protect his house from burglary, so the unwritten law allows him to kill to defend what is called the sanctity of his home. As his house is his property, so the women of his family are his property, according to the assumption of this "law." This, of course, is a primitive survival from the time when the savage male fought off any other male who threatened to carry away his mate. The most intelligent women of the present do not regard the unwritten law as admirable or protective. On the contrary, they condemn it as plainly degrading to the women whom it pretends to protect. Women are not property. They are people. They should scorn—as many of them do heartily scorn—any "protection" which they share in common with a ten-dollar bill or a set of furniture. Let woman have redress under the written law, like any mature, responsible individual, and she has no need of, and she should have no desire for "protection" by, a survival of savagery in which she was enslaved.

In writing of a group of "Tainted Tar Heels," like Walter Hines Page and John Spencer Bassett, who "swam against the current of contemporary opinions" and were "badly tainted with the spirit of revolt against old, outworn Southern shibboleths," Miss

Lewis suggests that there must have been many others not so well known, and exclaims:

> How vastly different they must have been from the objects of local apotheosis—and to me so much more attractive! What a joyous company they seem to me, those persons of shocking individuality, good Democrats who fell from grace. . . . Oh, there must have been some! They deserve their Bradford. Who were the stout spirits in this state who lived and died protesting against the herd in full cry? Where are their outrageous histories? Only the unusually able ones are remembered, but they are not the ones who interest me most. I want to know about the humble ones who wasted their shrill protests on the hot and desert air, the comparatively mute, inglorious Walter Hines Pages, the obscure, uncelebrated John Spencer Bassetts, male and female. I want to know about those nameless, savoury antis whose perverse opinions have composed that little trickle of salt and vinegar in North Carolina's thick, saccharine brew. God rest their rebellious souls—that is, if they want rest, which I doubt. Would I might write of them—that small and traitorous band of the dissenters, lost to sight, to imagination dear!

In this spirit of revolt she breaks many an idol of the state. In the midst of the apotheosis of O. Henry she has the temerity to suggest that he is a bit sophomoric, and that his characters are "stagey." She will not join in with the procession that is celebrating the triumphs of the Babbitts and the cities that they build "with commercialism as the first consideration and ugliness an inevitable corollary"; good roads may be the shortest distances between the homes and business offices of the Babbitts. She even comes to the defence of Mr. Mencken, who is despised by people who "pant for panaceas, for short cuts to the promised land, for everything that bolsters and inflates their self-esteem." She rejoices in his meat-axe when it is demolishing buncombe and pish-posh. His exaggeration and violent language are needed to awaken people from their torpor. She dares make light of the Mecklenburg Declaration of Independence, which is really based upon folklore rather than history, and adds:

> If there is a state in this Union that needs de-bunking as sorely as North Carolina, I don't know it. It just cries to Heaven to send in someone like John D. Wade, who "took down the great shirt of Georgia history and ripped open the seams."[1] A really first-class de-bunker in North Carolina would find enough to do to keep him busy for six lifetimes.

She is always ready to champion the group of liberal leaders at the university, and especially the editors of the *Reviewer*. Commenting on Paul Green's "The Devil's Instrument," she says:

> It seems to me that Mr. Green's hand is lighter in this story than in some of his other work. I liked that. He draws an accurate picture of that barbarous religious orgy so common in the South, the revival. This is the sort of thing that is easily overplayed, especially by a person not in sympathy with it. I don't think Mr. Green does this. He seems to me to present it truly, and whatever satire his story contains is subtle and not blatant.
>
> Mr. Green's "sinner," a North Carolina boy who loves his fiddle because crudely and blindly he loves the beauty of which it is the instrument, as he loves the beauty of evening skies beyond the fields he ploughs, is a taking fellow, as I imagine many sinners are. His groping after something ineffable and lovely that he cannot name seems much more religious—as I am sure Mr. Green means it to appear—than the hell-fire-and-damnation thunderings of the revivalist, or the shouts and moans of his converts.
>
> In "The Devil's Instrument" North Carolina finds her voice.

This characterization of a certain type of revival in the city which had just witnessed one under the leader-

---

[1] She refers to Wade's "Life of Longstreet."

ship of the most notorious evangelist of that section is not the only example of her interest in religious questions. One of her most frequent targets is the Ku Klux Klan as the fomenter of intolerance and law-lessness. In commenting on the last National Democratic Convention she alludes to the Georgian who revolted from his delegation and flayed the Klan and was thereupon kissed by a woman for the heroic deed.

If I had been in the Garden [says Miss Lewis] and could have reached him, I am happy to announce, he would have been kissed by two. I can't answer for the other, but one kiss, at least, would have been resounding and fervent.

When the Anti-Evolution bill was introduced into the North Carolina Legislature, she was one of the most vigorous opponents, using every weapon in her armoury, and saying, among other things:

There is at present no spectacle more pathetically ridiculous than legislatures of little Canutes and little Joshuas passing judgment on the natural order and telling the Life Principle how it ought to behave.

She repeatedly returned to the subject when Tennessee passed the law and made a spectacle of itself at the Dayton trial. In answer to Mr. Bryan's question, "Why are our legislatures not competent to decide what kinds of schools are needed, the requirements of teachers, and the kind of instruction that shall be given?" she said:

"Because, Mr. Bryan, the freedom of the human mind is the most precious possession of the race. Because through the exercise of that freedom all human progress, spiritual, intellectual, social, political, scientific, and material, has been accomplished.

Because to defend so dear a liberty great and gallant persons have suffered and died. Because when in the past this liberty has been curtailed by church or by monarchs or by tyrannical assemblies of the people, evil and confusion have invariably resulted. Because no body of men or women, since its members grope and are fallible like the rest of us, is qualified to dictate what other men and women shall or shall not think. Because for them to presume to do so is the unforgivable sin against the Holy Spirit by denial of faith in that Spirit to lead us profitably and to good issue through Its expression in the individual mind and heart. Because, Mr. Bryan, "nothing is at last sacred but the integrity of one's own mind." And because this principle is sealed with the blood of the martyrs of all races, all ages and all creeds."

Nor does she fail to see the significance of the whole Fundamentalist movement throughout the country:

This attempted union of Church and State by the Fundamentalists, this attempted dictation of legislation by a wing of the Protestant Church has nothing to redeem it. It is to be wholly condemned. It is not to be countenanced for a moment by persons who value religious freedom and who are educated and sensible enough to know that ecclesiastical interference in government has never been productive of anything but evil. The time is past to plead ignorance and mistaken zeal in defense of the Fundamentalists. They are in the open now to "put God in the Constitution" —which means, of course, to put Fundamentalism there—and they are unmistakably dangerous. They are especially dangerous to the already backward and priest-ridden South where they are most numerous. With the Scopes trial, the menace to religious liberty represented by the Fundamentalist effort to control legislation becomes obvious. It should be clearly denounced and stoutly resisted by everyone who subscribes to this government's constitutional guarantee of full religious freedom for all its citizens of whatever creed, and who holds to the constitutional provision of complete separation of Church and State.

In answer to a letter which had accused her of constantly sneering at Christianity and of being an "out and out infidel if she had the nerve to come out and say so," she wrote words that show her fundamental reverence and her discrimination. It would be difficult to find in so short a space a better analysis of the religious situation in America to-day than her conclusion:

> I do not consciously sneer at Christianity. There is, however, in my mind a clear distinction between the religion of Jesus and the organized Christianity of the present. These do not seem to me at all the same thing. And my infidelity is such that I consider the religion of Jesus far the more important. Moreover, I frankly and strenuously disapprove of all dogmatic theology that would substitute itself for the true religion of heart and life that Jesus exemplified. I am firmly convinced—along with persons as distinguished as Dr. Harry Emerson Fosdick and Glenn Frank— that the Church will never be the spiritual power in the world that it should be until it strips itself of its impedimenta of centuries of theorizing and dogmatizing and the weight of its present materialism and returns to the beautiful simplicity and divine humanity of Jesus Himself. If there is to be a new Reformation, so sorely needed, it must be this. I have the nerve to express this "infidelity" whenever and wherever I think there is the slightest possibility of its doing any good.

If Miss Lewis is an illustration of the free mind of a woman playing about all sorts of subjects and throwing on them a flood of light, Miss Frances Newman of Atlanta is the best illustration I know of a prodigiously well-read woman with a critical mind that is as brilliant and as incisive as that of any of the younger writers of America. She, too, has the inheritance of the old order, her family on both sides having a high standing among the people of several states; and she is still cared for by her "black mammy." Her education was of the conventional type, but her real training is perhaps due to the fact that she has been for several years an assistant in the Carnegie Library of Atlanta, and that she has travelled and studied in Europe. One of her duties in the library was to prepare the semi-annual bulletins, in which she published, at first, pertinent comments by the leading reviewers on current books, and later her own general comments on types of books and special comments on individual books. One wonders, even in these formal bulletins, at the range of her reading, her critical taste, and the subtlety of her style. Some of these comments she published in a regular column in the Atlanta *Journal*. These reviews began to attract the attention of writers and critics: she became a regular contributor to the *Reviewer* in Richmond, and lately she has been a regular reviewer for *Books,* the Sunday supplement of the New York *Herald–Tribune*. She astonished the reading public, but not those who had been following her development, when she published in 1924 "The Short Story's Mutations," with some sixty pages of introductory matter, which revealed a comprehensive knowledge of European literature and an apt phrasing of literary judgments. It is no wonder that Mr. Cabell speaks of her as "the most opulently gifted of all the younger women now publishing in America."

Miss Newman is, in her literary judgments, a completely emancipated woman. She might sit for the portrait of the Southern Woman of the New Freedom: Model, 1925. She is an emancipated Georgian, daring to write about Atlanta with sarcasm and irony not altogether characteristic of a booster of the New York of the South. She rejoices in Wade's "Longstreet" as "the first biography ever written in the state which was not as respectful to its subject as a funeral sermon," and as "the first absolutely unfettered prose ever written in the state"—the forerunner, she hopes, of a whole literature that will be as far removed as possible from "the strangely directed energy and imagination which have sometimes disgraced the state in the eyes of some of its fellows." That she is also an emancipated Southerner is evidenced in a brilliant article in *Books* of August 16, 1925, on the "State of Literature in the Late Confederacy." She maintains that the publication of Cabell's "Jurgen" in 1919, and of Mr. Mencken's "Sahara of the Bozart" in 1920, was the beginning of a literary activity that extends from Dallas to Richmond. With deft hand she sketches the groups of poets, critics, and writers of fiction, who, as if to refute the animadversions of critics as to the dearth of genius, set about writing novels, plays, and poems. Like a good many of the younger critics, she overemphasizes, I think, the work of the last five years at the expense of what had been done before with more moderation and discrimination, if less art.

That she is even an emancipated American of the most pronounced type is abundantly evidenced in her "Short Story's Mutations." A significance attaches to the stories selected, ranging as they do from Petronius to Paul Morand and including Voltaire, Boccaccio, Sherwood Anderson, D. H. Lawrence, and James Joyce. The idea of an Atlanta librarian reading some of these stories, much less advising others to read them! Noteworthy also is the fact that they are all translated by Miss Newman, who in addition to knowing Greek and Latin reads with ease French,

German, Italian, and perhaps Russian. Most significant of all is the critical comment scattered throughout the volume, concise, felicitous, suggestive. The whole book is as unconventional as her own mind. There is not a suggestion of pedantry that one finds so often in such anthologies or in the discussion of the technique of the short story, and yet she strikes one as being conversant with the whole range of literature, and even of music, art, and philosophy. Apt references to Wagner and Freud, Croce and Anatole France, are as frequent as the phrases into which she condenses her estimates of the writers of fiction.

Miss Newman has left behind every trace of Victorianism and Puritanism. She says of Henry James that he escaped from the England of Tennyson and Browning and Carlyle to which he had fled from the America of Longfellow and Emerson and Hawthorne, and adds:

Even after Darwin and Strauss had split the century in half, Longfellow and Tennyson went on writing limpid numbers to announce that the grave is not our goal, and Browning went on acquiring his more distinguished reputation by announcing the same thing in lines that give a sensitive reader the sensation of riding on a train with one flat wheel, and Charles Dickens went on announcing the same thing—in prose that was displeasing to the ladies of Cranford.

She dates the rise of important American fiction from the year 1917, which witnessed the emergence of Cabell, Hergesheimer, Anderson, Willa Cather, and others. She was one of the first in this country to have an autographed copy of "Jurgen," and I have no doubt she has one of Joyce's "Ulysses." Her knowledge of contemporary English and French fiction is almost uncanny, and she has the sympathetic attitude toward the most radical departures from the form of fiction as well as from the conventional standards of content. Sherwood Anderson is Gothic in the same way that Giotto was Gothic—"Gothic with the discovery of the bones and the sinews of the American mind and with the struggle of killing the smooth conventionalism of the story America inherited from England."

Her general attitude to life as well as to fiction may be gathered from her generalizations with regard to modern thought:

> The eighteenth century passionately denied everything except the three unities and the rhyming couplet, and the nineteenth century passionately denied everything without exception. The twentieth century is left with no beliefs and no disbeliefs—it has only tastes and distastes and a certain interest in its unconscious.

Speaking of writers like Joyce, D. H. Lawrence, Rose Macaulay, and the recent Americans, she says, with some degree of satisfaction:

> They know, among a vast number of other things, the things that we know, and they think the things that we think. . . . I1 they are decadent, we are decadent with them—without the waiting to go through the most agreeable stage between rudeness and decadence.

The quotation reminds me of a retort that Gilbert Chesterton once made to an inquiry as to what he thought of Lady Astor: "She has gone a long way from Virginia." Miss Newman has certainly gone a long way from Georgia! Too far, I am inclined to think.

If I have written in this chapter nearly altogether

of unmarried women, who have found places for themselves in various callings, I am not unmindful of the influence of modern life and thought on marriage and the home.   Has the revolt against chivalry had any effect on the most cherished tradition of the South; is there any substitute in the new conditions of living for the women and homes of the old order?   The best answer to that question in fiction is Miss Glasgow's "Virginia," and more particularly in the contrast between the tragic life of the heroine and the rich abounding life of her friend Lucy Treadwell.   Virginia at fifty has finished her life and is a lonely woman without inner resources to fall back upon, so absorbed has she been with her family and her household duties. Lucy's marriage had none of the glamour of Virginia's, but it was rooted in reason as well as in emotion. She was a large, young, superbly vigorous woman with an abundant energy that overflowed outside her household in a dozen different directions.   She had kept her mind as alert as her body, and the number of books she had read had always shocked her friend, who felt that time for reading was obliged to be subtracted from more important duties.   One finds even middle life boring; the other is radiant in the prospect of the years that are to come.   This slight reference can give no idea of the insight and depth of a novel that sounds the depths of the whole woman problem.

Perhaps an observation of my own may suggest the answer to the question I have just raised.   Harding Road is an old road leading from Nashville to "Belle Meade," which was one of the most magnificent of ante-bellum estates—one of those places that still suggest the social life of which I spoke at the beginning of this chapter. All along the road now are splendid houses which the well-to-do people of Nashville have built, with the background of the hills and valleys of middle Tennessee. One of these is a house of an Elizabethan type, first dreamed and then planned by those who had travelled in England. Around it are thirty acres of monumental oaks, gardens—vegetable and rose—and pasture lands for sheep. After a period of struggle and helpful coöperation, husband and wife realized in their home the dream of years. It is the custom of this family to entertain upon the lawn friends from the city, who are often reminded of England with its afternoon garden parties. Here literary clubs come, all of whom feel it a rare privilege to breathe for a while the atmosphere of such a place. The library, the slow accretion of years, with books well marked and well used, is the best indication of real literary taste. All these—house and lawn and gardens—are but the outward expression of the soul of the man and woman who have made this haunt of ancient peace. The father, one of the most prominent lawyers of the city, was the honour man of his class at the university, and has kept in later years the intellectual habits of his youth. The mother, a social leader in her younger days, is president of the Drama League and the friend of every cause that promotes the culture of the community. They have four children, three boys, who are honour graduates of the university, and a daughter, who is a student at Bryn Mawr. Is there not something in this home which need not suffer comparison with "Belle Meade" or any Virginia home of the olden days?

CHAPTER X

IT MAKES no difference how far the South may go in its progress toward liberalism, or how optimistic one may become over the outcome of the struggle with the forces of reaction, there is the everlasting race problem to shake the confidence in the future. Like a thunderbolt out of a clear sky will come some utterance of a leader, or some outbreak of primal passion. The national spirit may seem to be running at high tide when an anti-lynching bill in Congress will awaken all the old bitterness that characterized the debates of the 'seventies. John Sharp Williams, who said in his campaign against the unspeakable Vardaman, "In the face of the great problem it would be well that wise men think more, that good men pray more, and that all men talk less and curse less," will mar his farewell days in the body which he had so long adorned, by an almost blatant defense of lynching, which might have been spoken by Vardaman in his palmiest days. Churches may seem to have caught the vision of a new day of interdenominationalism and coöperation, until the race question becomes involved, and then a great denomination will defeat a simple plan of federation that would merely eliminate "South" from its cumbersome name. The Solid South periodically is declared ended as a substantial fact in American politics, but there still remains the ancient fear, the established tradition, that will not down; and the flag of white supremacy waves again. Let a man be never so liberal in politics, religion, or education, and you may find a sudden flaring up or explosion of racial prejudice.

It was not a Southern fire-eater, but William Garrott Brown, one of the best of recent historians and one of the most thoughtful publicists, who said:[1]

> We must take up every new plan with the chastening knowledge that most of our devices have failed; that nothing which can be quickly accomplished will go deep enough to last; that no sudden illumination will ever come. . . . Africa still mocks America from her jungles. Still she jeers: "With the dense darkness of my ignorance, I confound your enlightenment, still, with my sloth, I weigh down the arms of your industry. Still with my supineness, I hang upon the wings of your aspiration. And in the very heart of your imperial young republic I have planted, sure and deep, the misery of this ancient curse I bear."

And yet the most significant fact about the race situation in the South to-day is that more Southern whites, men and women, are actively and aggressively working for the improvement of race relationships than ever before. They are not willing for outside agencies to carry all the burden of thinking about it or of doing something for the amelioration of the Negro's lot. Atlanta, which is known far and wide as the capital of the Invisible Empire, is the headquarters of the Southern Interracial Commission, composed of representative men and women of both races from all the Southern States. Organized immediately after the Armistice to meet the conditions produced by the return of Negro soldiers, it has gradually undertaken a

---

[1]William Garrott Brown, "The Lower South in American History."

comprehensive programme that has been extended into fourteen states and eight hundred counties. Definite efforts in the direction of improved labour conditions, educational opportunities, justice in the courts, and recreational facilities, have not been more noteworthy than the good-will that has been engendered by the members of both races meeting for the candid discussion of mutual problems and for mutual helpfulness in improving difficult situations. They are under no illusions that the problem has been solved, but they are confident that real and substantial progress has been made in building a bridge across the gulf that exists between the intelligent white man and the intelligent Negro. Indifference and actual opposition have not discouraged them, but have rather heartened them to continue the work until the fundamental principle of coöperation and conference has been established as the basis of future development.

Such is a brief outline of the aim of the organization, but it gives no conception of the quality of the men and women who have been its leaders. The Chairman of the Commission for the first years of its existence was John J. Eagan, one of the foremost industrial leaders of Atlanta and Birmingham, who had worked out in his business a plan of industrial democracy in line with the most enlightened ideas of social leaders—all the more notable because the great majority of his employees were Negroes. Since his death in 1923, the Chairman has been Rev. M. Ashby Jones, pastor of the Ponce de Leon Baptist Church of Atlanta, who with Dr. Plato Durham of Emory University, Rev. C. B. Wilmer, and others, had initiated what is known as the "Atlanta Plan" of interracial co-operation between the churches of that city. Doctor Jones has for many years been one of the most liberal leaders in the South. In his church he has stood, as has already been seen in this volume, for progressive policies and ideas; at many civic celebrations he has interpreted the Civil War from a broad national point of view. Thoroughly identified with all movements looking toward the future rather than the past, he has been in a peculiarly fortunate position to lead in the work of the Interracial Commission. He has brought to it wide experience, the most careful study of all the facts involved, moderate and statesmanlike ideas and plans, and, above all, the Christian attitude to the Negro people. His power as a speaker and writer has made his influence far-reaching. When a prominent white man said to him, "I never sat down and talked to Negroes in my life, and I never will," Doctor Jones replied, as he has often said to large audiences: "Whatever you think of this question, in the interest of good sportsmanship, you have got to hear the coloured man and hear him with open mind."

The man most responsible for the executive work of the Commission has been, from the beginning, Rev. W. W. Alexander, a prominent minister of the Southern Methodist Church, and an intelligent student of modern social problems in the light of the best knowledge of the age. Turning aside from many attractive offers of all kinds, he has devoted himself with rare intelligence, courage, and tact to the organization of state and local committees. He has travelled extensively in all parts of the South, has kept in touch with all agencies that mould public opinion, and has lost no opportunity to bring to bear on critical situations the whole force of the Commission and his own personal influence. He has been greatly aided by R. B. Eleazar, who supplies five hundred newspapers twice each month with interesting and significant information of all kinds that indicates progress in better race relationships. In sixty Southern colleges courses have been given on the race problem, many of them using Dr. W. D. Weatherford's excellent books on the subject. A fine summary or recapitulation of all this work and its organization may be found in T. J. Woofter's recently published book entitled "The Basis of Racial Adjustment," but a still better idea is gained from a reading of the reports from the field by the secretaries in the various states. It is no wonder that Northern cities, now struggling with the new conditions produced by the Negro exodus from the South, are adopting the Southern plan of interracial committees, and that British communities in South Africa have seen the wisdom of the plan.

Along with the work of the Southern Interracial Commission in affecting public opinion and in the achievement of tangible results, is the intelligent and sacrificial work of a group of Southern men who have become the executive officers charged with the administration of funds appropriated by the General Education Board, the Slater Board, the Jeanes Board, and the Rosenwald Board for the improvement of Negro education. Northern philanthropy is not a new thing; what is noteworthy is that the men who have provided these funds have called into consultation wise Southern leaders to be members of the various boards and have chosen as executive officers the best types of Southern men. They have felt that the whole country is responsible for the mistakes of Reconstruction and that much indiscriminate philanthropy has done more harm than good. They have, therefore, sought to undo some of the mistakes of the past and to establish channels through which the most intelligent coöperation between all the forces that are interested in the right training of the Negro race may flow.

The man who has played perhaps the largest part in this adjustment is Dr. James H. Dillard, President of the Slater and Jeanes boards, a member of the General Education Board, and an adviser of the other agencies that have been mentioned. Doctor Dillard is by inheritance, training, and temperament an almost ideal Southern gentleman. A native of Virginia, a professor of the classical languages at Washington and Lee and later at Tulane, a leader in the movement for the improvement of educational standards throughout the South, he must have hesitated to give his life to a field of work that has not lain within the sphere of Southern ambition. The decision once made, he has displayed an intelligence, a statesmanlike grasp of actual conditions, a tact in working with all sorts of people, and a whole-hearted devotion to the cause of Negro education that entitle him to rank with the builders of a new order. Not so eloquent as was Dr. J. L. M. Curry in pleading before state legislatures and larger assemblies for the right training of Negroes, nor so forceful in speaking to the religious conscience of the churches as was Bishop Haygood— men who, as agents of the Slater Board, did a monumental work as pioneers in a new field—Doctor Dillard has over a longer period of time displayed rare gifts of patience, unceasing energy, and courage. He has had the confidence of the best Southern people, and has thus been enabled to help secure county and state appropriations to meet the propositions of the boards he represents. He has impressed men of the North as understanding better than anybody else what is the wisest distribution of funds; and he has won the co-operation of the Negroes themselves, and especially of those who are more concerned with progress, however slow, than they are with airing their grievances. In the face of all theorists and all radicals he has maintained that a little progress is encouraging and that true wisdom is found in taking the next step rather than in anticipating an ideal programme. "Because a thing is reasonable it cannot always come to pass at once," is the philosophy of a man who believes in getting back of words to things.

Men of like calibre are: Jackson Davis of Virginia, who, after much experience in his own state in dealing with local problems of race relations and real improvements in agriculture and education, was chosen by the General Education Board as its special representative in the distribution of funds throughout the entire South, and more particularly in assisting various state supervisors of Negro schools; Leo M. Favrot, noted for his practical achievements in Louisiana, and now active as agent of the General Education Board in extending his ideas and plans to the entire South; B. C. Caldwell, also of Louisiana, the special assistant of Doctor Dillard; and S. L. Smith, who, after being for several years the supervisor of Negro schools in Tennessee, is now the General Agent of the Rosenwald Fund for the building of Negro rural schools, and who, with the funds at his command and with the appropriations of state and county boards as well as the contributions of white and black citizens, has been largely responsible for the expenditure of more than twelve million dollars.

All these men, and others who might be mentioned, are in constant touch with each other and with the Commission on Interracial Coöperation and its committees, state and local, which have often helped them to accomplish specific results. It is quite patent that such committees can be of active aid in bringing individuals and organizations to help the public take advantage of the funds that are available, while at the same time the committees find their work made easier and more substantial by the concrete objects that the representatives of these funds have in mind.

Furthermore, all of these agencies are vitally related to the leading Negro institutions. Principal Moton of Tuskegee, Principal Gregg of Hampton, Dr. Isaac Fisher of Fisk, and President John Hope of Morehouse College, Atlanta, have been from the beginning active members of the Southern Commission and have helped to mould its policies and execute its plans, while a host of men in various states and counties have manifested the same spirit. The work of the General Education Board in helping provide coloured demonstration agents in farming and in domestic science, or of the Slater Board in providing special high schools for industrial and teacher training, or of the Jeanes Board in supplying supervisors of Negro rural schools, would have been impossible if these higher educational institutions had not supplied trained workers.

The recognition of their valuable service is the explanation of the fact that at this present moment the

Southern people are giving money to the Hampton-Tuskegee Endowment Fund. The headquarters of the campaign in the South are in the office of the Inter-racial Commission, and the committees, state and local, are the agencies through which the campaign is being conducted. After half a century of the work that these institutions have done along the very lines that white Southerners have emphasized as fundamental for the race, the response has been liberal. The same spirit caused the white citizens of Nashville to subscribe $50,000 to Fisk University a year ago.

One can get just a bit nearer to the working of all these forces by considering them, not in the aggregate, but as seen in a single county. Six years ago Miss Mary Sanders, who had been teaching for several years in Southwestern University at Georgetown, Texas, was elected superintendent of the schools of Williamson County. Born and bred in the South and trained at the University of Chicago, she brought to her strenuous duty of looking after the interests of seven thousand school children fidelity, intelligence, and consecration. She soon saw that the schools for Negroes were totally inadequate, that the buildings were either dilapidated shacks or almost equally dilapidated churches, that one teacher was sometimes in charge of ninety pupils, and that the white people, many of them members of the Ku Klux Klan, were actually antagonistic to any kind of education for the coloured race. She found also that in some districts the Negroes were paying more taxes than they received for their schools, and that the state funds that were apportioned to Negro schools were actually being used by white schools.

She set to work to remedy these distressing conditions. Knowing of the Rosenwald proposition to supplement public funds for building Negro schools, she went to the Chamber of Commerce of the county site to interest them in securing a good high school that would teach industrial arts and at the same time train teachers for the other schools of the county. To her amazement she found the mayor and a leading banker, and even a professor in the college, opposed to the building of such a school on the ground that it would cause the town to be known as a Negro town and would attract other Negroes there. Undismayed with this first affront, she induced a neighbouring town to take up the proposition, she secured the additional funds by personal solicitation among members of both races, and soon had a school that ranks with the best in the state. She met the proposition of the Jeanes Board, whereby she secured a supervisor of Negro schools, a graduate of Tuskegee, who has worked with her in the consolidation of schools and in the improvement of teaching. She will tell you by the hour of the eagerness with which the students responded to her efforts and of the progress of the race in that county.

All such coöperation as I have here indicated is offset, to be sure, by the opposition of extremists of both races. There is nothing new in the extreme Southern position. The men who now represent it are the descendants of those who defended slavery against the rising moral sentiment of the world; and of those who, taking advantage of the mistaken idealism and the partisan passion manifested in Reconstruction times, inflamed the popular mind. The leaders of a later generation have as politicians or as writers found the

source of their power in appealing to the racial prejudices of the uneducated masses.   Such leaders, as well
as a large part of the general public in the South,
have been quick to seize upon any evidence of the
Negro's reaction from the recent war, and, suspicious
of his increasing aspirations, have been ready to do
battle against any man who questions the South's divine right to rule and even to oppress the Negro.

And now the Ku Klux Klan is busy in parts of the
South; the very name of the organization is a source
of terror to the Negroes, even where there has been
no aggressive action.   Aside from any organized opposition to the Negro's advancement is the loose thinking indulged in by many Southerners.   Think of the
paradoxes involved in the following generalizations of
the mayor of a Southern city: (1) Old Negroes in
slavery were a good lot, but the Negroes nowadays
are worthless; (2) The best labour the South ever
had; (3) Education destroys the value of the Negro
by making him unwilling to work; (4) The South
makes great sacrifices to educate them; (5) The Negroes on the farm often do well, but these are the
old slaves; (6) The pure Negro is much superior in
character to the mulattoes; the mulatto is rapidly
dying out; (7) Three fourths of them have some white
blood; (8) The educated fill the prisons; (9) Booker
T. Washington has good ideas; (10) Negroes must be
kept in their places.

What is distinctly new in the immediate situation
is the voice of the Negro, North and South, speaking
in no uncertain terms against injustice of all kinds.
Of the many books written in recent years by Negroes
themselves or by Northern sympathizers—books from

the leading publishing houses—the most significant is "Darkwater," by Dr. W. E. B. DuBois, whose "Souls of Black Folk," published some fifteen years ago, had stamped him not only as a remarkable writer, but as the leader of a large section of his race. In both volumes we have the expression of the pathos and the tragedy of the highly educated and radical Negro. There could be no better evidence of the change in point of view within those fifteen years than the difference in tone between the author's two books—a change from melancholy to bitterness, from reasonable moderation to extreme propaganda, from the consciousness of defeat to the confidence of struggle and victory. In his editorials in the *Crisis* not only is he bitter toward the South, but he criticizes severely the report of the Chicago Commission, appointed to investigate the race riots in that city and to make recommendations for a future programme of racial adjustment. More recently Walter F. White's "Fire in the Flint" has tended to inflame the members of his race.

Of more importance than even these volumes as showing the mind of the Negro race at this time is the compilation, in a volume entitled "The Voice of the Negro," of a large number of extracts from Negro newspapers published in all parts of the country, and especially in the South. Not the least significant fact is that a Southerner, Professor R. T. Kerlin, formerly of the Virginia Military Institute, should have, after four months' careful study of several scores of Negro newspapers, made this exhibit of "angry protest and prayerful pleading." His purpose is that the whole nation may know just what the Negro press, which has become the greatest single power in the Negro race, is at the present time thinking and saying. That he should have published this book without any unfair or prejudiced comments, that he should even at times indicate a certain sympathy with the views expressed, is the best possible indication that many Southerners of the present generation are willing to face the facts, and even to confer with those who hold the most extreme views. He insists that only those who read these editorials, the summaries of sermons and addresses, the news items which so often go so far as to correct the false reports of white newspapers, the reports of the proceedings of conventions, and conferences, their petitions and resolutions, can have any idea of what is passing through the mind of the Negroes.

Throughout all such books and extracts there is evidence of increasing bitterness toward the South, and an increasing lack of confidence in even the liberal and progressive Southerner. To Southern prejudice and passion the Negro leaders attribute the poisoning of the mind of the nation. It is the inactivity of the best Southern whites that gives the opportunity for the extreme Negro to berate the moderate leader, who had hitherto expressed confidence in the ultimate triumph of a true and better South. It is apparent that the big stick of Negro opinion is often held over the heads of those leaders of the race who counsel moderation and patience. Among such would be placed the leaders of Hampton and Tuskegee because, as is alleged, they desire to keep the Negroes hewers of wood and drawers of water.

Not long ago, when I had been surfeited with the indictments and generalizations by unfriendly critics of the South, I went to the office of S. L. Smith, General Agent of the Rosenwald Fund, whose headquarters are in Nashville. On the wall was a big map of the fourteen states in which the fund has been used, with red tacks to show the places where Rosenwald schools have been built. Smith was happy over the fact that on October 6, 1925, money had been appropriated from his office for the building of the three thousandth school. Out of a fund of $12,729,922 expended on these buildings, he said, state and county taxes had amounted to $7,151,059, the Rosenwald fund to $2,267,292, while Negroes had given $2,706,292 in voluntary contributions and the whites $605,299. As a Southerner he rejoiced that 60 per cent. had come from taxes. But the figures were the least significant part of his story. He showed me pictures of the schools, the teachers' homes, the school gardens, farms, and shops, and students and faculties at work or at play amid delightful surroundings. Architectural beauty was combined with usefulness and efficiency, sanitation and recreation with opportunities for study and practical work. For the guidance of local boards plans are drawn for all these buildings, and they have often been used for white schools as well.

Smith held me for two hours telling the stories of how communities in all parts of the South have awakened to the need of Negro schools and have vied with each other in meeting the conditions for appropriations from the Rosenwald Fund. The largest number —fifty-seven—of such schools is found in Shelby County, Tennessee, which has one of the most efficient systems of schools in the country. Farmers of the

Delta region in Mississippi and Arkansas, seeing what had followed from such schools in making the Negroes happier and more efficient workers, have been quick to follow suit.

I had just read in the *Southern Workman* an article by Leo M. Favrot, on the development of a system of Negro schools in Coahoma County, Mississippi, under the leadership of the County Superintendent, P. F. Williams. Smith added many personal details that enlivened and gave colour to the statement of facts. He had first heard of the plans in a five-hour conversation with Williams in Memphis one night, and had promised the superintendent his support. Coahoma is one of the richest counties in the Delta with a Negro population of 85 per cent. and with one hundred planters owning 90 per cent. of the land. It had been hard to wake the latter up to the necessity of providing adequate schools, but once aroused they had gone forward with amazing energy. Before, they had tolerated the makeshift schools; now they decided to improve them. Already twenty-four primary schools, five junior agricultural schools, and a central agricultural high school have been built and organized and have teachers in all practical as well as academic subjects. A health unit has been established and diseases cut down. In connection with the extension departments of state colleges, education has been extended to adults. What has been done is but a part of a well-defined plan now supported by the landowners that looks to doubling and trebling the number of schools. Thus has come about the increase of the earning capacity and prosperity among all groups of Negroes; the improvement of individual and community health; and "the promotion of the well-being of all the Negroes in the county, who have a feeling of satisfaction and encouragement the like of which they have never felt before."

The example of this county has spread to others. Robert E. Lee Wilson, owner of a farm of forty-two thousand acres on the Arkansas side of the Mississippi, built a $60,000 brick high-school building for the Negroes on his plantation, only to have it burned the night before it was to be dedicated. He announced that they would begin the following day to rebuild an even better one. "These Negroes helped me to make my money," he said, "and I am going to see that their children get an education." Then Smith switched to South Carolina and told of the Lancaster Training School, built under the direction of Le Roy Springs, one of the most prominent capitalists of the state—a high school of twelve grades with the best type of teachers of domestic science and agriculture. In his continuous trips throughout the South, sometimes in company with the agents of the other boards interested in Negro education, he has come to know personally more educational boards and teachers than perhaps any other man in the South. With a smiling optimism he assures you that the whole situation is most favourable, and that there is little opposition to the programme of education now being fostered in every Southern state. Even the Ku Klux Klan leaders have been among the most active supporters of the new schools.

At about the same time that I had this conversation, I received the advance sheets of a history of Durham, North Carolina, by Professor W. K. Boyd of Duke

University. One of the most significant chapters in the book is on the status of the Negro population in a typical manufacturing town of the New South. The two leaders of the Negro race, often so opposed in their views to each other, agreed in their tributes to Durham as a home for the race. Booker T. Washington said:

> Of all the Southern cities I have visited I found here the sanest attitude of the white people toward the black. . . . I never saw in a city of this size so many prosperous carpenters, brick-masons, blacksmiths, wheelrights, cotton-mill operatives, and to-bacco-factory workers among the Negroes.

And he added that he found in Durham fewer signs of poverty among his race than elsewhere.

Similar is the judgment of W. E. B. DuBois:

> There is in this small city a group of five thousand or more coloured people, whose social and economic development is perhaps more striking than that of any similar group in the nation.

To make good these statements, Professor Boyd tells the story of the growth of real and personal property held by the Negroes from $644,376 in 1916 to $3,139,638 in 1923, of the development of insurance companies, banks, and public schools, of a college that was begun as a private training school and is now one of the system of state colleges, and of a public library supported in part by city and county appropriations. Especially noteworthy was the establishment of the Lincoln Hospital by the Duke family "in grateful appreciation of the fidelity and faithfulness of the Negro slaves during the Civil War," and the later enlargement of the hospital by gifts of the Duke family and other white and coloured citizens to the amount of $150,000.   It is maintained by appropriations from the county and the city.

The story of Durham might be paralleled in Winston-Salem, the other leading tobacco manufacturing city of the state.   A significant illustration of the attitude of the whites to the Negroes was that the late J. B. Duke, in establishing the Duke Foundation of $40,000,000, included among the beneficiaries Biddle University in Charlotte, and that his brother, B. N. Duke, has given large sums to other Negro institutions of the state.   More noteworthy still is the steady increase in the appropriation of the state Legislature to Negro schools and colleges.   In the *Southern Workman* (November, 1925), Lawrence A. Oxley, recently appointed as the director of the Negro Welfare Board, thus summarizes the progress of these institutions under the efficient leadership of Prof. N. C. Newbold:

North Carolina long ago took the lead over all the Southland in the matter of providing improved educational facilities for its Negro population.   During the past five years the state has spent over $15,000,000 on Negro education.   This amount represents a sum larger than the total appropriation for the education of whites and Negroes during the period 1905 to 1910.   A building programme of nearly $1,000,000 for the two-year period 1923–24 was recently completed.   This includes dormitories, dining-halls, homes for principals, administration and classroom buildings, shops, laundries, and homes for faculty members.   The salaries of Negro teachers in the quadrennium 1921–1925 will be in excess of $7,000,000.   New school buildings in cities, towns, and rural districts built in this period will exceed a total cost of $5,000,000.   Other special purposes such as supervision, summer schools, vocational training, county training, and high schools, will add $750,000, making a total expenditure in the four-year period of approximately $15,000,000 of public funds on the Negro schools of the state.

He tells also of the more recent organization of a department of Negro Welfare under the direction of the State Department of Public Welfare, whereby surveys are being made of delinquents of all kinds. Ten Negro social workers have been placed as family case workers, probation officers, and general assistants in county welfare work.

In the same issue of the *Southern Workman,* published, I should have said, by Hampton Institute, Thomas B. Parker, one of the most enlightened cotton-mill men of South Carolina, tells the story of the establishment of the Phillis Wheatley Centre in Greenville, South Carolina. In 1924, a committee of the Chamber of Commerce worked out the details of the plan by which $70,000 was raised to provide a handsome brick building for the Negro community centre, and a definite amount for its maintenance, both races making contributions. White people have not only given liberally of their money (about two thirds of the amount), but through various organizations have provided personal aid in making adult teaching, recreational facilities, family service, etc., effective. The city itself appropriates $1,500 annually for the library, an important feature of the Centre. The aim of the leaders has been to provide for the needs of the large Negro population and thus to turn them from liabilities into assets. The South is ready not only to say that it is the best place for the Negroes to live, but to do the things that will make the statement good. The economic aspect of the whole undertaking is subordinated to the humanitarian. It is proposed to study what other places have done and thus to continue the work to the greatest advantage.

Such undertakings—and they might easily be multiplied—Bishop Jones of New Orleans, one of the religious leaders of his race, had in mind when he spoke of the "multiplied instances of good will and of good fellowship which could not exist if there was not in the heart of a large element of the South a sense of genuine respect and love for the Negro." To the same effect writes Principal Moton of Tuskegee in a review of the Interracial Commission and similar movements in the South:

> I have not been unmindful of the injustice, discrimination, and unfair treatment which my people are too often obliged to take to a greater or less extent in all parts of the country, but I have here been trying to fix attention upon those strong, ever-widening currents of constructive endeavour which move forward with a swiftness that accentuates the eddies of passion and prejudice which appear along their course. Knowing as I do the inner workings of these movements which I have described, and the character and the spirit of the men behind them, I am satisfied that we have in them a force and an influence making for righteousness that cannot be defeated.

This last statement of Doctor Moton's is but one illustration of the spirit of conciliation and fairness that animates his autobiography, "The Way Out." He does not hesitate to state very frankly that the Negro should be permitted "to enjoy every right and privilege of the American citizen, that he should have a chance of growth and development, a chance for training and education, a chance to work, a chance to live and serve his race and country," but it is in tone and in spirit that he is sharply differentiated from some other leaders of his race. It is unjust to accuse such a man of sycophancy or materialism. He wants to build from the ground up; he deals with facts as they are and not as he thinks they ought to be. He has common sense and tact, and a sense of humour which is so often lacking in certain intellectuals of his race. He believes with his predecessor that an inch of progress is better than a yard of complaint. Such men as he—and there are many others who have found the way out as he has—are doing something better than talking: they are building institutions, projecting business enterprises, creating currents of thought and feeling. They have not lost confidence in the justice and the friendship of the white man, and are willing to coöperate with him in bringing about a better relationship. Theirs is a great task at the present moment; it is theirs to lead and not to inflame a race, to construct and not to destroy. They will be neither browbeaten by unsympathetic radicals of their own race nor humiliated by extremists of the other race.

Carefully weighing all the evidence from all sources that have been indicated in this chapter, one is impressed with the difficulty and the complexity of the problem. There is no absolute truth—only phases that need to be emphasized at different times and under varying conditions. There is no final solution; the best we can do, as a wise man who has done as much as any other man in this generation to improve conditions says, is to take the next step. Imagination is needed to visualize conditions, but we must see the difficulty that the white man has had to adjust himself, as well as the tragedy of the Negro who suffers from injustice and sometimes from persecution. Any man with a heart has sympathy with the black man who so often has been the victim of circumstances for which he was not responsible; but he should have sympathy also for the white man who has borne the burden of criminality, disease, and inefficiency. The only remedy is that all the human factors that make up the situation should feel their responsibility, and especially that they should coöperate in definite and constructive efforts. Out of conferences and coöperative efforts on the part of the North and South, white and black, will come gradual improvement. It was this that Doctor Moton had in mind when in his inaugural address at Tuskegee he recalled the fact that Tuskegee was due to the coöperation of an ex-Confederate soldier, a Northern white man, and a leader of the Negro race. This fact, he said, was a prophecy of a new day—"to the end that the white man of the North, the white man of the South, and the Negro should work harmoniously together in bringing forward that peace on earth which results when we have good-will."

CHAPTER XI

ECCLESIASTICS AND PROPHETS

PRACTICALLY all the men and women of whom I have written in this volume would be considered as liberals in their religious faith. In some cases I have indicated their attitude to the present evolution controversy and to similar questions that are involved in the adjustment of religion to modern scholarship and thought. Some few of the younger generation of scholars and writers have doubtless reacted rather strongly against the Church and orthodox creeds, but the great majority are openly and avowedly of the Centre Party in the conflict between the Fundamentalists and Modernists. They would insist on the necessity for defining terms before classifying themselves: they would call themselves "fundamentalists" if by that term are meant those who magnify the essential—really essential—points in the teachings of Jesus; they would call themselves "modernists" if by that term are meant those who accept the facts of modern critical scholars in their study of the Bible or who accept the facts and hypotheses of scientists in their study of nature. They would say to extreme conservatives and extreme radicals, "A plague o' both your houses!"and would insist that discrimination between ideas and types that are apt to be confused is the beginning of wisdom.

In a word, they believe that the South has the chance to make a real contribution to the nation and to the world by clinging to religion—yes, the Christian re-ligion—as the foundation of spiritual progress and at the same time by relating modern knowledge and prog-ress to the faith of the fathers. If I interpret their minds aright, they reject the deterministic philosophy of Haeckel and Bertrand Russell, the agnosticism of Huxley and Spencer, and the cynicism of Mencken and Cabell. They agree rather with the interpretations of Man and the Universe as found in the writings of Millikan, Osborn, and Conklin, and other scientists, who said in a signed statement of May, 1923:

> It is a sublime conception of God which is furnished by science, and one wholly consonant with the highest ideals of religion, when it represents Him as revealing Himself through countless ages in the development of the earth as an abode for man and in the age-long inbreathing of life into its constituent matter, culminating in man with his spiritual nature and all his God-like powers.

They would say that preachers like Percy Grant, Norman Guthrie, and Bishop Brown are not the rep-resentatives of true liberal progress in religion, but that Doctor Fosdick, Doctor Cadman, President Faunce, and Bishop Lawrence rightly divide the word of truth and are true prophets of the living God. On the other hand, they would repudiate without hesitancy the extreme statements and the ruthless methods of Doctors Straton, Norris, and Macartney, and the late Mr. Bryan, in making an irrepressible conflict between science and religion and in confusing the issues in-volved.

There are many preachers in all the churches of the

South who in their pulpits, and to a less degree in the assemblies of their churches, are seeking to lead the section into the right paths. Why is it they seem so often obscured in the public mind by noisier and more sensational evangelists and ecclesiastics? Why is it that they seem to have so little influence when great religious conventions are in session or when laws intended to suppress honest opinion are being considered by legislatures?

In the face of the fine opportunity that so many of its wisest leaders have seen, the South as a whole seems often to be the home of reactionary theology, the citadel of a narrow Fundamentalism. In the national consciousness its solidarity in matters of religion is quite as well established as its solidarity in politics. A Congregationalist minister in a leading city of the South recently gave an estimate of the strength of Fundamentalism in the various churches: the Baptists 99.99 per cent., the Presbyterians, 99 per cent., the Methodists 90 per cent., the Episcopalians, 85 per cent., and the Congregationalists 100 per cent. Fundamentalist in the country, and 100 per cent. Modernist in the cities. These figures are obviously exaggerated. Dr. Shailer Matthews, with perhaps different definitions and places in mind, gives the proportion between the two parties in the South and Middle West as fifty-fifty. I should account for the discrepancy by suggesting that at times when people are calm and when issues are not raised by some particular incident, or when one is thinking only of theological seminaries or preachers' institutes, Doctor Matthews might be right. But let some definite issue arise in which mob psychology may make itself felt, let some strong leaders speak out passionately while the moderates keep quiet, let some demagogue introduce a set of resolutions which it seems futile to resist, and then the figures of the Congregationalist minister seem nearer the truth. There are so many currents and counter-currents, so much progress and so much actual retrogression, that the real status is difficult to define.

Meanwhile the fight is on between conservatives and progressives in all the churches. The most definite and spectacular fight of recent years has just closed— namely, as to whether the Southern Methodist Church should reunite with the Methodist Church of the North. A plan of federation had been almost unanimously adopted by a joint commission of the two churches, the main features of which had been proposed by the Southern members. After many similar attempts at union, extending over twenty-five years, had been for one reason or another rejected by one or both churches, it seemed at last that the long cherished dream of many was about to be realized on the sixtieth anniversary of the close of the Civil War. The General Conference of the Southern Church in July, 1924, had passed the plan by a four fifths majority; nine out of the fourteen bishops were in favour of it, and with few exceptions all the connectional officers, the overwhelming majority of the pastors of the leading churches in cities, and nearly all the organs of the various annual conferences were advocates of the plan.

The acid test came when the annual conferences voted upon the proposition. It so happened that the bishops who opposed the plan presided over the conferences that had the largest number of votes, and that they used all their power, which is very great, to defeat unification. In the main, the rural districts and the conferences of the Lower South gave large majorities against the plan, while the Western conferences and those of foreign fields voted almost unanimously in favour of it. The final results show that, while a majority of the eight thousand votes were in favour of unification, the constitutional three fourths majority failed by nearly two thousand votes.

Many arguments were used by the opponents in propaganda that was spread abroad in pamphlets and leaflets, and by one paper that was the organ of the movement—a paper that spared no language of misinterpretation and abuse to carry its object. Fundamentally, the two main causes of defeat were: the recollections of the Civil War and of Reconstruction surviving after all these years of industrial and intellectual progress, and the fear that the Negroes of the Northern Church might in some way be forced upon the Southern Church. The flag of "white supremacy" was raised as in many a political battle of the past, and the spectre of social equality haunted the imaginations of men.

One of the most potent arguments used by Bishop Warren A. Candler, the main leader of the anti-unificationists, was that the Northern Church is dominated by Modernism. In an article on "Resolute and Revolutionary Rationalism" in the Nashville *Christian Advocate* (January 30, 1925), he exposed the adoption by the bishops of the Northern Church of six "rationalistic" books for the course of study for young preachers—an indication of a "rationalist drift" that is gradually destroying the faith of the churches of that section. Incidentally, he brings out the fact that the two Negro bishops of that church voted with the majority, and that constitutes another strong argument against union! He concludes with an appeal to the Southern Church to have no fellowship with such heresies:

> Modernism is prevalent in the Methodist Episcopal Church. It is there, and it is strongly intrenched in high places, so that it can project its principles and influences into the course of study which all the preachers, both white and black, are required to study. How rapidly will the leaven permeate the entire ministry of that Church!
>
> Moreover, it is in all the Northern churches; but, as Bishop Berry points out, it is stoutly opposed by many strong leaders of the Northern Presbyterians, Northern Episcopalians, and Northern Baptists, while it holds a commanding place among the Northern Methodists and with little opposition.
>
> It is too clear to deny with any show of reason that the churches of the South must save the cause of evangelical Christianity in the United States or it will be lost.
>
> The Southern churches are abundantly able to defend successfully "the faith once for all delivered to the saints" against the attacks of all the resolute and revolutionary rationalism now current in our country, *provided they are faithful to the trust reposed in them by Providence.*
>
> What is called "modernism" is not modern at all. It is but the superficial recrudescence of the teachings of Voltaire and the tenets of the English deists of the eighteenth century. Very much of what it puts forth as "the assured results of scientific criticism," about which "all scholars are agreed," may be found in Tom Paine's "Age of Reason." Every one of its essential heresies was proclaimed during the first three centuries of the Christian Era, and they were overwhelmingly refuted by the great Christian apologists of that period.
>
> The Southern churches have no slightest occasion for fear or shame in refusing and resisting all this aggressive rationalism Their position is as impregnable as their duty is unmistakable. But they must cease sending their young preachers to Northern seminaries and universities for education. Nearly every one of

the most wealthy and conspicuous of these institutions is sadly infected with rationalism, just as their predecessors were infected with liberalists before Timothy Dwight drove their skepticism from Yale and before the great revival of 1800 so nearly cleansed it away from almost all of the then existing colleges of the nation. The evil has returned in our day in redoubled strength, but it is no more invincible now than it was then.   Indeed, it is quite vulnerable, notwithstanding its boastfulness.

The great revival of 1800 began in the South, and the Southern churches should now seek another such gloriously saving visitation from Heaven.

But so great a work of grace cannot come to pass under the ministrations of rationalizing preachers.   Rationalism has never revived religion in a single parish nor turned one heathen tribe from the worship of dumb idols to the service of the living God.

Let the Southern churches beware of it.   Where it falls it blights.

Let the evangelical churches of the South stand in their lot, walk in the faith of their fathers, seek only the favour of God, and thus fulfill their high mission of saving evangelical Christianity for the blessing of the American nation.

Bishop Candler's point of view as expressed in this article and in scores of sermons and addresses is characteristic of the pride that Southern churchmen take in their conservatism.   The logic is inescapable. The hope of the world is America, the hope of America is evangelical religion of the most orthodox type, the hope of the American Church is the Southern evangelical churches, the hope of these churches is the Southern Methodist Church, and the hope of this church is its denominational colleges.   A member of another church might come to a different conclusion as to the divinely appointed church, but this point of view is the basis of ecclesiastical arrogance and of immense satisfaction in the presence of a ruined world.

Corra Harris, in her "My Book and Heart," pays

tribute to Bishop Candler as "the greatest churchman of his times," who comes as near "as any mortal man ever did to being an autocrat before the Lord." She recalls his triumphs as a pulpit orator and feels a pride in him as a representative Georgian. "Nothing will ever make me believe," she says, "that he really accepts the Scriptures as literally as he claims to do, but he does it for the church's good and for conscience' sake." She thought at the time when she was writing that he was nearing the end of the journey and was far up the ladder toward the Celestial City, for "he cannot catch a great audience by the neck as he used to and shake the money and tears out of it." The reason is that he is becoming "more scrupulous"; the rhetorical power of the stump speaker that he used to have is passing away. He is still "rumbling." And then she adds: "Heaven help us if he takes a notion to come back down and fetch another surge at this perverse generation! I do not think he has got it in him; but if he has, and decided to make the fight along evangelical lines, something would happen."

Well, he did come back down from the ladder, and something has happened. He wrecked the unification plan of his church, and he is writing and speaking as never before for "the faith once for all delivered to the saints." He is constitutionally opposed to every progressive movement of his time. "If it is true, it isn't new, and if it's new, it isn't true" is his dismissal of every new idea. He is a man of unquestioned power of pen and of tongue, and he is reënforced by a powerful religious organization, of which he has been a leader for a quarter of a century or more. He has the gift of ridicule that enables him to sway large audiences and a power of eloquence that stirs the emotions of the masses. Conservative in his thinking, he is radical in his methods of interpretation and utterly reckless and irresponsible in his weapons of warfare. Able to speak with ease upon any subject without preparation, he delights in hasty generalizations and extempore half-truths. No actor ever enjoyed a stage performance more than the Bishop does his playing with the emotions of an audience, and no prize-fighter ever enjoyed more the knockout blow for an antagonist. He fascinates, even while he infuriates, the intelligent auditor. When he writes, as somebody said of Horace Greeley, he "dips his pen of infallibility into his ink of omniscience with as little self-distrust as a child plays with matches."

He is most powerful as a preacher. In a typical sermon on Christian education he denounces state universities as centres of infidelity, prevented by constitutional limitations from even suggesting the truths of religion. Independent institutions, once the property of the Church, have forgotten God. Responsible to no organization or opinion, they threaten the welfare of the Republic. New England, under the leadership of apostate institutions like Harvard and Yale, is the breeding place of infidelity. He would rather be a poor Puritan preacher like John Harvard than all the Eliots with their moonshine religion. Jonathan Edwards was better than all the cultured preachers that have been produced in "emasculated seminaries." The only hope for the country is that the church colleges, which produced the giants of other generations, and which by their very nature are committed to evangelical religion first and foremost, shall arouse themselves to the need of the hour. To the policy that the Church ought to control institutions, and can control them, the Methodist Church is committed. A Columbia professor said not long ago, "You in the South don't need to build universities; we will furnish them." Such a statement is a gratuitous insult to this section. "We can and we will build them, in order to preserve our evangelical religion and the greatness of our section."

One of his former colleagues in the Episcopacy illustrates even better the effect of ecclesiasticism on a powerful leader. I never read Browning's "Lost Leader" that I do not think of him. In the prime of his life, he was the head of a college which he found small and unpromising and which he led into the light of a fuller day. By wide reading and by association with members of the Faculty, who had had better advantages of training than he, he came well into the currents of modern thought. With remarkable power of assimilation and of interpretation, and with a certain creative sense in the building of an institution of learning, he inspired his colleagues and students with a love of truth that was to lead them into all fields of human knowledge, a love of freedom that would break the shackles of the mind, and with a love for the nation that transcended sectional loyalty. I recall as among the most vivid memories of life his addresses and sermons, which were milestones in the lives of many men. I seem still to hear him saying, as his eyes glowed and his imperial voice rang out in the old chapel:

He who limits truth by any method, or, for any pretence, hinders men in their fullest rights to know it, fights against God. Christianity has never produced infidelity, but ecclesiastical creeds set forth as the final formulation of faith and sanctioned, not by reason but by prejudice, have been the breeders of infidels. Voltaire hated Romanism, not Christ. Ingersoll rebelled against harsh decrees and arbitrary wrath, not against the holy spirit and divine life of the Son of God. . . . The only protection that the kingdom of Christ claims is that which a truth assures. . . . The Church dishonours Christ when it trembles before any new proposition of science or literary criticism. Truth can never harm anything except falsehood, and the measure of strength in the faith of men must always be the truth. Instead of a blind assault made on such men as Darwin and Tyndall, the Christian world should patiently investigate their theories, and rejoice over all the light they can give to men. Higher critics cannot be overcome by a sneer from the pulpit. The worst sceptic is the man who refuses to have his faith examined.

It is the province of Christian education to make you lovers and searchers after truth, and if it fails in this it has no other grounds upon which to defend its cause. The Christian college must be a place where truth, all truth, must feel at home and have supreme authority.

At another time he spoke of the need for wise progressive leaders in the South, and his hearers applied the words to him:

The leadership of these last days is too often the shrewd calculation of the coward as to the trend of events, and a cautious hanging on to the rear of the unthinking multitude. It is not the man who knows what our people are, but what our people should be, that we most sorely need. . . . When any set of men assert that one dead man is stronger to shape an age than all living men, the declaration is the verdict of national death. . . . The world does not want the echoes of the past, but the fresh words and the prophetic notes of a real voice. . . . Only at the threshold of a new and open kingdom of truth should any man discard his former faiths. But once at such a door the duty to do it is supreme, and with reverent fidelity the step should be taken, not in secret but with a clear voice that echoes down the valleys and along the hills, till the assembled multitudes shall know of the higher order.

Nor were these mere words. In a great fight that has already been described in this volume he practised what he preached; his sword was unsheathed for the freedom of the college. At another time he became convinced that the Southern Methodist Church ought to be reunited with the Northern Church. In June, 1906, in his final message to the graduating class he chose as his subject, "A Plea for the Union of Methodism." Published in the July *South Atlantic Quarterly*, the address attracted national attention by reason of its statesmanlike and broad-minded views:

> The chief issue before Methodism in America [he said] is not a defense of the past, nor to prove the rights of differing bodies. The supreme question is a reunion into a permanent fellowship. The time has come when separation cannot be justified. . . In all matters of vital importance Episcopal Methodism is at one, and its complete union seems to be justified and suggested by every consideration.

The issue thus clearly and vigorously stated, he proceeded to dismiss one by one the difficulties in the way. The Negro, he held, should hasten rather than delay the union; our border warfare is a strong argument for it; federation has been a failure; union alone will eliminate competition and contention; the economic argument is all on the side of union; our religious and moral influence is seriously hampered by the emphasis placed upon non-essential differences.

> Why unite in the Orient and remain divided in America? This question is all the more pertinent in view of the growing national spirit in this country.

In conclusion, he said:

> The mightiest Protestant force in this republic cannot escape the just censure of the world if it weakens its usefulness in an unholy contention and wastes its energies in perpetuating an unnecessary division.

And then something happened! It gradually dawned upon the college community that the note of progress was no longer heard from him. He made a study of the pioneer heroes of Methodism as the theme of an address for a great religious assembly, and became so infatuated with their religious zeal and with the marvellous results of their preaching that he swung into the rôle of an evangelist, more intent upon swaying the masses than leading the institution that he had brought to a new life. A sermon preached by one of the bishops at annual conference, making light of the higher critics and evolutionists, had an influence on him out of all proportion to its real value, and especially suggested the way in which church leadership lay. Worst of all, it must be said, ecclesiastical preferment began to be suggested by his friends. He was elected bishop, and for the remaining years of his life he was allied with all the reactionary forces of his Church.

He never recovered the rapture of his creative period; broken in body and mind and spirit, he spent his last years in futile obstruction and in bitter lamentation over the signs of the times. He might have been one of the great leaders of his church if he had continued the course to which he set himself in his earlier years. He could have carried men with him and not lagged behind in the ways of progress. He missed his way on the road to leadership.

That the Methodist Church has not been altogether under the influence of such leaders is due in a large degree to the brave and broad leadership of such men as Bishop Edwin D. Mouzon. Despite the limitations of the Episcopacy, he has been a prophet, an interpreter of truth as well as a great preacher. As Chairman of the Commission on Unification he wrote and spoke unceasingly in behalf of the cause. It is largely due to him and his co-workers that a majority was given for the plan. Although defeated, he has the consciousness of having made a persistent warfare on the forces of reaction, passion, and prejudice.

He has rendered an even more important service in standing for a liberal interpretation of Methodism and Christianity. In the main he has stood for the progressive point of view—a fact evidenced in the attacks that have been made on him by the conservatives. In a little volume on the fundamentals of Methodism he emphasizes the view that Wesley did not insist on a hard-and-fast lot of doctrines but rather on experience and life. Again and again he has quoted in sermons and articles the words of Wesley:

The distinguishing marks of a Methodist are not his opinions of any sort. His assenting to this or that scheme of religion, his embracing any particular set of notions . . . are all quite wide of the point. . . . As to all opinions which do not strike at the root of Christianity, we think and let think.

And again:

The Methodists alone do not insist on your holding this or that opinion; but they think and let think. It is not an opinion, or any number of opinions put together, be they ever so true. A string of opinions is no more Christian faith than a string of beads is Christian holiness.

And the Bishop explains as he thinks of the new emphasis on creeds:

God pity us if, sent as we are upon a great mission, we fall out among ourselves by the way and take to disputing about things which are not essential to the gospel and have no relation to the great facts of Christian experience and life!

He has with all his executive and administrative duties, and with all his love of preaching, found time for study. He reads the most modern books, not for the purpose of refuting them but of learning from them. The result of his extensive reading and study may be seen in two series of lectures given at Southern Methodist University and at Vanderbilt University during 1925. The latter series on the "Programme of Jesus" is especially noteworthy because of the fact that he was willing to accept the invitation of the University to deliver the lectures when his church had withdrawn from all connection with it. Some of the bishops had even refused to appoint students to its School of Religion. The lectures, furthermore, had been identified in the public mind with the utterances of some of the most progressive religious leaders of America, notably Doctor Fosdick, who, in 1923, had spoken on "Christianity and Progress."

Waiving aside all possible criticism that might come to him, he established as the main theme of his lectures the social aspects of the teachings of Jesus. With a thorough knowledge of critical scholarship even as applied to the New Testament, he contends for the

supremacy of Jesus over all the other teachings of the
Bible that may seem to be out of harmony with his
teachings and life.   His criticism of the apocalyptic
literature, which with all its puzzles and symbols has
been so emphasized by Fundamentalists in their
prophecies of some cataclysm that will end the world,
is worthy of the best modern scholarship.   He goes
so far as to admit that some of the passages in the
Gospels may be due to the failure of the Apostle to
understand the meaning of their Master, and asks, "Is
it not extremely likely that the minds of the disciples
were so filled with thoughts of a spectacular apocalyptic sort that certain sayings of Jesus took on a
somewhat different character in their thinking from
what he had originally intended?"   In the chapter on
"Jesus not a Lawgiver but a Teacher," he says, evi-
dently with the present-day controversy in mind:

> Ever and anon in the history of Christianity we see professed
> followers of Jesus turning the Way of Life into a System of Dog-
> matics—and measuring a man's fidelity to the gospel, not by the
> beauty and Christlikeness of his life, but by the soundness of his
> metaphysical theories and the accuracy of his intellectual state-
> ments of the things that must be believed.

On the subject of revivals he has much to say:

> Certain professional evangelists have gone through the land
> outraging every reverent feeling and driving from us the modest
> and the thoughtful.

There are some conversions which

> convert a man *from nothing to nothing* . . .   Doubt and denial
> can never be overcome by compulsion and display. . . .   The
> soul of man can be won by instruction and appeal, but can never

be carried by assault. . . . Dogmatism and denunciation will never make Christians out of unbelievers.

And again:

Mere revivalism will not get us anywhere unless preceded by teaching and followed by teaching. Revivalism alone will never save the world. Christian education is necessary to furnish a basis for any worthwhile revivalism; and Christian education alone can conserve the results of revivalism.

Striking at those who look upon Christianity as having only individual salvation as its aim he says:

It is time to cease our pious talk about "only conversion can save the world," and "the soul of all improvement is the improvement of the soul"—self-evident platitudes both, which are often used by men obsessed with the individualistic conception of the gospel.

What are the conditions in human society that make it well-nigh impossible to "convert sinners"? The only religion that counts is that which has to do with conditions that may be remedied by Christian citizens. The difficult problem is to apply the principles of Jesus to industrial, racial, international problems. In a comprehensive survey of some modern problems and conditions, he asks with repeated emphasis, "Dare we be Christians?"

One of the great sermons preached in this country during the past decade was Bishop Mouzon's sermon in Nashville just after a series of five addresses on the "Virgin Birth" by a representative of the Moody Bible Institute of Los Angeles and William J. Bryan's address on "What Is the Bible?" had aroused much discussion in the city. There appeared to be concerted action on the part of the Fundamentalists to stampede what Mr. Bryan called "the centre of Modernism in the South." The Bishop took occasion the following Sunday to deliver his mind. With clear exposition he defined terms that had been confused; he took the main articles of the Fundamentalists and tore them to shreds, especially the doctrine of a literally dictated Bible, the belief in the scientific accuracy of Genesis, the legalistic and commercial theories of the Atonement, and pre-millenarian doctrines. He did not leave his hearers in any doubt as to what he meant; he called names, suggesting that while Mr. Bryan had formerly carried religion into politics, he was then carrying politics into religion. With sarcasm, eloquence, and spiritual power he spoke for an hour holding the rapt attention of his hearers. It was one of those deliverances that one hears now and then that impress one as deeds.

I have spoken at some length of the Methodist Church because it is typical of the entire South, and because I am more familiar with it. As I analyze the situation in this church, the liberals are growing in number and influence every year. The colleges and universities under the control of the Church are for the most part free to teach what they want to, some of them boldly, others softly. Southern Methodist University, despite the enforced resignation of Prof. John A. Rice on account of his book on the Old Testament, still has in the main a liberal faculty somewhat nagged by the patronizing conferences. Emory University, despite Bishop Candler's public utterances, has a theological department that ranks in ability and in liberal thought with the best. Duke University has just called to the head of its school of Religious Education Doctor Soper of Northwestern University, who is one of the outstanding leaders of liberal thought in the country. The connectional officers of the Church are, with few exceptions, modern in their point of view, while at the same time devout and spiritual. No man in America has written with more freedom and wisdom about current religious problems than Gilbert T. Rowe, the editor of the *Methodist Review*. His editorials, if collected, would rank well with the best religious writing of the day, while the articles that he has inspired have sounded no uncertain note as to the general policy of the magazine.

The same may be said of the Episcopal Church, which represents the old Southern traditions better than any other church. One might expect that it would be the most conservative, but it is not. It has the unique distinction of having been reunited with the Northern Church immediately after the war. The bishops of the South answered the first roll call, and there was no further question as to the unity of the Church in America. It has had the most liberal attitude to its Negro members and bishops. An astonishing event was that in Memphis a Negro bishop took part in the consecration of the late Bishop Beatty. And yet it does not appear that any disastrous results have followed from such Christian fellowship. It is no wonder that two of the most prominent workers in the Southern Interracial Commission have been Bishop Bratton of Mississippi and Bishop Reese of Georgia.

Judging from recent utterances of the leaders of the Episcopal Church, I should say that on the whole it is better represented in its administration by liberal lead‹ ers than any other church in the South. Bishop Gailor has been for several years president of the Council of the entire American Church and is known everywhere to be aligned with the progressive element of his church. Bishop Maxon, his colleague in the diocese of Tennessee, is a capital illustration of the enlightened leader. He has a scholar's knowledge of the problems of Biblical study, and does not hesitate to state his position on evolution and higher criticism. Bishop Mikell of Atlanta, in delivering the address in behalf of the Trustees of Peabody College for Teach‹ ers to the graduating class in 1924, gave as clear an exposition of the theory of evolution as it relates to religion as it has been my privilege to hear. Conscious of the fact that the teachers would be confronted with the problem in many Southern states and communities, he sought to interpret for them an attitude which would "safeguard Christian principles and at the same time find a place for scientific truth and all the results of a real education and culture."

An even bolder and more significant statement was the Commencement sermon preached at Vanderbilt University in June, 1925, by Rev. C. B. Wilmer, now Professor of Practical Theology at the Theological School of the University of the South (Sewanee) and formerly rector of the first Episcopal Church of Atlanta. The Anti-Evolution law had just been passed; the excitement was rather tense as the audience realized that he was making the controversy that had been engendered thereby the subject of his discourse. Speaking at first in general terms, he said:

Christ did not come into the world to dictate to scientists what they should think about atoms and evolution and the motion of the heavenly bodies; to interfere with the liberty of thought and investigations of physicists, geologists, astronomers, and the like. . . . Nor did he come to tell philosophers what to think; to furnish ready-made systems of truth . . . to be accepted on authority.

He then denounced the most recent attempts to control scientific truth through legislative action, adding that "most people have abandoned the Bible as an authority on astronomy, but still claim it as an authority on and against evolution." Recalling that the real cause for the death of Jesus was a time-serving, truculent civil power, yielding to the demands of an ignorant and corrupt priesthood who really thought they were saving religion but were mainly interested in saving their own popularity and prestige, he concluded:

It is for scientists and not for civil legislatures to say what is science; just as it is for mathematicians and not for politicians to say what is mathematical truth.

The Church must render unto Cæsar the things that are Cæsar's and also unto science those things that belong to science; and must under no circumstances undertake to force the state to do its bidding in order to put over its religious views or to interfere with the states giving to our boys and girls scientific teaching confined within the limits of the scientific realm.

He was so bold as to suggest the canonization of some scientists as the servants of God:

The Church owes an apology to a long roll of scientific men: Galileo, Darwin, and many others; and ought to make it publicly. As a tardy amends, the Church ought to include a number of these men in its list of saints; canonize them; and in order that this be not misunderstood, classify them under a special head: "Servants of the truth of God," with perhaps this passage of Scripture: "Inasmuch as ye have done it unto one of the least of these my brethren ye have done it unto me."

As one heard these brave and wise words he could not help wishing that they had been uttered while the Legislature was considering the passage of the bill. What would have been the effect if Bishop Mikell's address had been delivered at the same time? Or if preachers in all parts of the state had made known their point of view as the leading Nashville ministers did in a letter of protest to the Senate? Or if all the leading dailies had followed Mr. Finney of the Columbia *Herald* in denouncing such legislation as a violation of the fundamental principles of the patron saint of Democracy? Or if the Academy of Science of the State had become as aggressive in the expression of their opinion as they were six months after the bill had become a law? Would the Legislature have listened to an appeal from the President of the University of Tennessee as similar legislatures listened to President McVey of the University of Kentucky or President Chase of the University of North Carolina?

Nobody can tell what might have happened, but everybody knows what did happen, and everybody ought to know that the children of the world were shrewder and more powerful than the children of light. Perhaps nobody thought that such a thing could happen. Somehow, leadership was lacking to bring to bear the pressure of enlightened opinion, and the blind push of the intolerant multitude triumphed. Just when the state was beginning to recover from its surprise and hoping that the Governor was right in his idea that the law would pass into a state of innocuous desuetude, came the Dayton trial with all its comic and tragic aspects.

It is not my purpose to rehearse the events connected with the Dayton trial.   Already the presses of the country have been exhausted in printing accounts of it and even the cables felt the undue pressure of the world-resounding news.   But certain aspects of the whole episode cannot be ignored.   There was at first practical unanimity of opinion among professional and business men that such a law should never have been passed.   But when the criticism from without began to pour into the state, when the Civil Liberties Union took up the case, when Clarence Darrow was chosen to lead the fight for the defendant, aided by a local attorney, an often defeated politician of ordinary ability, there arose in the minds of many a disposition to treat the whole thing as a joke, a comedy or farce, as real as ever was pulled off in a puppet show.   At the end of the trial the Fundamentalists had a new monster in Darrow and a new martyr in Bryan.   The issue seemed to them so clearly defined that all could read its meaning.   If you want to know what science leads to, here it is: agnosticism or atheism.   There is no middle ground.   If you want to see what religion is, the only pure and undefined religion, here it is, too: the last message of the Apostle of Fundamentalism, given a new glory by his martyrdom for the truth.

Now that the tumult and the shouting have died away, and the reporters have returned to their dens and the editors have all had their say, and the mistakes on both sides have been duly appraised, there remain only the words of young Scopes as he spoke to the Judge:

> I believe that I have been convicted of violating an unjust statute. I will continue in the future, as I have in the past, to oppose the law in any way I can. Any other action would be a violation of my ideals of academic freedom—that is, to teach the truth, as guaranteed in our constitution, of personal and religious freedom. I think the fine is unjust.

Whatever may be eventually adjudged as to the constitutionality of the law, Tennessee cannot be acquitted of the verdict contained in those words. It is not merely a question of whether a state has the right to pass such a law, but of whether it ought to. The fundamental issue as to the relation of science and religion is before a higher court than any judicial tribunal. Tennesseans cannot evade this issue by hurling back contemptuous remarks about the radical thinkers of other states.

A goodly number of Southern newspapers gave enlightened expressions of the true point of view. Some of them, not attempting to decide as to the truth or falsehood of the evolutionary hypothesis, contended that no state should enter upon a policy of proscription of opinion. Others, convinced of the truth of the theory, sought to interpret it in the light of a larger and more vital faith. Of these latter none wrote with more force or penetration than Douglas Freeman, the editor of the Richmond *News-Leader.* He drew a clear distinction between the two groups of evolutionists: those materialists who "would make science their religion and evolution its only creed"; and those who find in evolution "a more awe-inspiring and ennobling

interpretation of that God-created miracle men call
'life.' " On July 9, 1925, just after Bryan had made
his sensational statement at Dayton that "the contest
between evolution and Christianity is a duel to the
death," Mr. Freeman said:

> The ultimate effect of Mr. Bryan's attack will, of course, be
> *nil.* Truth will go on, undisturbed by his challenging. That is
> the way of truth, despite inquisitions, Spanish or American. But
> for the day, Mr. Bryan may do great harm to many young men
> and women.
>
> He presents them cold alternatives. He tells them they must
> take evolution or religion, as he defines it. He says they cannot
> have both science and religion. He thinks they will draw back,
> when the issue is plain, and that they will return to the old state-
> ment of faith. The tragedy is that now, as usually, Mr. Bryan is
> mistaken. Thousands of young students will accept the evidence
> of science and may become out-and-out materialists, solely because
> they are told there is no middle ground.
>
> When Mr. Bryan's ranting is over and the Tennessee law is
> buried, along with ten thousand earlier attempts to set a limit to
> human progress, most of these students will come back and will
> see that Bryan was wrong and that there were no inexorable al-
> ternatives. Meantime these young people will wander so unhap-
> pily, so restlessly, and will miss so much of the joy of the new reli-
> gion that accepts scientific truth as the larger revelation of God!
> For while Mr. Bryan has been fighting a rearguard action in the
> darkness, grappling with imaginary foes, the vanguard has been
> "marching into the dawn"—into a more wonderful world of a
> fuller revelation of God. Men who believe that God speaks in the
> stone as certainly as in the commandments written on it, men who
> are convinced that growth and progress are part of a mighty plan
> proclaimed in star and in sea—as surely as in law and in gospel—
> these men find evolution a help rather than a hindrance, when it
> is properly interpreted. They have much of the thrill that comes
> to those who begin to see in daylight the form and the meaning of
> things that were mysterious and affrighting in the dark. Mr.
> Bryan cannot take from these men and women the happiness of
> their religion, but by his dogmatism he is trying to keep young

people, for his little day, from fellowship with the company of those who do not say "God *or* evolution," but "God *and* evolution."

That is just the point of view of the churchmen already quoted and of many others who might be quoted. In spite of the declaration of the Southern Baptist Convention that "one can understand both the Bible and evolution and believe one of them, but he cannot understand both and believe both," ministers like Dr. Ashby Jones, of Atlanta, have not hesitated to interpret the two as not essentially antagonistic. Dean O. E. Brown of the Vanderbilt School of Religion in an illuminating and comprehensive survey[1] of the controversy now raging in all the churches over various questions, agrees with Dr. Edwin E. Slosson that "the real conflict is not between science and religion as such, but rather between dogmatic and intolerant religionists and scientists on the one side and liberal and tolerant religionists and scientists on the other side." Dr. Wilbur F. Tillett, Dean Emeritus and Professor of Christian Doctrine of the same faculty, in 1924 published a noteworthy volume entitled "Paths That Lead to God" in which he makes a new survey of the grounds of Theistic and Christian Belief. He has taught more Methodist preachers than any other man in his church, and has had a wholesome influence in leading men into a more liberal interpretation of religion. In his latest volume he has gathered the fruits of a lifetime of study and reflection and leaves no doubt as to his position on the many perplexing problems of the day. A valuable feature of the book is the large number of quotations from outstand-

[1]"Modernism: A Calm Survey," *Southern Methodist Review*, July, 1925.

ing thinkers and leaders; it is a veritable storehouse for seekers after truth. Patiently and tactfully the author masses his material and draws his conclusions. Especially noteworthy are the chapters, "Evolution and God," "The Progressive Revelation of God in the Scriptures," and "Through Christ to God." A typical passage will serve to interpret the spirit of the whole volume:

> The time is long past when faith in a personal God . . . must be regarded as incompatible with faith in evolution as the method and process by which things have come to be what they now are. . . . Many of the strongest and most devout of present-day Christian theists found in all the churches, not only believe in evolution, but believe that the theory of evolution adds greatly to the strength of the arguments drawn from the created universe to prove the existence of a personal God and the power and wisdom of Him who preserves and governs all created things.

These words might have been written of Dr. William Louis Poteat, who for more than twenty-five years has been a teacher and an advocate of the theory of evolution in Wake Forest College—a leading college of the Southern Baptist Church. In May, 1925, he delivered at the University of North Carolina a series of lectures entitled, "Can a Man Be a Christian To-day?" Of the circumstances attending these lectures and of their general point of view I have already written. What needs to be emphasized now is that they were delivered about the time the Southern Baptist Convention was declaring war on men in their colleges who were in any way teaching evolution. The same convention endorsed the passage of the Tennessee Anti-Evolution law and prescribed articles of faith for all members of the denomination. One of the outstanding speeches of the Convention was by Reverend J. Frank Norris of Fort Worth, Texas, one of the national leaders of the Fundamentalist movement and a special guardian of the faith of the colleges. With the ridicule of a demagogue he referred to Doctor Poteat in the following words:

Once there was a little animal that lived in the mud. There came a little freckle on the side of his head. He turned it to the sun, and it grew and grew until it was an eye. Another little freckle happened on the other side of his head, and it grew and grew until it was another eye. And a wart came on the under side in front, and it grew and grew until it made a foreleg. Another wart came out in front, and it grew into another foreleg. The two hindlegs were made out of two more warts. The little animal crawled up the bank and was a quadruped. His tail grew out and he climbed a cocoanut tree. He wanted to eat, and so he pulled off a cocoanut. It was so heavy that when it came loose it gave him a violent jerk which broke his tail off. He slipped down the tree, stole a suit of clothes, and became president of Wake Forest College. [Prolonged laughter and applause.] I didn't say that the president of Wake Forest College stole a suit of clothes. He's a nice man and wouldn't steal. I was telling about his ancestor.

Doctor Poteat has grown accustomed to such ridicule. He had been exhorted by his own friends and the friends of the college to keep silent. Ecclesiastical statesmen had counselled peace or a truce on both sides. Imagine the consternation in certain quarters when he took advantage of the opportunity to state even more fully and more forcibly his views, when he, in effect, defied his opponents and critics. The offense was all the greater that the lectures were delivered in a university already under fire for its heresies; it was giving aid to the enemy: Baptists outside the state could not understand the praise lavished upon the lectures by the leading newspapers and by representative and prominent citizens. The guns were silenced for the time, but were unlimbered at the State convention in November. Resolutions were passed defining the faith of Baptists in such words that seemed to make a show-down inevitable between the College and the convention. President Poteat refused to resign, and gave as his reason before a body of enthusiastic alumni that he could not let his Alma Mater surrender on so vital a principle. The Convention sidetracked the whole issue, largely, I suppose, because of the determined support of Poteat by all who are in any way connected with the college.

Aside from all the details of the controversy, the lectures as read to-day in book form[1] may well be considered as the most authoritative discussion of the relation between science and religion that has ever been written in the South. The important point is that the author was speaking directly to a large body of students with the evident desire to help them adjust their inherited faith to the best thought of to-day. The book is divided into three parts, entitled respectively: "To-day"—a succinct and penetrating analysis of contemporary thought based upon a study of the best current literature, philosophy, and science; "Baggage"—a frank and searching delineation of the things that have been in the way of a true and vital religion; and "Peace"—a constructive attempt to reconcile the teachings of science with the real fundamental spirit of the Christian religion.

The chief virtue is that Doctor Poteat knows how

[1]University of North Carolina Press, 1925.

to discriminate. He denounces alike the rationalism of science and the rationalism of orthodoxy, the latter because it is "compromising Christianity before the intelligence of the world." He has as little sympathy for the "earnest and capable but misguided men who, in the effort to protect our most precious possession, are in reality putting it in peril," as he has for the extreme modernists who would give up all because reason has forced them to give up some of the Bible, or for the scientists who "set down as absurd what it is unable to explain or handle." While he rejects the account of Creation in Genesis if taken as literal or scientific, he accepts it as a great hymn, rich in suggestion and melody. He distinguishes between belief, which is a purely intellectual process, and faith, which in science and practical life, as well as in religion, is the creative power by which man achieves all his greatest aims.

There are four passages in the volume that seem to me spoken in a peculiar way to the young men and women of the whole South. They are filled with intelligence and spiritual insight. Here is the voice of the real South, the South of the future. The first emphasizes the desire to keep the younger generation as children of the Christian faith:

Its standards and sanctities and inspirations have made us what we are. They are the refuge and guide of our personal life. They are the origin and security of our social order, the dynamic of our social activities. I am concerned most of all to inquire whether your culture is going to be at home with your religion. This adventure of the growing day—it is likely to intoxicate a spirited youth and absorb his enthusiasm. Will it dim and then put out the candle of the spiritual life? And the general situation outside university life, the spirit and atmosphere of the time—is it favourable and friendly, or chilling and hostile to the faith of our fathers? Is religion still possible? Can a man be a Christian to-day?

And the answer to the question is succinctly put in these words:

> The agencies and institutions of Christianity are not Christianity, but its tools. And remember, Christianity must have its tools. The Book of religion is one thing, men's theories of its origin, purpose, and interpretation are quite another thing. Accordingly, a man may be a Christian without being attached to any of the historic churches. A man may be a Christian, and worship in the solitudes where no pomp of chanting processions and stately liturgy intrudes upon the secret session of the soul with God. A man may be a Christian and not know any more of what has occurred in the deeps of his nature than that a radiant peace has followed there upon a new personal attachment and a new alignment of interests. A man may be a Christian and not understand the phrases of your theology and be wholly unable to subscribe to its main propositions.

The point toward which he moves is the supremacy of Jesus. In words that have not a suggestion of cant, he exclaims with passionate conviction:

> If you ask me what is a man of intelligence to do in this scientific period to preserve peace in the family of his ideas, I answer in one word: Consider Jesus. Press through a thousand professional interpreters to Him, see Him at His gracious ministries, hear His original, unamended word. If A or B or C or D intervene and protest, "Who are you to ignore the succession of the rabbis and set aside the ancient formula?" answer, "Only a lover of the Truth bent upon lighting my taper at the Master light, only a limping follower trying to keep in sight of Him, only a happy slave responsible to his Master alone and not another."
> The Master Himself recognized the competency of the individual when he asked, "Why even of yourselves judge ye not what is right?" And Paul complains, "Why is my liberty judged by another conscience?" James exhorts us, "So speak and so do as men

that are to be judged by the law of liberty." Press through to Jesus. You will find Him the type of the manliness and beauty of the race irradiate with supernal goodness and power.

And the parting word is the vision of the light shining in the minds and hearts of the young:

And never lose faith in light. It is the condition of life. It is the best medicine, the best policeman. There is no foulness and festering in the light, nor any tyranny. Light is emancipation. Did not the King of the truth-seekers say, "Ye shall know the truth, and the truth shall make you free"? There is no fear in light, for all light is of God, and those who fear are in darkness. The deepest of all infidelity because it comprehends all other forms is the fear lest the truth be bad. Do not be afraid of the effect of enlarging knowledge upon acquisitions already made or upon long-cherished beliefs. That sort of timidity is an impeachment of the majesty and harmony of the sum of things. Besides, the old knowledge, after the manner of all life, will organize itself about the new revelation. Establish, if you can, outposts in every province of the intellectual domain. Dare to look into any dark recess, to walk on any far-looking crest in God's universe.

That Doctor Poteat's church in its soberer moments can rise to his enlightened point of view is evidenced in the action of the State Baptist Convention of Virginia in opposing and defeating a bill before the 1926 State Legislature providing for the compulsory reading of the Bible in all schools. Aside from the merits of this particular question was the strong statement of the Convention on the whole question of the separation of Church and State—a statement that cuts the ground out from any anti-evolution law that was ever framed. A widely read sermon by Dr. G. W. McDaniel of Richmond, endorsing the policy of his church in this matter, was all the more notable in that he is now the president of the Southern Baptist Convention.

Of equal significance in the Southern Presbyterian Church—a church noted for the conservatism of its seminaries and its official organs—is the recent publication of a book entitled "Forbid Him Not," by Dr. James I. Vance, the most distinguished minister of that denomination. In its plea for tolerance, and in its emphasis on the real essentials of religion, it may prove to be a rallying point for the liberals of his church who believe with him that "Christ is greater than all the creeds and that Christianity is better than any interpretation of it." Here are veritable signs of the coming of what has been called the New Reformation.

CHAPTER XII

A GLANCE AT THE FUTURE

AS I have considered the leaders who are to-day reshaping Southern life, I have often thought of those who for various reasons left the South to find in other sections the larger opportunities that were denied them in their native states. Such men are found in all the large centres of the country—outstanding leaders in industry, in education, and in the professions. What the nation has gained, the South has lost. They suggest another aspect of the tragedy that one so often associates with the thought of the South —the potential leaders who were lost in such large numbers during the Civil War, and those who were arrested in their development by reason of untoward conditions or of certain defects of temperament.

Many of those who went away retained their affection for the old land. Gildersleeve, who always cherished the memories of Charleston and of Virginia, is buried at the University of Virginia, his grave a sacred shrine to all aspiring scholars. Barnard, world-famous astronomer, requested that he be buried in Nashville, the home of his boyhood and college days, near the small observatory where he discovered his first comets. Others, like George Foster Peabody and Norman H. Davis, have contributed largely of their time and money to the development of the South.

This volume has made clear, I trust, that there are less compelling reasons why men should leave the South. Conditions are rapidly changing, the tide has turned. Poverty, ignorance, stagnation, conservatism, and extreme individualism are yielding to the determined efforts of the Poes and the Crawfords. Newspapers are becoming more and more the interpreters of large opportunities for men of training and vision. With all that there is still to discourage one, there is a substantial basis of hope. The Ku Klux Klan is still here, but it is waning, not having the united support of the South and being strongly opposed by pulpit and press. The evolution controversy of a generation ago scarcely touched the South, so engrossed was it in the reordering of a broken life, but to-day there is a strong and intelligent body of liberals ready for battle. Industrial progress has brought in its wake an increasing number of broad-minded men.

Best of all, the younger generation in the best colleges and universities is freer of traditions and prejudices and feels the stirring of the impulses that are surging in the minds of all other young people of the world. When a very wise leader of Southern education read the chapter in this volume on the development of the University of North Carolina, he said:

You have given an admirable example of an institution that has had the support of a progressive state, and under the guidance of able leadership has achieved an outstanding position in our educational world. However, the University differs from many other institutions, not in spirit or in essence, not in ideals or in ambition, but only in the achievements made possible by better financial support.

At the same time that North Carolina has been working, tremendous improvement has been made elsewhere in the South.

Other state universities have also moved forward notably in recent years. Much might be said too of the development of agricultural education. Private institutions have also increased their resources many fold during the past twenty-five years. Denominational colleges have all carried on campaigns for endowment, and in some cases have met with remarkable success. In my opinion, some of the achievements of small colleges are worthy of the same credit that is given to an institution like the University of North Carolina. When the Association of the Colleges and Secondary Schools of the Southern states was founded in 1895, there were only half a dozen institutions in the whole South able and willing to accept its standards. Since then, in spite of the fact that the standards of the Association have been .greatly raised, there are now nearly one hundred colleges and universities that have qualified for membership.

And then he added:

There is no one fact so outstanding and so significant in all the story of Southern higher education as this. We are now in the midst of a movement that is lifting all colleges and universities to a distinctly higher plane of achievement than they dared to hope for a few years ago.

And I knew that he was right. These institutions, each with its distinctive history and traditions and with its own particular constituency and service, are the hope of the South. They kept the light of the altar of truth burning through many a dark night, and now eager-hearted young men and women are bearing this light to the dark corners.

With the growth of scholarship in the South, and with the scholar's recognition of his place in a democratic order, there have come and will come more and more freedom of thought and freedom of speech. Scholars—an increasing number—are bringing to bear upon Southern life the influence of modern ideas and insisting on open-mindedness and cosmopolitanism as the prime virtues of a progressive people. Teachers of literature are bringing young men into a larger world of thought—"an ampler ether, a diviner air." Teachers of history, with scientific accuracy and a sympathetic attitude to the past, are bringing the experience of the world as a guide for the future, and are writing the history of this section, not according to the demands of sentiment, but with the accuracy of truth. Teachers of political and social science are giving due interpretation to the new industrial order now so manifest, and are bringing to the new social problems engendered thereby the best results of the experiences of England and the North. Teachers of science—applied and theoretical—are familiarizing the Southern people with scientific principles and methods. Teachers of Biblical literature, loyal to the essential truth of the old faith, are yet brave enough to accept truth from whatever source it may come and to abide by the truth wherever it may lead.

If the present generation shall meet all Southern problems and national problems with the spirit that has characterized the men who have figured in these pages, we shall see the coming of a new day in Southern history. No one can have too high a hope of what may be achieved within the next quarter of a century. Freed from the limitations that have so long hampered it, and buoyant with the energy of a new life coursing through its veins, the South will press forward to a great destiny. If, to the sentiment, the chivalry, and the hospitality that have characterized Southern people shall be added the intellectual keenness, the spiritual sensitiveness, and the enlarged freedom of the modern world, the time is not far off when scholarship, literature, and art shall flourish, and when all things that make for the intellectual and spiritual emancipation of man shall find their home under Southern skies.

THE END

INDEX

Date Due